RAISING TOMORRW'S CHAMPIONS

What the Women's National Soccer Team Teaches Us About Grit, Authenticity and Winning

BY JOANNA LOHMAN AND PAUL TUKEY

To: Hannah
keep loving the game!
M. Joanna #15

INSPIRE MEDIA LLC
OAKTON, VIRGINIA

RAISING TOMORROW'S CHAMPIONS
What the Women's National Soccer Team Teaches Us About Grit, Authenticity and Winning

© 2021 Joanna Lohman and Paul Tukey. All rights reserved.

Published by permission by Inspire Media LLC, Oakton, Virginia

Edited by Allen Lessels

Art direction, cover design and interior page design by O'Brien Design, Freeport, Maine

Photography credits as noted throughout

ISBN: paperback 978-0-578-81692-0

Printed and bound in the United States 10 9 8 7 6 5 4 3 2 1

Library of Congress Control Number: 2020924505

For club soccer team, bulk sales or wholesale sales, visit www.rtcsoccer.com

COVER PHOTO: BRAD SMITH/ISI PHOTOS

FIRST EDITION

To Melodie and my future child. We are here to support you to be anyone and do anything you set your heart to. — J.L.

Thank you, Katie, for the gift of time. To Christina, Duke and Aimee, you exemplify grit and authenticity and give your little sister, Angie, amazing examples to live by. To Levi, the sky is the limit. And to Havana and Joanna, your friendship means the world. — P.T.

CONTENTS

COURTESY OF RUTH HARKER

CONTENTS

WENN RIGHTS LTD/ALAMY STOCK PHOTO

COURTESY OF RUTH HARKER

by Carli Lloyd

THE 2007 NATIONAL TEAM: (Front row, from left) Natasha Kai, Lindsay Tarpley Snow, Heather Mitts Feeley, Christina Frimpong Ellertson, Joanna Lohman, Heather O'Reilly, Lori Chalupny. (Back row, from left) Leslie Osborne, Kate Markgraf, Briana Scurry, Lauren Cheney Holiday, Casey Nogueira Loyd, Yael Averbuch, Carli Lloyd, Angela Hucles and Hope Solo

Introducing: My Friend, Jo

A S I TOLD THE WORLD IN MY OWN BOOK, "When Nobody Was Watching," I've always been a strange mix in the self-belief department — and that goes all the way back to the beginning of my story as a youth soccer player in New Jersey. Moments of supreme confidence were too often followed by doubts and an endless loop of self-criticism. That negative cycle was front and center when I made it to the Olympic Development Program's regional team for the first time, not long after feeling enthralled by watching the U.S. Women's National Team's iconic victory in the 1999 World Cup. I was so excited and wanted to believe I belonged, that I was a National Teamer in the making. During regional camp at the University of Massachusetts, however, there was a girl from Maryland who was putting on a daily clinic on and off the field.

Joanna Lohman was big-time. Everything she did seemed easy; she could run all day long. I remember meeting her for the first time and seeing the size of her quads. Wow, this girl is jacked! Even though we were similar in age, she was someone I looked up to because she could do it all. She would attack and score goals. She had great vision on the field. She was good at defending. And even as Jo's greatness triggered my own issues with self-confidence — because I didn't think I could ever be as good — I was smart enough

Joanna Lohman, spreading goodwill from Malaysia . . .

to know that this was a person I needed to study closely. What probably struck me more than anything was that Jo was always full of smiles, always enjoying herself and making everyone around her feel good, and nothing really ever seemed to faze her. If you lose, a possession, a drill, or a game, you get back out there and try harder next time.

Fast forward two decades and, for dozens of reasons that define the razor-thin line between anonymity and fame, most people outside the National Team probably don't know much about my friend, Jo. This book changes that. Revealing the trust and respect the soccer community feels toward this trail-blazing pioneer, more than 150 players, parents and coaches share their personal stories, life lessons and photographs in the pages that follow. Jo begins with our mutual heroes, women like Mia Hamm and Michelle Akers, who allowed us all to dare to dream, and also includes our contemporaries of modern times in an unprecedented insider's guide to what it takes to become a champion. Jo's own journey, of overcoming adversity and injury, of being out and proud long before most of her teammates had the guts to join her, is revealed here, too. Her words are real, based on poignant and authentic behind-the-scenes examples of what it truly takes to become a winner — and, most importantly, a good person.

My husband, Brian, and I dream of starting a family of our own someday, but we also worry. It's a daunting time, for a parent or a young person, to try to become the best version of themselves in the midst of all of society's pressures. That's why we need people like Jo Lohman more than ever. Positive. Smiling. Leading by example. Never a household name, but respected by anyone who played the game. That's a hell of a legacy for someone who just wrote a hell of a book. I wish I could have read it all those years ago.

. . . to Niger and around the globe

PROLOGUE

AT ALL OF 7 YEARS OLD, ANGIE WAS ALREADY OBSESSED by a soccer dream shared by millions of other girls: She was planning to play someday for the U.S. Women's National Team. On Opening Day of the season, April 15, 2017, she was feverishly rooting for two role models, one who had already been a member of the National Team, and another who seemed really close to making it. There was Joanna Lohman, the self-anointed "Rainbow Warrior" known for her distinctive bleach-blonde mohawk — aka "the Jo-Hawk" — for whom this promised to be the best season of her 16-year career. Then there was Havana Solaun, aiming to get back on track with our hometown Washington Spirit, in her third year as a professional. Angie was conflicted. Joanna, who maneuvered a soccer ball in the furious manner a bee works freshly opened flowers in the springtime, had captured Angie's imagination since she was 5. But Angie was also now part of Havana's host family for the season — an arrangement necessitated by the fact that most professional women's soccer players don't get paid enough money to afford their own apartments. Angie and Havana ate breakfast and dinner together every day, even if Angie was so starstruck she could barely breathe the whole time. "Can I have two favorite players, now?" she asked.

Fast forward four years. Joanna has retired and has co-authored this book, Havana is still chasing her career around the world and — like millions of girls and boys across America — Angie has a whole team of favorite players, with names like Julie Ertz and Crystal Dunn, Megan Rapinoe and Alex Morgan. At age 11, her dream of following in their footsteps is no less vivid, but she's beginning to understand the degree of difficulty. She remembers that Joanna's 2017 season lasted all of 11 minutes before a devastating knee injury abruptly wiped out the entire year. She knows Havana's career veered right, then

11 Plus 1 Who Changed the Rules

At the end of 2020, a total of 241 women had appeared in at least one game for the U.S. Women's Soccer Team, aka the National Team, since its inception in 1985. In addition to winning more World Cups and Olympic gold medals than any other team in the world during that period, the USWNT and its members have recrafted the very definition of what it means to be female in the 21st century. Few have made more of a collective difference than these trendsetters whose successes and challenges are reflected in the pages that follow. And, we submit, every good team needs a captain. We picked one for the ages.

MICHELLE AKERS — Appearing in the National Team's second-ever international women's soccer game and its most famous game 14 years later, she quickly became America's first dominant player, proving we could compete without embarrassment on the world stage.

APRIL HEINRICHS — Ferociously and unapologetically prowling the soccer field like no woman before her, she infused the team with the DNA for tenacity that would span generations, and she later became the National Team's first full-time female coach.

MIA HAMM — Discovered as a high school freshman and placed on the national team a year later at age 15, she would become America's first female sports superstar and the reluctant face of soccer the world over.

BRANDI CHASTAIN — Others scored more goals and drew more fanfare until the instant in 1999 when she became forever known as "the one who took her shirt off" and landed women's soccer on nearly every front page in America.

BRIANA SCURRY — The first truly transformative yet misunderstood minority player, the self-left, then stalled and started again. "Do you think I can make it?" Angie now asks, less certain than before. "Do I have what it takes?" She also knows that female athletes can draw massive crowds, yet be criticized by their own President. She watches women inspire huge television audiences, while loving whomever they please, and she asks why some people think that's wrong. Her heroes can shave their heads, tie back their blonde ponytails, or dye their black hair pink. They can blur gender lines, or profess their devotion to Jesus, Buddha or nothing at all, and then go celebrate like mad when they score 13 goals in a World Cup game. Angie is old enough to notice that some people still take offense if the women seem to have too much fun. "The men celebrate like crazy, even when the goals don't mean anything . . . Why aren't women and men treated the same way?" she asks.

"Those are all really good questions," I told my daughter. "Joanna and I will ask Mia Hamm what she thinks. Michelle Akers too. And then we'll ask Abby Wambach, and Carli Lloyd and Jessica McDonald. We'll try to ask all the women who have ever played for the National Team, and let you know what they say." Of all the girls who have shared my daughter's fantasy of playing for the U.S. Women's National Soccer team, only 241 — about seven per year on average — have actually achieved that level as of the year 2020. An American girl would be more likely to be struck by lightning, at 500,000-1 odds, than to play soccer in a World Cup. But amazing things happen when girls dare to dream, when they give it their all, and even when they hurt and cry and sometimes fail. They overcome. Lieutenant CoCo Goodson did. So, too, did Dr. Ronnie Fair Sullins and Yasmine Sanchez. To truly inspire tomorrow's champions, we present those stories as part of an interwoven fabric, one that both reveals and honors the winners of yesterday and today. — Paul Tukey

described "fly in the milk" led the National Team as goalie through some of its greatest triumphs and most controversial moment.

ABBY WAMBACH — A trascendent youth soccer player who dominated on the field despite her lifestyle and inner demons, she became the first Generation X and out team superstar as the sport entered a new century.

HOPE SOLO — The girl from the wrong side of the tracks parlayed scholarships and the generosity of strangers into a singularly dominant, yet controversial career as the nation's female anti-hero.

CARLI LLOYD — Originally derided as lazy and unfit, then cut from the National Team with unnerving regularity, the Jersey girl doubled down on effort every single time and became the proverbial lunch pail hero in the process.

ALEX MORGAN — Late to the pay-to-play soccer culture by modern standards, her knack for scoring big goals in huge games and girl-next-door smile made her the first-ever soccer pin-up model and Generation Y superstar.

MEGAN RAPINOE — Once known in soccer's inner circle as a dependable player who showed up most in the biggest games, she emerged in the past decade as the out-and-proud voice of an entire generation in its fight for gender, racial and compensation equality.

MALLORY PUGH — Still in high school when she scored a goal in her first-ever National Team appearance in 2017, she set what some see as a new example by walking away from a full scholarship at UCLA and turning professional at age 18.

JULIE FOUDY (captain) — Taking the lead from her mentor, Billie Jean King, the first female recipient of a soccer scholarship at Stanford led her fellow National Teamers on the field, and has remained one of the world's most important voices in sports and gender equality.

NATIONAL TEAMERS FEATURED IN THIS SECTION

Michelle Akers

Thori Staples Bryan

Cindy Parlow Cone

Stephanie Cox

Marian Dalmy Dougherty

Crystal Dunn

Stacey Enos

Adrianna Franch

Mia Hamm

April Heinrichs

Angela Hucles

Ella Masar

Jessica McDonald

Megan Rapinoe

Briana Scurry

Danielle Slaton

Abby Wambach

Saskia Webber

Staci Wilson

Kim Wyant

A Triple-Edged Sword?

All girls face disadvantages, some more than others

Kick It Like a Girl

The National Team has Proven Women Have No Limits When it Comes to Competing

MIA HAMM SEEMED CRANKY IN APRIL OF 2018. Not 1992 mad, mind you. Not as pissed off as when Joe Elsmore called her offsides against Duke in the NCAA women's championship game when her team, North Carolina, was already leading 6-1. Never mind that almost no one understands the offsides rule in soccer. Surely on that day, Joe, a young sneaker and cleat salesman moonlighting as a referee, must have been a fool for the mere suggestion that Mia might have broken the mysterious rule by sneaking a half step behind the Duke defenders. She had already scored three goals in the game, but when you're attempting to become the best player in the world you never stop trying for more.

Fast forward to this particular spring day in California, more than a quarter century after Mia had begun to launch her sport into the forefront of our collective psyche. The most recognized American soccer player of all time — don't call her the "best ever" if you want to keep her engaged in the conversation — was annoyed about the double standards that girls still face in relation to boys. The occasion was the gathering of the Positive Coaching Alliance, one of the dozens of organizations dotted across America trying to deal with the two most conflicted forces in youth sports: coaches and parents. "I guarantee you that you will hear more, "Don't!" and "No!" at a young girls' practice or game than you will a boys'," said Mia, doling out advice in the panel discussion that included the father of her three children, the former professional

Mia Hamm, with her husband, Nomar Garciaparra

baseball all-star Nomar Garciaparra. "Boys get encouraged to be personalities, and yet girls get encouraged to be better teammates, rather than be encouraged to express their individuality. That was a constant battle for me when I was young and playing mostly co-ed sports; the boys could be individuals and celebrate like crazy when they scored, but if I did that I was considered a hotdog, a showoff, by the other parents."

IF MIA WAS PERTURBED in 1992 or 2018, Michelle Akers was positively indignant in the spring of 1975. For physical education class one morning, the boys were sent to the baseball field for a game of kickball; the girls were brought to the playground to play on the swings. "No!" exclaimed Michelle from the park bench in the Seattle suburb of Shoreline. "I am not doing that!" With all the other girls gliding back and forth in dresses with ribbons flowing from their hair, the third-grade teacher, Mrs. Ericsson, was not about to relent to the wild-maned child in blue jeans. "Michelle, if you don't get on those swings with the other girls, you're going to the principal's office." Michelle roared again. "No! I want to play kickball!" The gray-haired educator, as promised, marched the girl — who would become Mia Hamm's lifelong nomination as best soccer player of all time — straight back into the principal's cauldron. "Girls don't play kickball!" she said.

ERICA LANSNER PHOTO COURTESY OF MICHELLE AKERS

"I had been there before!" said Michelle with a hearty laugh in 2020, still a towering figure in blue jeans and flannel at the Georgia animal rescue farm she runs with her teenage son, Cody. "I had given a report on sharing day. I was so excited. I wrote my story about how I wanted to be a Pittsburgh Steeler when I grew up; I had my Mean Joe Greene jersey with me. When I finished, the teacher says, 'Girls don't play football!' Well, I was shocked and I defended myself: 'Yes, they do!' She says, 'No, they don't!' So I got even louder: 'Yes. They. Do!'"

Revered among soccer purists the world over for marauding across soccer fields the way Mean Joe played defensive tackle,

Michelle Akers, on her farm

Michelle knows she's relatively anonymous these days, especially when compared to the America's sweetheart with whom she won two World Cups and an Olympic gold medal. But if it was Mia who garnered most of the endorsements and got to play anything you can do I can do better with Michael Jordan in a make-believe televised statement of gender equality for Gatorade in 1997, it was Michelle who put a ragtag group of soccer neophytes on her shoulders and carried them into international soccer respectability.

"I've seen a lot of these studies that go out, or these polls that list the best player that's ever played our game, and it seems that Marta (from Brazil) for some reason always wins that contest," said Kim Wyant, Michelle's teammate at the University of Central Florida. Kim has the distinction of starting in the first-ever game as goalie for the U.S. Women's National Team (see sidebar), which began its official existence at a four-game tournament in Jesolo, Italy, in August of 1985 against England, Denmark and the host county. "I played against Marta. Great player. But let's be clear: These people don't know what they're talking about. There is no one that was ever better than Michelle. No one. I'm sorry. She taught us all how to play, she taught the Chinese, the Italians, everyone, how women can play this game."

When people attempt to compliment Michelle by saying she "played like a man," they'd better be out of harm's way. "I kicked most men's asses," she told us in a tone that left little doubt. She was particularly perturbed during our chat about what she sees as an inappropriate softening of physical expectations for girls and women that persists to this day. "At my son's junior ROTC (Reserve Officers Training Corp), they do a lot of pushups and I always ask questions about it," said Michelle, with her voice rising. "These men talk to me like I have never done a pushup, or sit-up, and I could do 50 more than they could. Then they tell me they have these certain standards on how they're graded. For the guy to get an excellent evaluation, he had to do 50 pushups in two minutes. For the girls, it was 10 pushups in two minutes! Why are they keeping the girls down and not challenging them?"

BIOLOGICAL REALITY TELLS US that physical differences exist between the sexes that make average men run faster, jump higher and, yes, grow stronger enough to complete more pushups, than average women. Yet the data shows the chasm isn't as wide as one might

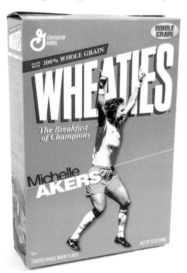

think — generally only about 10-20 percent — among the best male and female athletes who are either genetically predisposed to compete well or possess the will to get the absolute most of their bodies, or both. It's the age-old discussion of nature vs. nurture. Are you great in sports because you were born to be, or because you worked hard? In women's soccer, no one has studied the topic more ferociously or for longer than Albert Anson Dorrance IV, at once the most successful and among the most polarizing male figures in the sport. Born to an American oil company executive living in India, Anson believed the activist author Gloria Steinem and every other contemporary book he had read about women prior to accepting the new position as the head coach of the women's varsity soccer team at the University of North Carolina in 1979. Just about the only thing he likes more than books, in fact, is debating their content. He has co-authored several, and has been profiled or mentioned in at least a dozen others.

"I was a product of early 1970s feminism that said men and women are exactly the same," said Anson, who told us he had been raised in all-male boarding schools and didn't yet possess much first-hand knowledge about the opposite sex when he added the women's team to his resume at age 28 after having coached the Tar Heel men for two years prior. "The books said the only reason there were any differences is because of environmental

Are Men and Women Really All That Different?

KIM WYANT HAS ALMOST ALWAYS BEEN IN THE LEAD WHEN IT COMES TO SOCCER. She was a goalie in the first NCAA women's championship game, the first starting goalie of the National Team in 1985, and soon after posted the team's first shutout. She's been playing, and now coaching, almost every day since. With some strong opinions about how to get the most out of today's young athletes, she thinks North Carolina coach Anson Dorrance has it about right. "You've got to have this level of authenticity with them, and transparency, and you have to develop a certain level of trust," said Kim. "Until I show my players that I care about them as a person, and they know that in their hearts, I can't get them to move in the direction that I want them to go."

COURTESY OF NEW YORK UNIVERSITY

Today's players, she explained, are more sensitive than ever. "These kids lived through the great recession; they've seen their parents maybe lose their homes, maybe lose their jobs," she said. "There's a skepticism rampant among these kids about everything, about what the government does, what any leaders do. So you, as a coach and a leader, have to spend hours

Kim Wyant, far right, with the New York University men's team

and hours taking a massive interest in their lives." Kim, however, stands alone in another category: she became the only current female head coach of an NCAA men's soccer team when New York University hired her in 2015. She is among numerous coaches — and the one with the most first-hand experience — who told us the psychological differences between males and females are dissolving, or maybe they were never that pronounced in the first place.

Said another way: Maybe Anson Dorrance, with his 22 national women's championships to show for it, is spot on with his views about women, coaches and trust. In 12 years of coaching the University of North Carolina men, however, his best outcome was a single Atlantic Coast Conference title. That suggests to some in soccer that he didn't understand men as well as he would come to understand women. "I've coached a lot of young women in my time and, let me tell you some of those women are really tough, tough players to coach in terms of being demanding and outspoken, and elbowing each other for room on the leadership level," said Kim. "I've had to separate female players in fights, pull them off each other. Same on the male side. So, yes, there may be subtle differences between men and women, but they're not as drastic as one might think."

influences. I thought, 'This is great; the fact that men and women are the same will clearly make coaching women easy for me because I was very comfortable coaching men.'"

Anson has a habit of telling people that his early results in coaching North Carolina women were "disastrous," even if the record of his first four years, 73-9, didn't exactly look that way on paper. He admits he yelled a lot, barked orders, and made generally impersonal commands toward his players, just as he would do with his men's team, and just as the generals would behave in his most favored books detailing the military. He was obsessive about giving women the same opportunity to compete as men — the birth of his first child, Michelle, caused Anson to miss the first-ever North Carolina women's soccer game, Sept. 12, 1979 — yet he was perplexed when some women left his practices and game fields in tears. "When I coached men, I consciously tried to dominate them with my personality, to fire them up with the intensity of my voice," he told one of his biographers.

Then, in October of 1982, Anson was tipped off about a player another coach had just seen at a club soccer tournament at Brown University. His recruiting budget in those days didn't allow for much more than phone calls, but that February he scratched together the

---

COMPETE WITHOUT APOLOGY

Since 1985, the members of the National Team have redefined how the nation, and the world, perceives females in the previously male dominated world of team sports. Here is some perspective from the professionals for today's aspiring competitors:

NO HOLDS BARRED — "When I joined the National Team it changed my life being surrounded by other women who were like me who wanted to compete, who wanted to sweat, who wanted to tear someone's head off," said **Kristine Lilly** (USWNT 1987-2010). "We were taught it was OK to try to win and not feel bad about it. And those are the lessons that I want my girls to feel — like they can do anything."

NICE ISN'T ALWAYS NECESSARY — "I try to teach girls to accept and take direction and criticism," said **Janine Szpara** (USWNT 1986-87). "That's hard for a lot of girls because we're not indoctrinated into a culture of accepting criticism, and of being accepting of that person that's pushing them. Society typically speaks to girls in different ways by saying, 'Hey, we need you to be loving and caring and sensitive.' And the other message they get is to be nicer to each other. It's a constant reinforcement of characteristics that society wants out of girls — and sometimes girls just need to ignore all of that."

PLAYING WITH THE BOYS — "Everyone says that boys are bigger, faster, stronger and quicker," said Tiffany Weimer, who played with youth national teams and professionally from 2006-2019. "Well, some boys are, and that's why I think girls should be playing with them, especially when they're younger, to get faster, stronger and quicker themselves."

NO EXCUSES — "My parents told me they never wanted me to use gender as a crutch, to say I couldn't do something because I was a girl," said **Lauren Cheney Holiday** (USWNT 2007-2015). "They wanted me to show the world it didn't matter if I was a boy, or a girl."

IF YOU CAN'T HACK IT, LEAVE — "I'm glad my Dad had this philosophy whenever I came running into the house saying, 'The boys are being mean, or they're too tough, or they're not letting me play,'" said **Tiffany Roberts Sahaydak** (USWNT 1994-2003). "He didn't have any sympathy. He'd say, 'Then go do something else.' It taught me to roll up my sleeves and get tougher. My Mom, on the other hand, was from the Filipino culture where they value beauty. She had these visions of me being in the entertainment industry and had me take singing lessons. I was terrible!"

money for a plane ticket to Colorado where the young woman lived. In a scene reminiscent of Marla Hooch's workout in "A League of Their Own," Anson first watched April Heinrichs play soccer in a high school gym because it was way too cold and snowy to play outside. The fire and fury of this 19-year-old woman, then playing freshman basketball for a local community college, was like nothing he had ever seen in a female, or male.

Though Anson didn't know it at the time, she had dreamed of a soccer scholarship for years. Born April Minnis, the fifth of five sisters with four different fathers involved, April never knew her own biological father and was left to be raised by her step-father, a firefighter named Mel Heinrichs, when she was 15. "I found a note on the kitchen counter from my mother, who had left in the middle of the night," April told us. "She wrote that I would be better off with Mel, and she was probably right." Sports had long been April's emotional and physical outlet, her potential pathway to a far better life, but she held off from committing too quickly to her new college suitor — who was one of the few people in the country of that era offering women money to kick a ball. Anson would call and promise scholarship dollars and playing time and she would reply with the question: "Does your team get along?" He'd call again and again, and each time she'd ask about team chemistry.

National Teamers Megan McCarthy, left, Tracey Bates Leone and April Heinrichs in Haiti in 1991

"I told her they got along great, but the truth is I realized I didn't know and didn't care," said Anson, who would become the National Team's head coach from 1986-1994 in addition to his duties at North Carolina. "It's not something I had ever thought about when coaching a men's team; it's not something I cared about when I played." Through that spring, as the recruiting dance continued, April's question began to open a window into female sports psychology that he'd only begun to suspect: Maybe Gloria Steinem and the feminists weren't exactly right. Women, he said, would generally respond better to his criticisms if he worked hard to make them trust him first. "It turns out that it's sort of this liberal myth that everyone wants to cling to that men and women are exactly the same," said Anson, who knows his views can be highly controversial. "We all live on a spectrum of behavior, but the psychological differences between the sexes are actually quite profound."

BY THE FALL OF 1983, with 11-year-old Mia Hamm still playing tackle football and every other sport she could find in Texas with the boys, and high school sophomore Michelle Akers dominating on adult male and female soccer teams in and around Seattle, the future DNA code of the U.S. Women's National Soccer team was already spawning on the campus of the University of North Carolina. What Anson named "the Competitive Cauldron," initially forged around April Heinrichs' desire to win everything — from the sprints, the passing drills, and the one-on-one matchups, to the pushups, sit-ups and crunches — has become the stuff of legend in women's sports. Anson has since told variations of the same story in hundreds of speeches in the past nearly four decades:

"When I watched April's first preseason practice in 1983, I was in shock. From the first minute this woman was an absolute shark. She chewed everyone up. She didn't care what anyone thought of her. She had no hesitation at any minute against any player. She was going to win. It didn't matter what it took. She was going to bury every player. I was ecstatic!"

Soon, Anson said, the upperclassmen would be lining up at his office door. "What are we going to do about April?" they asked their coach, hoping for intervention. Bemused, he answered with a question: "Clone her?" The coach also finally understood the significance of April's constant question about team chemistry. If the Tar Heels didn't get along prior to her arrival, she knew it would only get worse with her style of play in the mix. She knew that cliques, the smaller groups that can form within teams, can be destructive. She also knew that some young women resisted competing in practice against teammates they considered friends — she had experienced that all her life to that point on the sports fields and courts of Colorado and had to find boys and men to play against instead — and that creating a culture of winning required a heavy dose of the masculine energy typically attributed to boys' and men's teams.

REUTERS/ANDY CLARK/ALAMY STOCK PHOTO

Head coach April Heinrichs, with Mia Hamm in 2003

Looking back, April believes she and her coach were a dynamic duo, one that would shape the attitude and spirit of the National Team likely forever. April was injured for that first four-team tournament in Italy in 1985, and Mia was still too young, but by the time April teamed with Michelle and Mia and 13 others in 1991, they would fulfill Anson's vision and beat Norway in China to become the first-ever champions of a women's World Cup. So what if barely anyone in the United States noticed, or that chronic knee injuries would force her into retirement by age 27, long before the American public started filling stadiums for women's soccer. April knew she helped her coach open doors for women to compete that will never close.

He's an "intellectual giant," she said, with a remarkable ability to take subtle cues from women that can help teams win games, in Anson's case more than 1,000 and counting. But she contends that Anson does get one thing wrong when he gives that well-worn speech.

Joanna, in Botswana

Shoes Mean More the Farther I Travel

MEMORIES DON'T GET MUCH BETTER THAN 1992 FOR ME. As fifth-graders, my buddies were kings of the elementary school hill, I was always the first-picked tomboy queen of their playground, and I was blissfully unaware of all the issues of gender, race and religion about to hit me across the forehead in years to come. I did, however, think I already understood something about socio-economic status: the boys all had Air Jordans and I didn't. "Please Mom! Please!," I pleaded. "Dad! Dad! Dad! I'm begging you!" They knew well enough that, at age 10, I'd outgrow the cultural badges of honor in about two months. But I was persistent. And man, when my besties, Curtis and Joharri, saw me glide into school with my new pair of kicks, they lit up. I was a girl living large in the boys' world and I don't think I'd ever been any happier.

Nearly a quarter-century later and halfway around the world, that memory would gain new perspective. The privilege of my American birth and refinement of those playground skills had afforded me an amazing career that, along the way, took me to more than 40 countries. Professional seasons in Spain, Sweden, Cyprus, Japan and the U.S. were sandwiched around sports diplomacy programs in India, Malaysia, Argentina, Thailand, Indonesia, Botswana, Côte d'Ivoire, Niger, and Nigeria. I have used soccer to battle sex trafficking, promote conflict resolution, and keep kids off the streets. Most of all, I've been able to use my stature in the game to help improve the plight of females, as I was trying desperately to do on behalf of a state department program known as Girl Power on Nov. 8, 2016. When I arrived at the soccer field, just as the girls from the local village were being bused in, the sun was blazing. The air was stagnant and humid; the thermometer might have read 100 degrees, but the heat index must have been 110. One by one, as they stepped off onto the scorched earth that served as a soccer field, I realized they had no shoes. None whatsoever. Their feet, almost literally, were on fire.

Alas, there is no Michael-Jordan-appearing-with-free-shoes happy ending to this story. We just played soccer despite the swelter, with girls from Africa in jaw-dropping wonderment of what a Jo-hawked woman from America could teach them to do with a ball. I left them in awe of their resilience, reminded that I've been so damn fortunate. But I left there, too, with memories that haunt me to this day. Until we live in a world where every girl has the same opportunities as boys, we have so much more work to do. — J.L.

She did care what people thought of her; having your mom leave town when you're a high school freshman will do that to you. "The way Anson portrays it, I was friendless at North Carolina, but I had very good close friends on the team and I'm still close with a couple of them today," said April, who would be named the female player of the decade for the 1980s in the U.S. and later became the first woman ever elected to the National Soccer Hall of Fame. With 35 goals in only 46 National Team games, she still holds the highest goals-per-game average of any woman who has scored more than two. "I do think what myself and my teammates taught Anson about coaching women is that you can be demanding, you can set expectations, you can challenge women, you can raise the bar, then raise it again — and then raise the bar again — and you can communicate with women in a direct manner. If you treat women with respect, then they can be all in on the team and competition concept."

THERE WAS, ULTIMATELY, AT LEAST ONE KEY PERSON paying attention to that 1991 World Cup and the world of women's soccer in general. Remember that referee in the NCAA championship game? Joe Elsmore didn't need any convincing that women could and should compete on equal footing with the men. He had been a soccer player himself, all-conference at North Carolina State, after growing up in the town of Kearny, N.J., which prides itself on the self-anointed moniker Soccertown USA. He considered a North Carolina women's game a plum, albeit exhausting, assignment. "You can tell right away who is the best player, the fastest, the most aggressive, the goal scorer, the vocal leader," said Joe, who had started his professional career selling soccer equipment at his

COURTESY OF JOE ELSMORE

Referee Joe Elsmore, right, with Mia Hamm in the foreground in the 1992 college national championship game

own sporting goods store. Trying to keep up with the woman who was the focal point of the game taught him that the line between elite male and female athletes was razor thin. "What happened with Mia and me through the years is that, as a referee, I had to be close to her when she got the ball because people are constantly trying to foul her. Every time she touched the ball the crowd would get up out of their seats; you could feel the tension. Through all of that, we developed this great rapport on the field."

Unbeknownst to Mia, Joe's career had been progressing — and he had been formulating an idea that he wanted to bring to his new bosses at Nike. He approached her at the end of the championship game and handed her his business card. "Before you make your next move in life, promise me you'll call Nike," he said. Though the company was at the top of the footwear world, riding the popularity of another Tar Heel alum named Jordan, it wasn't even involved with women's soccer products at the time. Joe was in sales, traveling store to store in retail management, with absolutely nothing to do with marketing or product development. He was playing several hunches: that girls were ready to compete on the soccer fields across America and the rest of the world, that Mia Hamm was the one that would show them how, and that he could somehow convince Nike to buy in.

"There's just something about this girl that we need to connect with," he told the sultans of the swoosh after a flight to the company headquarters in Oregon. Most of them had no idea who he was. "She needs to be part of

ELIZA SCHEER

National Teamer Marian Dalmy Dougherty, with senior Nike executive Joe Elsmore at the Mia Hamm Building in Oregon

our brand, part of our company . . . and lead us." The man who would help launch millions of girls' soccer dreams waited for what seemed an eternity until a Nike executive named Steven Miller came back into the room with a directive: "Go ahead, Joe, and figure out how to get it done." Twenty-eight years later, in Beaverton, Ore., the largest structure on the largest sporting goods campus in the world is known as the Mia Hamm building — where a former youth soccer player from Colorado holds staff meetings. Product manager Marian Dalmy Dougherty was just 13 years old the first time Joe Elsmore's discovery appeared in a national television advertisement for Nike. "Mia changed everything," said Marian, who would go on to play 11 games herself for the National Team from 2007-2009. "I think it gave every single girl hope that she could be something more than what we thought we had to be, which was a man. To have Mia Hamm as an icon, for girls to look up to? I'm not even sure there are words strong enough to articulate what that means."

'You Can't Win Without the Gays'

After Building a Culture of Acceptance, the National Team Inspires the Current Generation of Youth to be Comfortable in Personal Expression

SOCCER, FOR MELINA DE LA CRUZ GONZALEZ, had always been her happy place with her father. While many of the girls in her extended family were content to watch the men and boys play, Melina jumped into the games whenever they would let her. By age 12, however, she began growing increasingly distant from her parents, who were in the midst of a divorce. With her body changing and her mind struggling to process new feelings, she began staying behind at the neighborhood park when her family left the games and headed back to their home in East Harlem in the evenings. Her first drink of alcohol that summer seemed like no big deal. Most nights, she was still hanging out with the boys who found their joy in kicking a ball. On other nights, though, the drinking soon escalated, as did the behavior of her expanding, fractured circle of late-night companions. Melina would have liked to have gone home and talked to her deeply religious parents about her realization that she was having romantic feelings for girls and not boys, but was certain they would reject her immediately.

"I kind of felt like that if I had come out at that time, it would affect the divorce in a certain way," she said. "I felt like I was the reason my parents were having all those problems." Throughout middle school she drank more and attended school less. By age 14 in 2015, with her father's own alcohol addiction worsening, Melina had joined a New York City gang, often chased through city streets and fearing for her life — yet still rationalized that was easier than owning up to her identity and dealing with chaos at home. "I felt like my mom wasn't going to accept me and my father and brother weren't going to accept me, so I kind of felt like I had no other place." At one of her lowest points, after lying drunk and bloodied on the pavement with a broken arm, a cousin brought Melina to Saturday Night Lights, run by New York City Football Club and City in the Community. The violence prevention and youth development program, funded by the Manhattan District Attorney's office, offers soccer in a safe environment for thousands of young people during evening hours when crime levels are at their highest.

Melina loved it. Surrounded by girls her own age, she didn't need to wait for the precious moments when the boys invited her to sub in. "It gave me a chance to actually play the game and communicate with females, and see other females who work with you and not

COURTESY OF NEW YORK CITY FOOTBALL CLUB

Melina de la Cruz Gonzalez, in New York City

against you," she said. "That's when I realized how fun it was." Unfortunately for Melina, however, Saturday was just one day of the week. On the other days, her alcohol addiction tightened its grip. She was missing more classes than she attended, showing up at home only at sunrise if at all. When she came to play soccer one Saturday, staggering and slurring her words, organizers later found her passed out on the floor of the women's restroom.

THE STATISTICS IN AMERICA STILL PAINT A GRIM PICTURE of the outlook of teenage members of the LGBTQ+ community, where suicide rates are up to four times higher than the general population. The Human Rights Campaign compiled data that shows more than 40 percent of these young people feel shunned by their families and neighborhoods, and LGBTQ+ children are only half as likely as their straight peers to participate in organized sports like soccer. More than 70 percent of LGBTQ+ youth feel sports are not welcoming of their differences, which is why 83 percent of gay males and 63 of lesbian females keep their sexual orientation private while playing youth sports.

Abby Wambach grew up believing her personal choices were no one's business but hers, either. When she dated a boy from McQuaid Jesuit High School while attending the all-girls Our Lady of Mercy High School in Rochester, N.Y., she snuck around like most teenagers, keeping her parents, six siblings and most friends on a no-need-to-know basis when it came to the most intimate details. When she dated women at the University of

Warriors are Born by Taking Baby Steps

N 2003, MY SENIOR YEAR OF COLLEGE, I was coming off a great four-year career on the Penn State soccer team. I was a three-time All-American, one of three finalists for the MAC Hermann trophy awarded to the player voted the best in the nation. Already having played multiple games for the National Team, I seemingly had all the ingredients of the American dream in my grasp — even the long blonde hair and the husband-to-be. I was also curious. Maybe . . . probably . . . definitely, and I had been for a long time. As boxing champion Mike Tyson once said, "We all have a plan until we get

punched in the mouth." For me, that moment was my first date with a woman. Bam! I joke now, all these years later, that I got hit by the proverbial "gay stick." Step one: break up with the guy. Step two: tell the parents.

I remember it like it was yesterday; my mother and I were walking around my neighborhood and she, acting on intuition, asked if my teammate had a crush on me. "Yes," I said, stunned. "Do you have feelings for her?" she asked. I knew I had to be honest: "I think I do, Mom."

Various takes on that conversation, with me trying to explain how whole and alive I now felt, lasted for months afterward. Then Mom told Dad and the topic was never raised again until months later when my father walked into my bedroom one night in tears. He had lost me, he said. In a way, I realized in those moments, he was right. There's no sugar-coating it when you shatter your parents' dreams; those conversations — the ones where you establish your true identity as gay or straight, man or woman, athlete or not — can send mothers and fathers into a painful process of mourning the person they thought they had created.

Joanna, with her father, Steve

Our bond, however, hadn't gone anywhere. I assured my father I was his same daughter and I promised I would include him in my journey of self-discovery. "I love you, Jo," and "I love you Dad" had never been more true. I credit both my parents; they took it well, without much time to dwell, as I came flying out of the closet — giving media interviews years before it became more commonplace among my peers. Two decades later, I have to pinch myself to remember I wasn't born draped in a rainbow flag while sporting a baby mohawk. Becoming the "Rainbow Warrior" was my destiny, one that started with that first coming-out step. — J.L.

Florida, she comfortably came out to teammates in a truth-or-dare type drinking game, but otherwise let other people on campus make their own assumptions. At 5-foot-11 and more muscular than most women, she usually let it slide when she heard the occasional offending comment. One afternoon, though — as detailed in her best-selling 2016 memoir "Forward" — she let a 300-pound Gator football player know exactly what was on her mind about his homophobic remark: "I don't recall what he said but I'll never forget his tone, the snide veneer coating his words . . . I hear a silent whistle and I'm off, scorching the field with my feet, running at him with all I have, as if each step might be my last. He's on bended knee, studying his foot, and doesn't even hear me coming until I'm on top of him, knocking him over and belly-flopping onto his chest. I am near feral, teeth bared, kicking and growling as we flip and fumble across the grass, and when he finally escapes, scrabbling away, I rise up and think: Victory."

Like Melina de la Cruz Gonzalez, Abby began to turn to alcohol more frequently to numb a deep pain as her career progressed. On the field, she was shining, teaming with her childhood hero Mia Hamm with the Washington Freedom for the championship of the Women's United Soccer Association. Abby would help the United States send Mia off to retirement with an Olympic gold medal in 2004, and emerge as a team leader for the next 11 years in which she amassed more goals than any woman or man to that point in history. She never drank before or during games, she said, but off days and, especially, off seasons were another story. "What I have learned in my recovery from alcohol is that secrets are what bring us down," she told us when we spoke to her on the fourth anniversary of her sobriety on March 12, 2020. "Shame is what brings us down and I was living almost these two completely opposite lives. I was living this alcohol life and this professional one and was really successful at it. And the two weren't, obviously, working together, and it made me feel like a little bit of a fraud."

For the first 12 years of her National Team career, Abby said she never felt the need for a true "coming out" moment. Confirmation of what most people assumed came on Oct. 9, 2013, with a modest social media announcement four days after her Hawaiian wedding to fellow National Teamer Sarah Huffman. Two years later, progressive columnists gushed about the social progress when international television

Abby Wambach, at the National Press Club in 2015

cameras followed Abby all the way to the sideline after America's 2015 World Cup victory when she kissed her wife in celebration — nor was it lost on Briana Scurry that the cameras had abruptly cut away 16 years earlier when Bri was similarly headed for a World Cup sideline lip-lock with her girlfriend at the time. "I guess America just wasn't ready to show two girls kissing back then," said Briana. "But Abby made me sit up straight in my chair."

By the time she retired from the game, Abby didn't want to leave any gray area whatsoever about the intentions of her future actions. "For so many years I never wanted to be this person who put myself on a mountain and screamed from the mountain tops about my sexuality because it didn't matter to the way that I played the game, but it does matter to who I am as a person," she told a National Press Club audience in October of 2015. She was ready to speak out on behalf of the Melinas of the world who "may not feel comfortable in their own skin. I want to advocate for them, because if they don't feel comfortable, I will be the person to tell them 'You are loved and you are heard.'" Divorced in 2016, Abby is now remarried to author Glennon Doyle, whose 2020 best-selling confessional, titled "Untamed," details how the two women met and soon formed a modern soccer family with Glennon's three children and ex-husband.

When they're not on the road promoting their books, or elevating myriad social causes from Black Lives Matter to gender equality, Abby and Glennon post near daily Tweets and Instagram stories about the most mundane details of their lives . . . from taking out the trash, to picking up the groceries, to Glennon sneaking into the refrigerator to steal a slurp from Abby's favorite smoothie. If all those scenarios seem normal, that's the point. "I'm living in my truth and what I call, in my sobriety, my peace," said Abby. "It's not an easy venture and it's not an easy task, but if you feel on the inside what you say on the outside, that's the key to all the success in the world."

"GO GAYS!" EXCLAIMED A NOW CONSPICUOUS Megan Rapinoe in the middle of battling the President and winning a World Cup in the summer of 2019. "You can't win a championship without gays on your team — it's never been done before, ever." More than just another one of Megan's provocative sound bites that resonated around the world, the statement is also true. We confirmed in our interviews that the United States has never fielded a National Team roster without multiple lesbian players, dating back to 1985 when,

among others, goalies Kim Wyant and Ruth Harker were out to their teammates, but still hiding that fact from most of the outside world. The same was true in 1999, when Briana and fellow goalie Saskia Webber, among others, were lesbian members of Mia Hamm's team that won the hearts and minds of America in the Rose Bowl. Science does definitively state that elite female athletes are somewhat more likely to straddle the gender line, with higher levels of testosterone, and therefore more muscle mass and capacity for strength and speed. The best athletes are also more likely to display variable gender expression and/or sexual orientation. Said another way: The further a girl progresses in soccer, or any other sport for that matter, the more likely she — and her family — will have to confront sexuality and gender issues that still run counter to certain cultural and religious acceptance thresholds.

"It didn't take much to look around the locker room and say, 'I get it. You're gay. You're gay. And you're gay.' But obviously people didn't feel comfortable sharing it back then," said Stacey Enos, a member of the 1985 squad who holds the distinction of being one of the first two of more than 60 National Teamers to have played at the University of North Carolina. "I'm going to be frank: That's one reason I had a hard time sometimes going to certain events where you didn't feel like you could be yourself and not get judged for it. Nobody wants to be judged."

$800 Gucci bag

Saskia Webber, in 2000 and 2019

Sometimes the Issues Aren't Easy to Understand

FOR THE TWO SEASONS WE SERVED as host family for Havana Solaun when she played for the Washington Spirit in 2017-18, we warmly shared the highs (starting lineups and game-winning goals!), the lows (frustrating injuries, curious coaching decisions) and the mundane: Havana likes eggs, cheese, spinach and sausage — every single day — for breakfast. We loved her instantly. I was selfishly eager to learn all I could about the game from my new soccer daughter so I could pass it on to my youngest daughter, Angie, who mostly lived in breathless awe of having a professional player in the house. Havana patiently answered questions about the importance of nutrition, fitness and keeping my zealousness in check. She also talked openly with my wife about cute men, and women, and the two of them spent more than a few mornings bantering in excited whispers whenever teammates caught Havana's eye.

I never considered any of that my business back then, but I asked her if she'd be willing to share her perspective on sexual orientation and gender expression for this book. Perhaps, I said, it could help a young girl, or boy, gain better understanding of the choices some will inevitably face. "When I was in middle school, there were probably two girls that were on the masculine side of the spectrum," she began. "It just seems that the further along I got in soccer, the more prevalent the masculine woman became. Now, I kind of have my own

Havana Solaun, with her mother, Sandra

theories that I've discussed over and over with teammates. Right now, for example, we are in the middle of a major women's equality and empowerment movement and society is teaching young girls that you don't need a man to feel pretty or to be strong."

Some people are most definitely born with their preferences pre-determined and fixed; others are more fluid. The transient soccer lifestyle, Havana said, complicates the issue of nature vs. nurture. "It is just easier to date your teammates than it is males, because you might live in a different country every six months, so how can you commit to a significant other if he's not doing what I'm doing? After soccer, that can change for some people. In college, I personally dated two females that have since married males; I think that's common."

In her late 20s, Havana told me she accepts that she's a masculine female, but really doesn't fully identify with either gender. She has gay members in her family, but admits the whole issue isn't easy to understand, especially for her mother. Havana's advice for children and parents mirrors her own coming out experience. "Parents want to help, to give you the answer, to fix a problem," she said. "They want to say, 'Honey, this is what you do.' But in this situation, you don't need their help; you need their understanding. You need them to listen. I remember my Mom said to me, 'Well, it's just very confusing for me.' I said, 'Cool, Mom, because it is for me, too.'" — P.T.

Dr. Janis Sanchez-Hucles, a renowned psychologist, empathizes with parents who have a hard time confronting the issue in their own children. "I'm the kind of person who does not like to be surprised," she said. "I like to be able to see things before they happen, or be prepared." When her daughter, Angela, came out to her before joining the National Team in 2002, Janis admits to being confused. "The important thing is to listen and to be accepting of what they say," said Janis, who noted that her daughter dated boys throughout high school. "When your children are opening up like this, I don't think that that's the time for the parent to do a lot of talking no matter what a child has to say. Your child wants to be accepted and loved for who they are." Her biggest fear was, and still is, what mother and daughter call "the triple threat" of oppression, based on race, sexual orientation and gender. "I'm black, gay and a woman," said Angela. "I know my mother was afraid for me and, to be honest, I have been afraid for myself. I feel very out now, but I still find myself in certain environments and situations where I'm checking for safety — and I don't know if that will ever go away in my lifetime."

Angela Hucles, with her mother, Janis, circa 1981

COURTESY OF ANGELA HUCLES

One thing Angela knows for sure, however, is that having Briana Scurry and Abby Wambach and other gay National Teamers of that era made her feel like she was never alone, and everyone else inside the locker room always made her feel like hers or anyone's sexual orientation never mattered. She still laughs at the thoughtfulness, yet irony, of Mia Hamm's gift welcoming her to the team: a T-shirt stating "Boy Crazy" on the front. "Later on Mia said, 'Oh my gosh, Angie, I'm so sorry, I didn't know! Why didn't you say anything?' I just thought it was cool that Mia Hamm bought me a shirt."

IT WAS, FOR MANY YEARS, considered a form of professional suicide for women in sports to come out publicly as gay. Tennis champion Martina Navratilova never earned anywhere near the endorsement dollars of Chris Evert despite winning more tournaments, and Billie Jean King, outed against her will as a part of a palimony lawsuit with a woman in 1981, lost nearly all of her sponsors when the truth of her sexual orientation leaked. After the 1999 World Cup, it was Saskia Webber who became the first female soccer player to throw caution to the wind as soon as she retired. Her agency, Wilhelmina Models, wasn't happy when Saskia revealed herself to be gay in a 2000 *New York Times* article, but the reveal did earn her an invitation from Al Gore's campaign manager to hit the trail on behalf of the Don't-Ask-Don't-Tell policy on homosexuality in the military — which she promptly declined on principle. "I thought that was a bullshit policy, so I said, 'No!'" With her sports, modeling and political careers all ending at once, her life was turned upside down by the loss of one identity and the revelation of another. "I went through an incredible time of post-World Cup stresses. I was incredibly depressed," said Saskia. "I was drinking way too much and just lost my way. Once those lights go out, once that ball goes flat, life goes from total Beatle-mania to zero. And how do you deal with that?"

It was about that same time when Ella Masar was asking some difficult questions of her own. Then a walk-on player at the Uni-

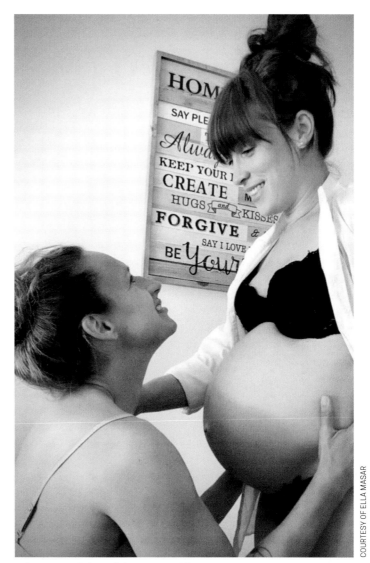

Babett Peter, left, with her spouse, Ella Masar

COURTESY OF ELLA MASAR

versity of Illinois, she had developed strongly religious views after a childhood with a bipolar mother, an alcoholic father, and the heavy influence of a homophobic boyfriend. She publicly crusaded against homosexuality for nearly a decade, even as romantic feelings grew stronger toward a female friend. "I literally spent an hour in the shower trying to wash myself clean," said Ella, who was still dating men by the time she started earning call-ups to the National Team. In 2009, at a party in Chicago where she played professionally for the Red Stars, Megan Rapinoe asked her when she was going to come out of the closet. "What are you talking about, Meg? You're so full of it," Ella replied. But by the time Megan and their National Team teammate Lori Lindsey revealed their own orientation to the public in 2012, Ella would soon be joining them in her own unabashed campaign — in hopes that she can help other young girls avoid the same shame she endured. "I've lived this life of feeling dirty for being with a woman and I've lived a life where I can, 110 percent, not deny what I feel for a woman. I deserve to be loved like everybody else," said Ella, who

WORDS MATTER

THOUGHTFUL INTERACTIONS BETWEEN coaches, parents and teammates are essential to making all players on a team feel comfortable, regardless of sexual orientation. "Having coaches and other role models using the proper terminology and language with young people is so key," said Lilli Barrett-O'Keefe, a two-year starter at Pomona-Pitzer college and founder of the Play Proud soccer program. "Having a coach saying, 'Hey, you're welcome to bring your boyfriend, or your girlfriend, to the team barbecue,' or having a coach ask about everyone's pronouns before practices goes such a long way. I think that's exactly what the National Team does by example." Here are other considerations from professional players:

OVERCOME BIASES — "I don't like any judgment of anyone," said **Briana Scurry** (USWNT 1994-2008). "I'm an African American lesbian. Being gay in the African American community is not well received. I have real issues with African Americans who have a problem with gay people. I say, 'Really? How in the world can you, as an African American person who's been basically persecuted under the feet of the man for centuries, say anything to anyone when you know how I feel? How dare you persecute gay people when you didn't like it when it was being done to you?'"

DON'T ASSUME — "I get comments all the time," said Army 1st Lieutenant CoCo Goodson (NWSL 2012-2015). "I'm not gay, but I have so many friends and family members who are. People just assume, because I joined the military and I played soccer, that I am gay. It just shows you right away what kind of people you want to be around and how ignorant people can be."

GET TO KNOW THE PERSON — "A lot of people at my church back in Birmingham, where they're not around a whole lot of outwardly gay people, just assume that every gay person is like the stereotype they've put in their mind," said **Cat Reddick Whitehill** (USWNT 2000-2010). "I'll ask them, 'Do you know anyone that is actually gay? And do you love them?' Some Christian people are hiding behind this weird ideal of what they think is right."

WELCOME COMMUNICATION — "My daughter was telling me about a speaker who had come to her school from the local LGBTQ community," said **Kim Wyant** (USWNT 1985-1993) "She told her classmates that she could speak personally about it because her parents are lesbian. She talked to me about some of the stereotyping and how that's being shattered in society. And I just thought to myself, 'Well, that's great. When I was a kid, we didn't talk about things like this.'"

CELEBRATE DIFFERENCES — "Seek out diversity on a global scale, not just in what you do, but in who you work with, who you spend time around," said **Whitney Engen** (USWNT 2011-2016). "I've watched some really cool relationships blossom between my friends who I never would have thought would be together. Try to just see people be comfortable in who they are, and own it, and get to be the best version of themselves. I think that that's something really special and I'm really grateful that I was part of the women's soccer world, one of the earlier arenas for women to come out and be comfortable."

SUPPORT UNCONDITIONALLY — "The game has definitely taught me this, that you're going to be around all kinds of people and you just have to love them for who they are," said **Mallory Pugh** (USWNT 2016-present). "They are your teammates and you support them no matter what."

played professionally in Europe for many years until retiring in 2019. She delivered her first child in 2020 with her wife, German soccer star Babett Peter. "I've had a lot of young women write me and say, 'Thank you for doing this because my family doesn't support me. I'm gay. I'm homeless. I have thoughts of suicide. You inspired me that I know it will be OK one day."

For Melina de la Cruz Gonzalez, that same kind of inspiration, fueled by soccer, might have saved her life. On that Saturday when she showed up staggeringly drunk at 6 in the evening, her coach and program director, Lilli Barrett-O'Keefe, opted not to send her

away from Saturday Night Lights for good. In her sober moments, Melina was becoming a respected young leader of the program, so Lilli brought Melina home that night and then made it a point to have a blunt conversation with her when the alcohol had worn off. "Traditionally, a club would obviously just suspend that player and kick them out of the program, but I saw something much deeper had to be going on," said Lilli. "When we sat down, she told me she was gay and was growing up in a very religious and conservative family."

For Lilli, the conversation hit home. Once an aspiring National Teamer herself, who played in the Olympic Development Program in Illinois and attended Anson Dor-

COURTESY OF NEW YORK CITY FOOTBALL CLUB/PLAY PROUD

Melina de la Cruz Gonzalez, far right, with National Teamer Lori Lindsey, Lilli Barrett-O'Keefe, Melina's mother, Maria, and Ethan Zohn, the co-founder of Grassroot Soccer

rance's summer soccer camps at the University of North Carolina, she had become disillusioned with a competitive soccer culture that she felt rejected her sexual orientation as a teenager. The one player on her youth team who had revealed herself to be a lesbian, according to Lilli, was treated like a pariah by her teammates. "The whole time the narrative around her was that she was sort of creepy and people didn't want to share a room with her, and she didn't really have a lot of friends," said Lilli. "She was none of those things; she was lovely. She just happened to be a lesbian."

Drawn to Pomona-Pitzer College's social justice programs, Lilli did play two years as a forward on the women's soccer team — but she became far more interested in her research grant to study the social impact of the National Team. Growing up, she said it was difficult for her to relate to the girl-next-door, conservative image of the 1999 World Cup team; the teams thereafter, however, presented what she saw as a revolutionary level of openness. "When you see Abby Wambach, or Megan Rapinoe, or a Lori Lindsey or a Joanna Lohman and their energy and commitment to inclusion, it becomes a transformational experience," said Lilli, whose other research grant work led her to create educational programs in Kenya and Saturday Night Lights, in her global work as North America's director of streetfootballworld.org, a global non-profit that uses soccer, aka football, as a universal language.

OPEN COMMUNICATION, IN THE END, is what led Lilli to invite Melina's mother, Maria, to the East 115th Street middle school gym on a Saturday night for an intervention of sorts. With girls of all ages kicking soccer balls just outside the door, Melina and Maria sat across the table from each other with Lilli in the middle. Everyone's faces were already reddened when Melina blurted out three words: "Mom, I'm gay." Tears came like a flood.

Melina de la Cruz Gonzalez, front, with her friends from Saturday Night Lights at a 2015 World Cup celebration with Alex Morgan

"I love you no matter what," said Maria, who hugged her daughter as if she'd found her again for the first time in years. "It's safe to say that Melina had never cried like that in her life," said Lilli. "Melina, she's fucking tough like so many of the girls that I work with in East Harlem. You don't crack them. But her mother had literally the textbook perfect reaction: 'I just want you to be happy, and I want you to be safe.'"

The transformation in Melina's life, she said, was like flicking a switch. She left the gang, quit drinking and returned to school regularly from that moment forward. She ultimately made it through high school as an honors student and began attending a local community college.

In 2015, she even rode as a guest on a float in a tickertape parade through the streets of Manhattan. Melina's National Team heroes had just won a World Cup and Lilli had an inside connection. "They are all such great role models for me, for my friends, and for the LGBTQ community," said Melina. "If they are able to be out and proud, it's more reassuring for us younger kids or people who have not come out yet."

Lilli has since moved on from Saturday Night Lights on a weekly basis, leaving the program in the good hands of Melina de la Cruz Gonzalez and a host of other homegrown leaders doing good things for their community through soccer. Lilli now focuses on streetfootballworld, Common Goal and other initiatives such as Play Proud, which endeavor to make the game accessible for everyone. Any little thing, from a public post, to a private kiss that happens to be shown on camera, opens the door another crack. "Even if you're not super outspoken like Megan Rapinoe, even if you're not on the first team, but you bring partners to games or kiss your partners after goals, it matters. When you post anniversary pictures on social media to just sort of normalize this, it helps. Parents, and coaches in levels from youth all the way up to the National Team, are all part of the solution."

3 : RACE

Uncomfortable Conversations

The National Team Finally Appears to be on the Right Track Toward Leveling the Playing Field for Everyone

"YOU GET TO THAT BUS STOP FIRST!" Ernest Scurry Jr. told his children in Huntsville, Texas, until a tropical storm literally washed away his home. "Always be first," he said when he sent his older children off to school in Minneapolis, Minn., where he had moved his family in search of a better life. Even when that home, built over a landfill, began to literally sink into the earth, Ernest never wavered in his message. After those two devasting setbacks, the Scurry family moved to Dayton, a small farming town 15 miles north of Minneapolis, where the youngest of nine children took her father's advice to heart. Morning after morning, Briana Scurry always stood out for being first in line at the bus stop. One morning in 1980 when Briana was 9, a boy took exception to her elevated standing and tried to take her place in line. "Get out of the way, blackie," he said.

Ernest and his wife, Robbie, were calm when Briana recounted the story later that evening at the dinner table. When her siblings suggested that a physical retaliation was in order, Ernest rejected the idea. He signed Briana up for Karate lessons to learn how to defend herself, but the veteran of the Korean War knew that, as the only black child in the school, Briana would likely be inviting conflict daily if she were to pick a fight of her own. In the end, however, Briana's older sister stuck to her original idea. When Daphne Scurry accompanied her littlest sibling to the bus stop the next morning, Daphne approached the racist boy and gripped his forearm so firmly with her fingernails that he's probably

Briana Scurry, making her legendary penalty kick save against China in the 1999 World Cup at the Rose Bowl

been bearing the scar for life. "My sister said, 'I know how to end this right here,'" said Briana, the only African-American woman inducted into the National Soccer Hall of Fame as of 2020. As with most things in her life now, she laughs easily and disarmingly in the telling of the 40-year-old story. She understands, however, that nothing about it has ever truly been funny. "Do I necessarily think that was the best way to handle it? Well, she had to speak to him in a language that he understood."

The issues of racial inequality and flat-out racism in soccer have, until recently, been the most difficult to put into words. In terms of representation, the National Team has fared much better in some areas than most people realize. From 1985-2020, about 12.5 percent of the players all-time, 30 of 241, have been of African-American descent (see Page 40), and black players have been on the field about 13 percent of the time, which is equal to the roughly 13 percent black population in America. On the other hand, only a small number of Hispanic players have ever been selected to the National Team, and even fewer Asians have ever made it — though that may be changing. Many of the best U.S. youth national teams of recent years have an even higher percentage of black, Asian and Latino players — and 23 percent of the players on the 2019 National Team World Cup roster were black — which could paint a brighter picture of inclusion and acceptance. But then there are the subtleties. Entire youth suburban soccer leagues often have little to no ethnic diversity, and certain members of the populous are still woefully ignorant. At a women's professional game in Utah, with the U.S. Women's National Team still basking

Silence Wasn't Working

In the wake of the murder of George Floyd in May of 2020, the world seemed to pause for a period of racial awakening. Here are just a few perspectives from National Teamers as shared with us, or on their social media posts:

Michelle Akers (USWNT 1985-2000):
"I gotta admit when (Megan) Rapinoe first kneeled, I believed staging a protest during the national anthem was disrespectful to the flag, our country, and those who protect our freedoms with their lives. Especially as a USA player. Today I feel differently. The anthem and flag do deserve respect, but so does each and every American citizen. Our country has a history of proclaiming specific rights for all and selectively applying them to a few. To protest (respectfully) for rights that aren't happening equally for all is what needs to be done."

Rose Lavelle (USWNT 2017-present):
"I realize my silence has not contributed to addressing these issues and, therefore, I am part of the problem of racism and inequality. Because, to spark change, we need everyone to do their part, speak up and demand better. I was not doing my part and I must own up to that."

Linda Gancitano (USWNT 1985):
"This racism and social justice discussion is part of equality. I think it's all the same conversation. I think treating every individual equally and with respect and kindness is the new consciousness — what the world is asking for."

Alex Morgan (2010-present):
"When will all Americans be treated and respected equally regardless of race and gender? We are yearning for true leadership and inclusivity from the top."

Midge Purce (USWNT 2019-present):
"Have I experienced overt racism? Yes. I was raised by my black father with my black brother,

COURTESY OF JOANNA LOHMAN

Joanna, with Rose Lavelle in 2018

so overt racism has been prevalent in mine and my family's experiences. But I think it's crucial to understand that open hate isn't the only way that racism manifests itself. Racism is complex, and it can be very nuanced. It allows you to like my Dad, and think he's a great guy, while simultaneously supporting, perpetuating and being indifferent toward systems and culture strategically designed to oppress him. Make no mistake, that's still racism."

Lynn Williams (USWNT 2016-present):
"The goal is not to say, 'I don't see color.' That's not the goal. The goal is for everybody to say, 'I see you, I accept you, we're equal.' That goes for all races, ethnicities, genders, sexuality, that's what the goal is. If someone ever said to me that they don't see color, then I would say, 'You don't see me.' Because this is who I am, I just want you to accept me."

in the afterglow of the World Cup victory, an appalling fan remark directed toward goalie Adrianna Franch led her to offer this public Tweet on Sept. 8, 2019:

"The situation surrounding our game Friday night is not a NEW issue, nor is it a first for me. RACISM is NOT okay in any form!! We as a HUMAN RACE can be better and should be better. We as a SPORT can help show the way."

TO REVEAL THE PRESENT AND FUTURE of racial issues in soccer, the evolution of the game may be best understood by focusing for a moment on the past. In the year that began with Ronald Reagan's second inauguration, and the release of the music video "We are the World," featuring Michael Jackson, Tina Turner, Lionel Richie and Diana Ross singing in harmony with other musical icons of the day to benefit famine relief in Africa, the United States Soccer Federation was invited to send a team to the Mundialito. Translated in Spanish to mean "Little World Cup," the four-team tournament would be lost among most lists of key events of 1985, but the invitation would lead to the first actual physical assemblage of the National Team that had existed only on paper since 1982. Sixteen American women would travel to a beach town known as Jesolo in Italy in August of 1985 to lose three games and tie one.

As 1985 progressed, "Back to the Future" would become the dominant film, Nintendo would be the preeminent game, and Windows 1.0 would begin to set the stage for computers' grip on our lifestyle. In the age prior to social media, however, an event in Philadelphia is notable today, if only because it was so unnoticed back then. A radical black environmental group known as MOVE, short for the Movement, had been sparring with city officials since 1972 about everything from caging animals at the local zoo, to clean air and water policies, to police brutality. When it all came to a standoff between police and residents, the local Philadelphia government made the unconscionable decision to drop explosives on a residential home with 13 black American citizens inside. When the fire from the bomb began to spread to nearby homes, the police commissioner, a white man named Gregore Sambor, ordered the fire department to stand and watch while more than 60 other houses — an entire predominantly black neighborhood — burned and left more than 250 homeless. Eleven people, including five children, were killed and yet white America never seemed to care. The only person ever arrested was a black woman who survived the bombing by hiding in the basement.

STILL ANOTHER NOTEWORTHY EVENT OCCURRED IN 1985. On July 5 — just six weeks prior to that first ever National Team game — baby Megan Anna Rapinoe was born to her parents Denise and Jim, 11 minutes after her fraternal twin Rachael got out of the way. The twins' grandfather would nickname Rachael "Muffin," while cheekily describing little Megan as "Ma Barker," in deference to the notorious mother of an outlaw gangster family from the Roaring Twenties. In the midst of a seven-child family, Megan said she always

Megan Rapinoe, next to Meghan Klingenberg, kneeling in support of Colin Kaepernick in 2016

fought unusually hard to have her voice heard at the modest dinner table in Redding, Calif., where crime became anything other than a laughing matter. Older brother Brian, the twins' hero and first backyard soccer coach, always seemed to be in trouble. On one memorable day when the twins' soccer exploits were being celebrated on the sports page, Brian would be profiled on the front page for drug-related offenses that would send him off to jail for much of the next two decades.

For a while, Megan felt as if she'd lost Brian for good. As he described in a 2019 interview with *ESPN* magazine, he had initially aligned himself in prison with a white supremacist gang as a way to survive the prison culture and maintain his drug habit. After years of solitary confinement, however, Brian emerged with a new perspective that he shared with his little sister in texts and letters: "You start relating to people beyond your hood, your area, your color. It doesn't take long before you start talking with each other, seeing how much you have in common. Back there, it's just you in the cell, and the man next to you is just a man himself." When Megan infamously became the first white American athlete to take a knee in support of black NFL quarterback Colin Kaepernick's stance on police brutality and racial injustice in 2016 — she stated to the media: "Being a gay American, I know what it means to look at the flag and not have it protect all of your liberties." That made Brian even more proud of Megan than winning World Cups in 2015 and 2019.

"I have so much respect for her. And not just because she's the shit at soccer," he said. "It's her utter conviction in the things that she believes in and the stances she takes against injustices in the world."

Speaking out and up has always been, according to Stephanie Lopez Cox, just a case of Megan being Megan. Stephanie, the first player of Hispanic heritage to play a significant role on the National Team, has known her ever since Megan and Rachael showed up as teenagers at their first Elk Grove United club team practice in California, with Megan already yelling at her twin. Stephanie won an NCAA national championship with the Rapinoes at the University of Portland in 2005 and would beat Megan to the National Team by a year. "She used to use that voice on her sister when we were younger; she was always on Rachael about something," said Stephanie. "But it's been so gratifying all these years later to see how she is using it for the greater good."

Ruth Harker, left, with fellow National Teamers Thori Staples Bryan, Staci Wilson and Crystal Dunn

While U.S. Soccer never blinked when Megan came out as gay in 2012, it took a zero-tolerance attitude toward Megan kneeling during a National Team match against Thailand in Columbus, Ohio, in 2016. Just as Colin Kaepernick was banned from the NFL, she was soon thereafter left off National Team rosters; Rapinoe SC, an apparel and training company that she co-founded with Rachael, lost sales. U.S. Soccer eventually skirted the issue by passing what was informally known as the "Rapinoe rule" that made it illegal to kneel during the anthem — and she was allowed to rejoin the team in time for the 2019 World Cup that would send her profile, and political platform, into the stratosphere. She became the tournament's leading scorer and most valuable player, all the while functioning as what she calls a "walking protest" in favor of equal pay and gender equality, as well as gay rights and racial fairness.

FOR CRYSTAL DUNN, IT WAS MEGAN TAKING A KNEE, and their private conversations beforehand, that will always stand front and center when she thinks of her teammate. Crystal told us she had never experienced any gross or obvious instances of racial discrimination growing up in Rockville Center on Long Island in New York. Though she was one of the few black students, and often the only black player on her soccer teams, she said her athletic prowess created a safe bubble. Teachers and principals, she said, always had her back. Yet she knew the horror stories of racism, and felt the stereotypes manifest

Fixing Racism Begins at Home

STACI WILSON, ACCORDING TO HER COLLEGE COACH, Anson Dorrance, is one of the few players he ever recruited in 40 years who could "change the temperature" of the game simply by being involved. To this day, he calls her "Buzzsaw" for the way she, at all of about 5 feet tall, took down opponents. I hit it off with her instantly when we met for the first time in October of 2018 on a State Department trip to Niger in Africa. We were surrounded by military personnel and guns the entire time. Truckloads of them. In Agadez, the gateway to the Sahara, we were assigned our own bodyguard, who slept in the next room. I was still playing, so Staci, a 1996 Olympic gold medalist turned strength and speed coach, trained me through 100-degree morning workouts. Then we'd work 15-hour days teaching children, sleep in weird places, and do it all again the next year in Nigeria. After those experiences together in Africa, I couldn't think of too many people I admired more.

So when Staci called me in January of 2020, I answered on the first ring. "Jo, I want you to be a panelist," said Staci, the first black female player at North Carolina. "And you're going to be the only white panelist." The occasion was the United Soccer Coaches Association's annual convention held in Baltimore, in other words a white event in a black city, where Staci would be moderating a panel discussion titled: "Inclusion Without Power: Black Soccer in America." I was nervous when the event began, so I listened. Lincoln Phillips, the first black professional coach in the United States, told the story of leading the Howard University men's soccer team to the 1971 NCAA Division I

COURTESY OF STACI WILSON

Joanna, with Andre Fortune, Lincoln Phillips, Lenny Taylor and National Teamers Staci Wilson and Thori Staples Bryan in 2020

championship, making Howard the first historically black college to win the title — only to have it stripped for bogus player-eligibility violations based in vile racism. I listened as a black coach in the audience recalled a game where the other team, white players from an upper middle-class neighborhood, refused to play against his mostly black team. I listened to stories of black players being called racial slurs and left off teams because of the "pay-to-play" system.

I realized I was no longer nervous. I was angry, ashamed, and hotter on the inside than that African heat made me on the outside. I knew in my heart that the individuals responsible for creating this injustice shared the same skin color as me and I thought of taking the microphone. Just then, though, I realized the most powerful thing I could do in that moment, as the only white panelist and among the few white people in the room, was just to listen and learn. To be present. When I finally did speak, it was brief, heartfelt, and with humility. I'll continue to go to Africa with Staci Wilson or anyone else who wants to come; it's important work. But I left Baltimore that day with another vow: to help fix what we need to right here in our own country. — J.L.

THE PIONEERS

To honor the achievement of overcoming barriers both real and perceived, we list the 30 National Teamers of known African heritage here, along with the date of their first appearance and career appearances* (through the end of 2020):

Sandi Gordon – July 9, 1987 7
Saskia Webber – Aug. 14, 1992......................28
Thori Staples Bryan – March 11, 1993..........65
Briana Scurry – March 16, 1994 175
Staci Wilson – Jan. 23, 1995...........................15
Tammy Pearman – Aug. 6, 1995.......................9
Danielle Slaton – Feb. 24, 1999.....................43
LaKeysia Beene – Jan. 7, 2000........................18
Nandi Pryce – Jan. 7, 2000 8
Keisha Bell – March 11, 2001 2
Angela Hucles – April 27, 2002....................109
Shannon Boxx – Sept. 1, 2003.....................195
Lindsey Huie – March 11, 2005 1
Tina Ellertson – July 10, 2005........................34
India Trotter – Jan. 18, 2006.............................2
Danesha Adams – Oct. 1, 2006........................1
Sydney Leroux – Jan. 21, 2011 77
Christen Press – Feb. 9, 2013 139
Crystal Dunn – Feb. 13, 2013 105
Jaelene Daniels – Oct. 21, 2015 8
Mallory Pugh – Jan. 23, 2016 63
Casey Short – Oct. 19, 2016 32
Lynn Williams – Oct. 19, 2016.....................29
Jessica McDonald – Nov. 10, 2016 19
Taylor Smith – July 27, 2017 10
Tegan McGrady – April 6, 2018........................1
Adrianna Franch – March 2, 2019..................4
Midge Purce – Nov. 10, 2019..........................2
Alana Cook – Nov. 10, 2019...........................1
Sophia Smith – Nov. 27, 2020 1

NOTE: Kim Crabbe made the 1986 roster, but did not appear in a game
*bold denotes still actively playing

themselves even in her most successful moments at the University of North Carolina and later the National Team. In the wake of the murder of George Floyd in May of 2020, she decided to step out herself and tell the world that words matter.

"My whole life people have been describing me as, 'You're athletic. You're fast. You're powerful," she told us. "It's true, I can be all those things, but I'm not just a body. I'm so much more than that. I think that black people are viewed by society as a threat for those same traits that the sports announcers talk about: 'Aggressive. Strong.' That's why we get the cops called on us, for no reason, just walking down the street. It threatens people for some strange reason." As the national narrative spawned a moment for racial inflection in the summer of 2020, Crystal called out her teammate publicly for the moment Megan had once again transcended her sport — this time in an even more powerful way than when Megan publicly revealed herself as a lesbian.

"She came up to me and said, Crys, 'I'm thinking of kneeling.' And I remember being filled with so much joy for her wanting to fight the cause," said Crystal during an open roundtable about racism broadcast by the *Bleacher Report* on June 17, 2020. "But at that time, I said, 'You have nothing to do with this.' Crystal said Megan made her understand that when racism is inflicted on one person, the inherent malaise impacts everyone around them. Crystal did not, however, feel she could join Megan with her knee on the turf during the anthem back in 2016. "I remember telling Megan, 'I have to stand, dude, because I don't know what's going to happen. I'm scared for my job. I'm scared that it's going to look differently if a black girl on the team kneels.' I just remember having really hard conversations with her about how I was internally conflicted.

National Team goalies through the years: Briana Scurry, left, with Siri Mullinix, Kim Wyant, Alyssa Naeher, Adrianna Franch, Ruth Harker, Jen Mead, Amy Allmann Griffin, Mary Harvey and Tracy Noonan Ducar

Then I saw the way that U.S. Soccer responded and treated Megan. They kept her out of some games, kept her out of camps, and I thought, 'Yes, that was bad, but they could rip up my contract.' I thought I actually was going to probably get it worse."

By the time Crystal played her next game after making those comments, at the Challenge Cup presented by the National Women's Soccer League in late June and July of 2020, the majority of the women's professional players were kneeling during the anthem; even the ones who stood were wearing Black Lives Matter T-shirts over their uniform jerseys. Two weeks earlier — with societal upheaval reaching a profound, almost breakneck pace nationally with the wake of George Floyd's death — U.S. Soccer, led by its new president, the former National Teamer Cindy Parlow Cone, had voted swiftly to rescind the Rapinoe rule. Cindy, among the most competitive people ever to represent our country on a soccer field with 75 goals in 158 games, admitted she had been wrong to chastise Megan Rapinoe in the first place. "Megan and I have had several conversations about this topic, and about what else she has done," Cindy told us. "I know that it wasn't easy for her to do — because she was ahead of the curve from the rest of us, including myself. And so I apologized to her for the policy about standing for the flag. I thanked her for being a leader. It took most of the country several more years to catch up to where she already was."

THAT LEVEL OF HONEST INTROSPECTION gives many people around the game hope for significant changes on many fronts. As U.S. Soccer's first female leader, now charged with leveling the playing field once and for all with regard to gender and race, Cindy has been a part of the sisterhood that's been fighting for social change for decades. She first hopes to settle years of acrimony about equal pay, and then work together with National Teamers past, present and future to demonstrate the game welcomes everyone regardless of race or socioeconomic status. "Right now, there are a lot of organizations that are doing great work in this space, but it needs to be bigger," she said. "And we need to figure out how to incorporate the inner-city kids, or lower socioeconomic kids, into our landscape

Briana Scurry, with Angela Hucles and Danielle Slaton in 2019

so they feel like this sport is for them — that club soccer or the rec league is open for them — regardless of geography, economics, or skin color."

As of 2020, 30 women of African descent had played at least one game with the National Team and their stories are poignant. Danesha Adams recalled being called the N-word on a youth field, and Thori Staples Bryan said she's been called that vile descriptor all her life. "That's just a fact of life in America when you're black; it still happens today," said Thori, who runs a youth soccer camp in North Carolina that attempts to empower young girls. The stories can be haunting. Staci Wilson is considered one of the greatest players in the vaunted history of University of North Carolina soccer, but believes the color of her skin limited her opportunities on the National Team. "I know I can't ever prove it, because no one tells you the truth," she said. "But it's a feeling I've had to live with all my life." Briana Scurry, who was writing a book, titled "My Greatest Save," just as we researched this one, said she is certain racism was in play during her career — even if people weren't calling her names to her face. She learned that no matter how hard she tried to be first and best, following the lessons her father taught her, that effort wouldn't always pay equal dividends. "I thought for the longest time that the reason why I seemed to be undermarketed and underacknowledged or not praised up was because I was a goalkeeper," she said. "And then Hope Solo came along and I realized it wasn't at all about being a goalie. They ignored me because of the color of my skin."

For National Teamers who are already mothers, the prospect of raising black children in America can be daunting, even from the moment of birth. Danielle Slaton and her white husband, John Albers, celebrated the delivery of their son, John Jr. in early 2020. "I remember thinking, within the hour of him being born, 'Thank goodness his skin isn't as dark as mine,'" said Danielle, who played 43 games with the National Team beginning in 1999. "That might keep him safe in a way that I can't." She said she empathizes with Jes-

sica McDonald, a member of the 2019 World Cup team, who talks publicly about being on the same field in Utah where Adrianna Franch heard the racial slur in 2019. In Jessica's case, police threatened to arrest her then 7-year-old son Jeremiah when he was trying to get down to the field to be with his mother after a National Team game. "It's particularly agonizing with black boys," said Danielle. "What is the time that they go from being cute, to a threat? And it happens in a day. I don't know what age it is. Age 8? 10? 12? But you look at her son and you see him out on the field throwing confetti with her, this cute, wonderful, amazing boy. And then at what point does society see him differently — as a threat? And why?"

Jessica told us she lives in fear of misunderstandings due to racism. "I am dreading the

DPA PICTURE ALLIANCE/ALAMY STOCK PHOTO

Jessica McDonald, with her son, Jeremiah, at the 2019 World Cup

day, just hoping to find the words, when my son truly realizes he's black," she said. The moment that has come the closest so far is the same moment that made so many people realize Megan Rapinoe was right to kneel. On May 25, 2020, while Jessica folded laundry one room away, Jeremiah was playing with his toys in the living room with the television on in the background. When she heard the video gone viral of George Floyd begging for his life — "I can't breathe" — she stepped into the space next to her son. She considered turning off the TV, but stood paralyzed. "I didn't know what exactly was happening in that moment," she said. "You see the knee on his neck. Oh, my gosh. You hear those last words, the simple fact that he was yelling for his Mom. And then just like that, he was gone." Jeremiah turned to his own mother, unsure of what they had just watched together. "Did he just die, Mommy?" he asked. Jessica slumped into a chair. "Yes," she said. Only days later, she fought back tears as she re-lived the agony of having to comfort her son. "I have to explain things to Jeremiah, in very simple words, because he's not understanding

The many faces of Crystal: with her husband, Pierre Soubrier, loud and proud, and powerful

the magnitude of things in life right now. Just for him to witness something like that was crushing. It truly was on a different level for me as a mother."

Jessica, also told us that, as the calls and texts began pouring in from teammates, the incident would prove to be cathartic. The level of openness within the soccer community was like nothing she had ever experienced. "Out of that tragedy came a very beautiful thing, as an African American, to see," she said. "Everybody is supporting us on this issue now, because it used to only be blacks fighting for blacks. My teammates have been asking a lot of questions and we've had a lot of chats with different teammates who are not black. I've been hearing a lot of apologies, and I've said, 'I don't need for you to be sorry. I just need for you to continue to be aware of what's happening, and continuing to talk about it, because we need this to change.'"

TRUE TO THE COLLECTIVE CULTURE that had been established on the National Team for decades, nearly every current team member spoke out in some manner during the aftermath of May. One of the captains, Becky Sauerbrunn, owned up to the shortcomings of prior dialogue. "I had not been in a lot of conversations when we talk about race with the group," she told us. "We talk a lot about gender, we talk a lot about LGBTQ issues, but we really haven't talked about race. Clearly that is an issue and it makes people uncomfortable, but we have to get through that and we need to start having substantial conversations and listening to one another."

Stepping forward in her own role as a team leader, Crystal Dunn held tightly to the belief that the summer of 2020 brought renewed clarity for an issue buried too long. "We have been getting together for hardcore conversation," she said. "All the black

Mo'ne Davis, in 2018

RICK CAWLEY

players shared their experiences, and I think it was so incredible the response that we got from our teammates. I think the meetings have also encouraged people to ask questions — because I don't think race needs to be a difficult discussion. I want people to ask me how I feel and what I'm going through for any challenge that I might face based on my race." Other players, even the ones who don't typically engage loudly, used their own platforms in their own ways. "We call for an END to systemic racism that allows this culture of corruption to go unchecked and our lives to be taken. See the demands. Sign the petition," re-Tweeted Christen Press on May 30, 2020.

Those collective words, it was clear, were not going unnoticed by the soccer playing youth of America. Thirty-five years later, it would be impossible to imagine something similar to the MOVE bombing in Philadelphia happening today without a majority of the nation taking the proverbial knee. "When you see your role models out there fighting for what's right, it makes you want to go out and follow the same footsteps in the future," said Mo'ne Davis, who told us that Christen, a Stanford graduate, is the player she most admires. Mo'ne plays soccer, softball and basketball. But six years earlier, in the summer of 2014, she became a cultural phenomenon in Philly as the girl who pitched a baseball team of inner-city boys to the Little League World Series with a 70-mile-per-hour fastball. In those heady days of breathless ESPN coverage and newspaper headlines, Mo'ne took an American history tour with her team, the Anderson Monarchs, south from Pennsylvania, through Washington, D.C., and into the Carolinas. All the monuments, the visits to museums, made her truly aware of the implications of the color of her own skin for the first time. It made her appreciate it all the more, three years later, when a player from her favorite sports team knelt down and spoke up.

Mo'ne Davis, in 2014

"When you have a female, a white female, kneeling for police brutality and racism, it sticks with you," said Mo'ne. "So many people aren't going to do that when they know they will be criticized for it. That was really cool to watch. And now you have people looking back on what she did and they're starting to realize, 'Colin Kaepernick was right. Megan Rapinoe was right. Christen Press is right.' I knew they were right the whole time, this team. It helps tell me how I want to live my life."

NATIONAL TEAMERS FEATURED IN THIS SECTION

Yael Averbuch

Lori Chalupny

Brandi Chastain

Marian Dalmy Dougherty

Whitney Engen

Julie Johnston Ertz

Joy Fawcett

Meghan Klingenberg

Kristine Lilly

Lori Lindsey

Alex Morgan

Leslie Osborne

Mallory Pugh

Danielle Slaton

Aly Wagner

Abby Wambach

Opposing Forces?

Parents and coaches can be the biggest factors in fulfillment

Sign Her Up? Not So Fast

Four Tar Heels Tell us that Early Entry into Organized Sports Should Never Replace an Old-Fashioned Outdoor Childhood

MEGHAN KLINGENBERG LOVED TO RUN. She chased after the other girls and boys in her suburban Gibsonia neighborhood just outside Pittsburgh. She sprinted from her parents' car straight into the pool at her grandparents' house in nearby Shaler, and was most often the last cousin in the door when the dinner bell interrupted the neighborhood games during the weekly four-generation family gatherings. She liked to run for her first youth soccer team, too, even if it wasn't always in the right direction. "Meghan! Meghan! This way," hollered her father, Dan, as he frantically waved her back toward her teammates in the fall of 1993. His first child, age 5, didn't have the first clue that scoring goals involved coordinating passes and shots with all the girls in the same color shirts generally swarming together in the same hive. Toward the end of the year, with a game on the line, Meghan's coach sent her teammates into panic mode when he motioned her from the bench and into the huddle.

"Nooooo!" exclaimed the little girls in a chorus of protest. They were bigger and taller than she was, all of them. "If you put Meghan in, we'll lose for sure!" Meghan shrugged her shoulders matter-of-factly. "They're right," she thought to herself. Later, when the game had ended, Meghan was neither sad nor mad as she approached her mother Kristen on the sideline. "Mom, can I just play softball, please?" she asked. "I'm just really not very good at this soccer thing."

Meghan Klingenberg, circa age 8

Whitney Engen could relate. At age 6, she loved her pink gymnast outfit and found little interest in chasing a soccer ball around the fields of Torrance, Calif., with a bunch of other children and parents who seemed far too eager. Never mind that most of her teammates came up to her armpits and she could play reasonably well if she felt like it, her father Chris would nonetheless have to ply her with candy to get her into the car for practice. Reese's Cups were her favorites, but even those failed to keep her inspired. At the end of every game during her first season, she told her father she wanted to quit soccer, too.

"The family rule is that you have to play a sport for two seasons before you can decide," Chris told his daughter. He was also playing a genetic hunch. By age 9, Whitney had already busted out of the tutu at 5 foot 7 with size 9 feet and the gymnastics coaches had levied the bad news that she was sim-ply going to be too big to become a bal-

Whitney Engen, circa age 9

lerina or a gold medalist on the balance beam. When sign-up season rolled around for her third-grade year, she decided to give soccer a go with no strings of candy attached. Besides, the car rides back and forth to the games were just so much fun. Chris loudly tuned his old car radio to the AM classical music station. For the half-hour drive each way, father and daughter belted out opera tunes, from the likes of Luciano Pavarotti, Placido Domingo or Maria Callas, at the top of their lungs.

MORE THAN A QUARTER OF A CENTURY LATER, with collegiate national championships, a World Cup trophy and a decade-long professional soccer career on their resumes, University of North Carolina and National Team teammates Meghan Klingenberg and Whitney Engen have a resounding message for parents everywhere: What's the rush? Absolutely introduce your children to the game, and all sorts of other sports, too, but not when they're too young and you're expecting too much. The right activities for your daughter, or son, will reveal themselves in time, or maybe even right away.

Lori Chalupny, who left the University of North Carolina one year before Whitney and two years before Meghan arrived, began playing soccer on the asphalt of her elementary school playground in St. Louis. As the only girl who self-selected into the informal pick-up games, she relished scoring goals, but also the opportunity to play goalie and frustrate the boys' scoring attempts with rolling, diving saves. More often than not, Barbara Chalupny would send her daughter to the restroom at the end of the school day to wash off the blood and black tar before she let Lori into the family car. "I played other sports," said Lori, a defensive midfielder and defender on the U.S. Olympic gold medal team of 2008 and the 2015 U.S. World Cup champions. "I played basketball and softball at a kind of a recreation

Benefits of Getting Outdoors

PLAYING ORGANIZED OUTDOOR SPORTS LIKE SOCCER is beneficial for children of all ages. To help children gain independence and problem-solving skills, however, parents are encouraged to prioritize at least as much unstructured outdoor play for their children as they do adult-mentored or coached activities. Here are the some of the other benefits of time outside, according to **Dr. Sara Whalen Hess**, a clinical psychologist who played 65 games for the National Team from 1997-2000, including a key role for the 1999 World Cup champions:

HEALTHIER CHILDREN — One out of three children in the U.S. are clinically obese and many, according to the American Academy of Pediatrics, have vitamin D deficiencies, both of which can be overcome with time playing in the sunshine. "All three of my kids, even my just turned 8-year-old, enjoy time on their bikes with their friends," she said. "It's so simple, but it's so healthy, emotionally, socially, and physically."

INCREASE ATTENTION SPAN — Studies show that children who play outside regularly in an undirected manner are more likely to become more curious, self-directed adults with an improved ability to focus on tasks. Time in nature especially helps in the treatment of Attention Deficit Hyperactivity Disorder. "One of my children has ADHD and being stuck inside during the COVID-19 shutdown was incredibly difficult for him, much more so than my other two kids," said Sara. "Every time he goes outside, then later comes back in, he's a lot more settled. He feels better. Anytime anxious kids are having a particularly difficult time, or feeling isolated, getting out in nature will help them."

OVERALL IMMUNITY — Outdoor light stimulates areas of the brain that regulate melatonin, involved in healthy sleep patterns, and the development

Dr. Hess, outdoors with her children

COURTESY OF SARA WHALEN HESS

of beneficial hormones that can improve everything from the health of the heart to our central nervous systems. Sara, who specializes in treating young athletes with anxiety, keeps this in mind every day: "I actually hate seeing patients in an office. Whenever the weather permits, my patients and I get up and go outside for a walk because it's just so therapeutic to be out there doing that rather than sitting in an office with artificial lighting. People feel better when they're outside, they function better, they work better. They are also more interactive and feel better emotionally."

Whitney Engen, with her parents Chris and Kim, and North Carolina head coach Anson Dorrance

level. But, honestly, I feel like soccer chose me. I mean, the first time I played it, the game came naturally to me. I really feel that was what I was meant to do; I loved it and it just kind of clicked with me from the beginning."

Oceans of research supports the phenomenon known as "sports sampling," modern parlance for trying every game in town depending on the season, from skateboarding to skiing, basketball, baseball, badminton and bowling. The results of that will lead to myriad long-term benefits including higher development of motor skills, quicker decision-making and a far higher likelihood of being great at a child's chosen sport later on in life. Even more research has found that youthful contact with nature, an activity sorely lacking in most modern children's lives, leads to everything from fewer mood swings, better eyesight, stronger immune systems and generally overall happiness (see sidebar). No research whatsoever supports a child attaining future athletic success from entering into organized sports prior to age 5 and a half — which, incidentally, is the average age the National Team players interviewed for this book started playing soccer for their community recreational teams.

Yael Averbuch, right, with her sister, Shira, and father, Paul

Gloria Averbuch said she knew all that instinctively. The family of highly competitive runners — her husband Paul Friedman entered the U.S. Olympic trials in 1980 and 1984 in the marathon — the Friedman-Averbuchs had grown up outdoors and were raising their children the same way. An author of several books on sports, health and fitness, Gloria wasn't in any hurry to have their oldest daughter, Yael, join the highly competitive community recreation teams of Montclair, N.J. Even at age 7, when Yael went to see her friend play soccer on a Saturday

Lori Chalupny, with Julie Johnston Ertz and Christen Press in 2015

morning, she declined a one-game invitation to join the short-handed team. The family soon found, however, that a seed had been planted and quickly rooted. The following season Yael not only joined her friend's team, but made the sport her obsession from age 8 forward.

"From the time she was very young, we felt like 'Let's not make this mistake and just do this one sport and be too singular-minded,' because we knew, and had read, that's a mistake," said Gloria, who counts her 2002 collaboration with North Carolina head women's coach Anson Dorrance, "The Vision of a Champion," among her most successful literary efforts. "Yael was stubborn; she would not agree to do anything else. We'd say, 'How about T-ball?' I remember saying, 'How about running? How about basketball? How about walking? How about . . . ' The answer was 'No, no, no and no.' So, because she

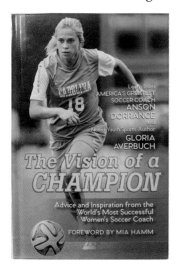

said no to everything else, because she was so interested in one thing, her dad studied to become a soccer trainer."

BRIDGING THE CAREERS OF FELLOW Tar Heels Lori Chalupny, Whitney Engen and Meghan Klingenberg at North Carolina, Yael Averbuch would go on to start a record of 105 consecutive games for the most successful women's college program of all time. She also represented the U.S. at youth team levels from U-16 to U-23 and appeared in 26 games for the National Team from 2007-2013. Even Yael, however, knows she's an exception that parents and players typically should not follow. Of all the National Teamers interviewed for this book, she's the only one we spoke with who concentrated exclusively on soccer throughout her entire childhood. "I don't think anyone should be restricted to one sport if they're

Winning is Never for the Faint at Heart

BAREFOOT, IN MY ONE-PIECE BATHING SUIT THAT wouldn't come off all day, is how I remember spending most of my childhood summers. We lived on Locksley Lane in a neighborhood called Sherwood Forest where the community pool was named, you might guess, Robin Hood. My friends and I were what you would call, "pool rats," whereby every morning we'd wake up early for swim practice. I was never a good swimmer, and always hesitant to jump into the cold water, but the coaches would spray me with a hose until I finally gave in. My older brother, older sister and all of my friends swam well. For me, the Robin Hood swim team was a rite of neighborhood passage that I endured until we would all go home and eat breakfast.

It was just before 10 a.m. when my favorite summer days truly began. My friends and I would jump back on our bikes to arrive just in time for the pool opening, then spend the rest of the morning and afternoon swimming, playing basketball, or ping pong. Not for the faint at heart, our favorite game was known as "hot box," which involved sprinting back and forth between bases while trying to dodge a tennis ball being thrown at your head by the "it" player. It was dodgeball on speed, and I was known to be one of its best combatants. No one (well, almost no one) could get me.

COURTESY OF JOANNA LOHMAN

Joanna, surrounded by her sister, Molly, and brother, Peter

The path to safety included running across the red-hot asphalt then through grass. Day after day, from Memorial Day weekend until Labor Day, my little feet would turn to leather, with the requisite stubbed toes, scraped knees and a sunburnt body to match. "Hot box" is where I learned the hard lessons of what happens when your knees meet pavement, of when your bare foot meets a sharp stick, and the pain of when a tennis ball nails you at fast speeds. Yes, I guess I did get pegged once in a while. But over time this primitive game, with no coaches or referees, taught me to maneuver my body, contort it into positions to elude getting hit, develop the speed to outrun the boys, and most importantly, take chances. "Hot box" was all about the dares and being the player in the middle risking everything to get to the other side. I was one of the few girls who dared.

When it was my turn, I'd also throw the ball the way Robin Hood fired his arrows, just as hard as I could. I'd revel when it connected with another player's skin; it was all part of the game that trained all of us to be teammates, friends, foes and, ultimately, athletes. Win or lose, we'd laugh either way, then jump into the pool for one last swim before the bike ride back to Locksley Lane. If it sounds like some sort of fairytale life, that's because it was. — J.L.

Rushing into Organization Offers Few Rewards

WE COULDN'T WAIT TO GET OUR YOUNGEST DAUGHTERS into their first organized soccer seasons. Aimee, who liked her powder blue uniform far more than actually kicking the ball, came first. At age 5, she would spend most of her recreational team's games holding hands with her little blonde friend while all the other boys and girls ran circles around them. Eager to get her to do something — anything — on the field, I offered Aimee a candy bar of her choice if she scored a goal. In her dreams-of-chocolate awakening, she dashed down the far sideline, stole the ball, and kicked it squarely into the net as if she'd been doing that all season. Yet even as I was jumping up and down in celebration, my daughter quickly ran back downfield to re-embrace her friend's tiny hand. "Don't you want to score another goal?" I yelled across the field. "Do I get another candy bar?" Aimee asked with a knowing smile. Alas, that would be the one and only goal of her season; she would much rather have been making sandcastles at the beach.

Aimee, age 5 and No. 5, holding hands . . .

PAUL TUKEY PHOTOS

Soon enough, it would be Angie's turn. In her pre-school activity known as sharks and minnows, or the two-vs.-Dad games with her sister in our front yard, Angie was always the aggressor. The instant she turned 5, we signed her up for Montgomery Soccer Inc., among the nation's largest youth organizations serving about 11,000 children a year. Arriving for her first game at the Herbert Hoover Middle School, however, she literally froze amidst the sea of girls dressed in blue, green, red, yellow or teal. Her little tears became full-on sobs as we approached her first coach. Angie would eventually calm down and kick in a few goals that season, but left the field in tears just as often whenever the other team tallied. "Don't worry about it, no one is keeping score," said my wife, Katie. "I am!" replied Angie. At the end of her six-game career, she quit soccer. "Forever," she said. Forever, as it turned out, lasted all the way to age 6. — P.T.

Angie, age 5, all tears

Yael Averbuch, with her husband, Aaron West, and daughter

interested in other things, and there are certainly benefits of being well-rounded and becoming a well-rounded athlete," said Yael. "I'm missing certain athletic qualities from not playing other sports, and I recognize that."

For most National Team players, their path has more resembled the one navigated by the Klingenbergs of Gibsonia and Shaler in Pennsylvania. While Meghan was still finding her sea legs in soccer, her father, Dan, enrolled his future National Teamer in taekwondo lessons to overcome her shyness. By the fifth-grade talent show, when many other girls wore dresses while singing and dancing, she adorned a black belt and white robe while tossing nunchucks in the air and splitting boards with her feet after flying leaps across the stage. She was still a slick fielding shortstop on the softball team, and played point guard on her basketball team, yet spent the most satisfying part of childhood squeezing every moment possible from her outdoor experience.

"The neighborhood had all kinds of kids my age; I would play outside from 9 a.m. after we finished breakfast, through 'til it was dark and I was expected to be home," said Meghan. "I think a lot of kids today don't understand what it will take to be a healthy, happy, passionate human that is successful in their older lives if they're not able to explore life in all of those ways. When you're playing with friends, you are having fun, but you're also learning what you like and what you don't like. You're learning different skills, and how to move your body, how not to move your body. You find out what hurts, what doesn't hurt, and how it feels to win and lose. Then you interact with those friends with no parents around. You're learning all of these things without direction, and I think that letting kids be creative and letting kids figure out how to deal with failure on their own is one of the biggest assists that we could possibly give them in their development."

As for improving in soccer for Meghan, that came the old-fashioned way, too. That pool at the grandparents' house was encircled by a stout wooden fence that took a constant beating from her soccer ball. "I'm not the type of person that likes to be bad at things and I just remember practicing," she said. "I remember crushing balls off the fence and annoying, like, everybody. I don't remember there being a time of me saying to myself, 'Oh, I'm good now.' But I do remember that by the time that I was 10 or 11 years old, people were starting to recruit me to their teams — because they actually wanted me on their team!"

Have Club, Will Travel

In America, the Pay-to-Play System Stands Between Every Player and Her College or Professional Dreams

SOCCER WAS NOTHING IF NOT AN ENIGMA to Steve Baldwin. He saw it as a throwaway sport that the gym teacher at Gaithersburg Junior High School forced the Maryland boys to experience one week a year in the 1970s when they'd really rather be playing baseball or basketball. Being told to kick a ball, with no hands allowed in the game, felt like punishment. "Honestly," he said while laughing, "I couldn't imagine why anyone would want to do that." Throwing his full attention into building information technology companies after graduating from the University of Maryland, he said he never thought about the game again until his daughter would rather wear cleats than tapdancing shoes by age 5. "Carlyn was suddenly, at least from my perspective, all excited about soccer," said the chairman of both Qbase LLC and Finch Computing based in northern Virginia. "We didn't play it around the house, so I wasn't sure where that passion came from. But you do what Dads do. Right?"

That meant a couple of years of cheering loudly for the Chantilly recreational soccer team, followed by two seasons of driving his daughter around northern Virginia for practices twice a week and games every weekend. Steve was a full-on soccer Dad by then, writing checks to the Vienna Youth Soccer Association, and offering boisterous encouragement and the occasional coaching pointer from the sidelines. He cheered even louder when goals were scored. When Vienna played the Braddock Road Youth Club one weekend at nearby Robinson High School soccer field in Fairfax, however,

COURTESY OF CARLYN BALDWIN

Carlyn Baldwin, with Braddock Road

Carlyn Baldwin, with the University of Tennessee

he was mesmerized even as Carlyn's team lost. The Braddock Road girls were playing the same game, but their pace and precision of passing seemed higher, even as the volume level on their section of the sideline seemed lower. Not long afterward, a father on the Vienna team offered Steve some unsolicited, yet serendipitous, advice: "The way your daughter plays, you need to get her to Braddock Road."

Steve Baldwin, tech guru, might have been on a pathway to join one of the largest and most anxiety filled groups of sports parents and young players in the country: the "club-hoppers," who are always looking for the grass-is-greener option. When Carlyn aced the tryout, the Baldwin family left Vienna — but never moved again. "Something about Braddock Road just looked and felt different," said Steve, whose world would center around that field in Fairfax for the next eight years. Carlyn made U.S. youth national team rosters at age 18 and again at 22, earned a scholarship at the University of Tennessee, and eventually left college early and moved to Europe in 2017, where she's been a professional player — still dreaming of making the National Team back home — ever since. "Braddock Road turned out to be one of the best decisions we ever made; it literally changed the course of Carlyn's life."

IT WAS NEVER THEIR INTENTION as they furiously worked to introduce women's soccer to the world in the 1990s, but Joy Fawcett and Kristine Lilly inadvertently helped to unleash one of America's most controversial industries as they rode off with Olympic medals and two World Cup championships tucked into their retirement resumes. Youth sports are now estimated to comprise a collective $17 billion machine in the United States — and girls' and boys' soccer "club," aka "travel," teams are the two biggest pistons in the massive "pay-to-play" engine that can be as competitive as they are expensive. Whereas the girls of today aspire to be the next Alex Morgan or Crystal Dunn, their mothers were often inspired by Fawcett or Lilly, or their teammates like Briana Scurry, Julie Foudy and

Joy Fawcett and her daughter, Katey, with Mia Hamm, left, and Kristine Lilly

Mia Hamm. Many of these same Moms, and Dads, are investing up to $10,000 a year in registration fees, annual dues, private coaching lessons, equipment and travel expenses to try to make their children's — and their own — National Team dreams come true. For every Carlyn Baldwin who scales the ultimate American soccer stepping stones by earning one of the 200 or so spots on a youth national team roster between the ages of 13 and 22, there are literally hundreds of thousands of girls each year whose parents might appear to be spending a whole bunch of money in vain — and millions more whose families can't even afford to try (see sidebar, Page 60). Of those most accomplished girls, only an average of about seven new players per year make it onto the National Team for a single game.

As the first child ever born to a National Team mother, Katey Fawcett was breastfed at halftime of National Team games and literally grew up on the soccer field with American icons as defacto aunts, National Team goalie Amy Allmann Griffin as a godmother, and a hero of the 1996 Olympics, Shannon MacMillan, as a live-in nanny. Katey was just 5 when her mother scored the second of five overtime penalty kicks that would secure the 1999 world championship against China. When Joy retired after winning the 2004 Olympics and it came time for Katey to play the game herself, however, her famous mother ran

almost screaming away from the hucksters who promised to deliver the soccer fantasy in exchange for a healthy fee. "Even back then, I took a look at the out-of-control club soccer scene in southern California and I just couldn't do it," said Joy, who had two other children in the middle of a career that spanned 17 years and 241 games. She retired as the all-time leading goal scorer among defenders with 27. "The soccer

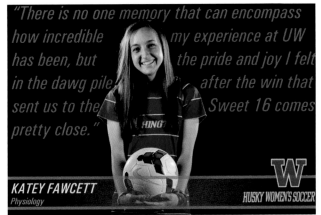

"There is no one memory that can encompass how incredible my experience at UW has been, but the pride and joy I felt in the dawg pile, after the win that sent us to the Sweet 16 comes pretty close."

KATEY FAWCETT
Physiology

HUSKY WOMEN'S SOCCER

Katey Fawcett, at the University of Washington

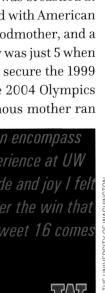

When Training Becomes a Nightmare, Walk Away

O N JAN. 15, 2020, I RECEIVED AN UNSOLICITED email at 5:14 p.m. under the subject line: "U-13 girls soccer — Young girls that deserve better." Intrigue quickly turned to disappointment when I read the issues weighing on a father, who had been referred by a mutual acquaintance who knew positivity is the number one trait of my JoLo Soccer mentoring sessions with young players. "A number of families have been having a difficult season at a local club," he wrote. "We're very unhappy with the culture we've found, and are dismayed by the negative experience our daughters are having. Rather than providing a positive, challenging environment, they've been exposed to seething negativity and shocking hostility. Where they once looked forward to every practice, now they struggle with having to go. It's unhealthy, and it's entirely unnecessary. My own daughter went from being proud and excited, to considering quitting soccer altogether."

COURTESY OF JOANNA LOHMAN

Joanna, training one-on-one

I wish I could honestly report this was a unique case, yet all too often I am hearing similar stories of club coaches going too far to push players and emphasize winning. In this case, I decided to get involved. I met with the father, then started training the daughter, keeping it all about soccer at first. As we began to talk, I heard — literally — about nightmares: "This is really scary . . . But at night I felt like I could hear him talking to me and giving us stuff to do. And I felt like if I didn't do it, if I didn't wake up and sit up in bed, he'd get mad at me." The young girl began to live in fear of the prospect of seeing the coach at practice. "I went down in my closet because that's where I keep my uniform stuff and I was telling myself, 'I don't want to go. I don't want to see the coach. I don't want to see my teammates.' And my dad came in and he saw me just crying on the floor."

When she had enough, she wrote a letter to the coach that she shared, reluctantly at first, with the teammates she was leaving. "Many girls said, 'Thank you. A lot of people needed to hear this. And a lot of people don't have the voice that you do. And some people can't speak up and say it because they're too afraid.'" After sharing her story, she has been bright, cheerful and among my most eager students of the game. At the age of 13, when 70 percent of girls have quit organized sports — mostly because they're not fun anymore — this girl was still envisioning a future with soccer, albeit for a different club. She agreed I could share her experience and advice, just not her name. "I think soccer is so beautiful," she said. "I love watching it and I love playing it. And I'd tell anyone going through what I did to stand up for herself. If anything bad happens, you have so many people to talk to and so many people who care. Don't let anyone bring you down or make you feel bad about yourself." — J.L.

culture down here became crazy. Parents are crazy. It's toxic because there's so much pressure for these kids. I could not find one single club that I thought would nurture the kind of fun that I think that most kids need."

Instead, she launched her own club with her husband, Walter. They told member parents on day one that college scholarships were definitely not the goal at Saddleback United, where practices emphasized fun and relationships were prized more than victories and goals. Even when her godmother and nanny weighed in with opinions that Katey was going to need a more competitive club environment if she wanted to play Division I college soccer, the Fawcetts held their ground. "I'm all for nurturing dreams. I mean, my dream was to make the Olympics, long before there was even an Olympic soccer team," said Joy. "But you need to be able to hear what your kid really wants and have that discussion."

Managing the Club Soccer Experience

More than 95 percent of collegiate soccer players come from some version of a "pay-to-play" club soccer environment, which has become virtually unavoidable in America. Here's some advice from National Teamers on how to navigate the journey:

KEEP IT LOOSE — Some clubs focus on competition, traveling and winning at young ages, as early as age 7 or 8, but no evidence suggests this helps with soccer success later in life. Rather, the data shows too much early stress and focus can lead to burnout, both for the child and the family. "I felt very passionately that, as long as I could keep bringing in good coaches for my daughters' teams, it was equally important that they're surrounded by their friends," said **Kim Conway Haley** (USWNT 1993). "Until age 14, we had a community team that was convenient and flexible enough so the girls didn't have to pick and choose what sport they play full time."

FIND THE RIGHT LEVEL — All children progress physically and emotionally at different rates and times. **Danielle Fotopoulos** (USWNT 1996-2005) advises not to worry about not making the "A" team right off the bat; just keep playing for whatever club team keeps you on the field to develop at your own pace and consider finding a trainer/mentor to keep you grounded (see Chapter 9). "Set your goals appropriately. If you

Kim Conway Haley, with Michelle Akers, in 2019

want to play in college, stick with club soccer and most likely you can find a college. It might not be the University of Florida, but there's Division 2, Division 3 and lots of other junior colleges. If you love soccer, hang in there."

OVERCOME REJECTION — At some point, if you're attempting to push yourself to the next level, you won't make a team. **Alex Morgan** (USWNT 2010-present) thought of quitting soccer at age 13 when a team cut her just prior

Katey decided to stay at Saddleback United, play for her high school team, and she ultimately appeared in 26 games across four seasons primarily as a reserve player at the University of Washington, where Amy, her godmother, served as an assistant coach. "All of my greatest friendships have come through soccer and my teammates," Katey told ESPN when it came calling for a 2013 feature story about the soccer legend's daughter with the grounded set of values. "That's just something that is worth all the work you do and all the time you put in. It's like a big group of sisters."

ONCE UPON A TIME IN A GALAXY WHERE SOCCER was barely known in the United States, Kristine Lilly told coach Anson Dorrance she would need to phone home. At age 16 in July of 1987, she had just been selected to something called a National Team and wanted

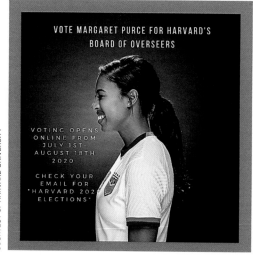

COURTESY OF HARVARD UNIVERSITY

Midge Purce, elected to the Harvard Board of Overseers in 2020

to the California State Cup tournament in 2002. Her parents encouraged her to keep trying. "Alex was devastated," said Pamela Morgan. "She thought, 'Maybe I'm not good after all.' I told her that coaches are human and they make mistakes in judgment, and that we would help find her another team."

COACH TRUMPS CLUB — Especially at younger ages, finding and sticking with a coach is more important than finding and sticking with a club. **Midge Purce** (USWNT 2019-present) credits former National Teamer **Shannon Higgins-Cirovski** (USWNT 1987-1991) with honing her development. "She's really talented at maximizing people's strengths and shoring up your weaknesses to the point where they're not

weaknesses. She was great at not trying to make everything about your game perfect. She taught me that if I can be really, really good at a few things, that's where I could start to set myself apart from others."

EVALUATE SATISFACTION — Given the investment, parents and children should have an open conversation once or twice a year about the fulfillment with the current club team, according to **Christie Welsh** (USWNT 2000-2006). "I had parents ask me, 'Is my daughter in the right place? Should she move?' My answers were always: 'Is she happy? Is she feeling like she's growing as a player?' If one of those is missing, then I don't think you're in the right place. If both of those are missing, you're definitely not in the right place."

ASK FOR AID — "Most clubs do a fairly decent job of doing fundraising and finding money for kids whose families can't afford the fees," said **Brandi Chastain** (USWNT 1988-2004). Discovered by her club coach at her brother's soccer practice, **Jessica McDonald** (USWNT 2016-present) benefited from the generosity of the families and benefactors of the Sereno Soccer Club in Phoenix, Ariz. "At the time, I didn't even realize (the scholarship) was happening. As I got older, everything hit me: 'Oh, my gosh, no wonder why I was always at my teammates' houses.' It was as if I had 18 other parents! I'm very grateful that people were willing to pay for my brother and me to play club soccer because we wouldn't be where we are today without it."

to ask permission from her parents prior to accepting the invitation to fly to China with a bunch of strangers. Scared to death, she brought her stuffed pet lion, Tamba, in her carry-on bag. "I'm still amazed all these years later that my parents said, 'Yes.'" said Kristine. A year later, the girl — who would appear in 354 international soccer games in 23 years to set the soccer record most unlikely ever to be broken by future women, or men — was still ambivalent about committing to just one sport. When Anson called to say National Team training camp was opening soon, she informed him she'd be a couple days late because there was a high school softball game she didn't want to miss.

"It was a different time, of course, but I played every sport, especially basketball and softball, and I loved it. I didn't want to give that up, even in college," said Kristine. Like her friend Joy Fawcett, she is making sure her own children have the same opportunity for a diverse childhood by running her own soccer academy that places college scholarships and winning individual games lowest on the list of priorities. Girls can play at the Kristine Lilly Soccer Academy through eighth grade and then decide if soccer, or some other sport, will be their focus. "I didn't want to spend all that money on club soccer; I'll be honest with you," said Kristine, who has been married to Brookline, Mass., firefighter David Heavey for nearly 30 years. "And my daughters, they're like me.

COURTESY OF LESLIE OSBORNE

Soccer Moms (clockwise from top left): Kristine Lilly, Aly Wagner, Heather Mitts Feeley, Leslie Osborne and Tisha Venturini-Hoch

They play basketball and lacrosse and gymnastics — and soccer. If one of my daughters gets to be 13 or 14 and says, 'Mommy, I'd really like to do more soccer,' then I'll say, 'OK, let's try it. Let's join a club that's a little bit more training and more commitment.' But the problem is, when you start to go down this path — and this is the fundamental problem with youth sports right now — you'll have kids who still want to play basketball and lacrosse, but the soccer club doesn't allow that. That's just wrong because so few kids are going to make it to college sports; the pay-to-play club system is so annoying to me."

Kristine believes her lifelong commitment to playing multiple sports, even recreationally as she played soccer professionally, was a major contributor to her most remarkable statistic of all: Even with all those years of playing all those games, she never suffered a major injury. "I have basically been cross-training my entire life and I think that helped," said Kristine. The research backs her thesis. Specializing in just one sport like soccer, especially prior to puberty, brings a 30 percent higher risk of injury than playing multiple sports each year. Some of the same research shows that, with the exception of figure skating and gymnastics, early specialization and joining club teams prior to middle school doesn't make a child any more likely to be successful in that sport later in life.

"People just assumed that the Tiger Woods model, where you put your child into a sport at a really young age and make them focus, was the ideal," said Tom Farrey, an ESPN journalist who founded the Aspen Institute's Sports & Society program in 2011 when his own sons were approaching the pay-to-play age. He has come to loathe the for-profit culture that has inadvertently reduced opportunities for lower-income girls and boys. "The Tiger model might lead to some really great outcomes. If the goal is to win a championship at age 8, then have your child join a soccer club at age 7. But we're now seeing the hazards of doing that, the burnout with most kids quitting by age 12

Kristine Lilly with her daughter, Sidney, at the 2012 Hall of Fame induction ceremony

or 13, plus the injuries from overusing the same muscles and ligaments over and over. There's also a lack of athletic creativity that comes from specialization and, ultimately, a failure to develop well-rounded athletes as they get older."

THERE ARE, AS SOCCER DAD STEVE BALDWIN WOULD DISCOVER, a few "I'm-playing-soccer-and-won't-take-no-for-an-answer" daughters in the world. In his case, he said, he found the most demanding, yet emotionally safe, environment and stuck with it. Taking Carlyn to the Braddock Road club, with a head coach named Larry Best, amounted to a second opinion that sounded valid. "I took the view with Larry, 'You've been coaching 30 years at this point, so that makes you the expert.' I saw him in the same way I see the kids' doctor, or their teacher. If Larry tells us to do something, we will do it." Right away, Steve said, his sideline support became more polite clapping than loud cheering. Larry taught him that winning games and tournaments meant little — until about age 16 — even if Steve occasionally had to help explain that to his own competitive child or some of the other mothers and fathers.

"A lot of parents went bat-shit crazy when Larry wasn't coaching to win every game, or their daughter wasn't getting what they thought was enough playing time," said Steve.

"My daughter hated to lose. Hated it. And there were times when Larry had to step in and calm her down. And a lot of parents yanked their daughters out of the club and left because they couldn't handle it. But Larry saw soccer development as a marathon and not a sprint; so many parents think a trophy or a game result at age 12 or 13 actually matters, but I learned right away from Larry to accept the fact that it didn't."

Icing a sore ankle, Carlyn had been awake most of the night prior to the Virginia State Cup finals in 2010. Filled with a mixture of pain and anxiety even

LASZLO SZIRTESI/ALAMY STOCK PHOTO

Carlyn Baldwin, left, playing in Europe for Sporting CP in 2017

Ability to Pay Should Never Impact Ability to Play

COMING FROM MAINE, WHERE ALMOST ALL OF MY YOUTH sports activities were either organized by the school, the Boys Club, or the other kids in the neighborhood, club soccer was part of the expensive culture shock of moving to Montgomery County in Maryland for my new job nearly a decade ago. Family budgets and priorities would need realignment; family vacations became the three-day weekends centered around my daughter's tournaments from Richmond, Va., to Gettysburg, Pa. We often find the lower-priced hotel option a few miles out of town and have skipped more than a few team dinners and eaten out of our cooler instead. Still, as my wife, Katie, always reminds me, we are among the privileged. She volunteers to help my daughter's club, the non-profit Potomac Soccer Association, raise money so that a child's ability to play soccer isn't hampered by the family's ability to pay the bills.

"We both work just one job, so we're lucky in that one aspect alone," Katie said. "We both have cars. What about the families with multiple jobs and one car, or no car? How can we make club soccer work for that family?" Those kinds of questions are a personal passion for our club's long-time executive director, Laurie Lane. Like many other club executives we spoke with for this book, Laurie places a priority on financial aid programs and fundraising events where every dollar counts toward the possibility of an underprivileged child advancing their love for the game. About 15 percent of Potomac's 600 players receive financial aid to offset the $2,300 annual dues. "I think when you're in soccer, you understand all the values that it brings to bear for the kids," Laurie said. "But it's not before the game with the Richmond Kickers, she was apoplectic 70 minutes later. Screaming and crying, Carlyn threw her soccer bag to the ground. As her teary-eyed teammates began to line up to congratulate their opponents on their victory, she picked up the bag and began to stammer toward the parking lot at the Ukrop Field in Richmond. Sternly, loudly, but not yelling, Larry simply said, "Carlyn." She dropped her head, then the bag, and begrudgingly took her place at the end of the line. "I was furious; it was the second year in a row that we lost in the finals and I thought we should have won," she said. "I was a little 13-year-old having a major attitude and Larry wasn't having any part of it."

Like Carlyn Baldwin, who played for Sporting CP in Portugal in 2020, her teammate Kaleigh Riehl wasn't interested in much athletically other than soccer. She rode horses with her older sister, but her father found his way to Larry Best even before Kaleigh was old enough at age 7 to be "carded" — which is soccer's universal identification form required for all tournaments sanctioned by any of the sport's national governing bodies. "My daughter wanted to be the best version of herself right from day one, and I thought we were lucky to have one of the most respected youth coaches in America right in our own back yard," said Mark Riehl, who had played soccer himself at the University of Virginia. He kept Kaleigh on the Braddock Road team and served as Larry's assistant coach for more than a decade, even after she enrolled at Penn State and helped win a national championship her freshman year. "Right away, Larry talked about a long-term

Angie . . . making the last shot count and coach Jason Travis getting wet

an easy thing to raise scholarships for soccer when you're competing against things like children's cancer programs for the same dollars."

Back in Maine in the 1960s, some of my fondest memories were selling lemonade and my mother's cookies to raise money for the Boys Club. It turns out that's one strategy that hasn't changed. Fifty years later, our family helped out at one of the Potomac Club's annual events, a bake sale and pizza party — complete with a dunk-the-coach tank at $3 per chance. Angie, my daughter, spent $15 of her allowance money attempting to kick a ball onto a small target 12 yards away. She missed on all five shots, as did every other player. Then she begged me for $3 more. When her coach, Jason Travis, landed in the water, Angie had scored a goal she'll probably remember forever. "When we do club soccer right, we're creating a family — an inclusive family," said Laurie. — P.T.

Steve Baldwin, far right, at a Washington Spirit meet-and-greet event featuring National Teamers Andi Sullivan, seated far left, and Rose Lavelle, seated far right

PAUL TUKEY

view, long-term goals, and gave the players the right mix of serious instruction — you focus when you're on the pitch — and the opportunity to have fun with your teammates between the drills and before and after practice."

As a parent-coach who stayed in the same hotels during the key tournaments as the other families, Mark heard earfuls about playing time in the fall of 2014, which was the sophomore year of high school for many of the girls. Kaleigh watched in frustration when several friends were dragged off the team by parents concerned about prospects for college scholarships; in the "DMV," an area comprised of northern Virginia, Montgomery County in Maryland, and the District of Columbia, about 25 different clubs compete for the same players. "Something I've always loved about Larry is his attitude: 'If you don't want to be on this team, if you don't believe in what we're doing here, that's fine. We don't need you,'" said Kaleigh, who joined Carlyn in leading Braddock Road to an national Under-16 championship that year despite the roster churn. Two years later she helped the United States to the U-20 World Cup, and in January of 2020 she became the 11th player picked overall in the draft for the National Women's Soccer League. We happened to talk with her on July 4, the day she celebrated her first professional game for New Jersey Sky Blue. "What Larry told us, and it proved to be true, is that to be great, and have a championship in the end when it matters, you need everyone on the same page with a common goal and vision."

LARRY HAD COME TO THE GAME IN A KINDER, gentler era, where sports junkies like him hung around fields because that's all there was to do. As an unpaid assistant coach in the late 1970s and early '80s, he had helped guide a bevy of pioneering and similarly unpaid

National Teamers including Megan McCarthy, Wendy Gebauer and April Heinrichs in a system of soccer that emphasized skill development more than athleticism. When a British protégée named Jill Ellis moved to northern Virginia at age 15, Larry helped mentor the future head coach of the U.S. National Team that won the 2015 and 2019 World Cups and exploded the game into the American psyche. He was aware of the game getting louder around him during his four decades as a youth coach, but Larry remained oblivious to all the noise once he blew the whistle to start a practice. His better players did get more playing time in important games, but he felt all players deserved the opportunity to improve.

"I think the kids that come to Braddock Road today are the same way they were back then; it's the parents who have changed," he said. "The kids want to play, to get better, to be challenged. The kids will listen, and appreciate the instruction. But parents today are 10 years ahead in their minds and they're constantly projecting, I might add, to the detriment of their children. It has become too cutthroat and not enough patience, a constant battle of winning now vs. where we were — always in the mindset of developing players and individuals. And Carlyn is a good example; Carlyn is a winner. When she loses, she's pissed, and those were always tough conversations. We were constantly talking about a bigger picture here in terms of what we're going after. We asked questions after every loss: 'Did you compete? Did you go out and give it your all? When you walked off the field, were you dead tired? If you couldn't walk, then you've done your job, win or lose.'"

For Carlyn's dad, the guy who once saw playing the game as punishment, a bigger picture than even he could have imagined was coming into focus by the time his daughter signed her first professional contract in Europe. In 2017,

Carlyn Baldwin, with Kaleigh Riehl and Braddock Road's 2014 national club championship trophy

Steve Baldwin had been approached by the owner of the Washington Spirit, one of the nine professional teams in the National Women's Soccer League, about providing a level of financial support. Two years later, Steve was asked if he'd like to become the team's majority owner. "Yes," he said, but on one condition: he insisted that his daughter's club soccer coach become chief executive officer of his new professional team.

"No," said Larry Best, calmly as ever. "I'm not interested. I am very happy in my space just doing what I do with kids." But Larry, who was inducted into the 20th class of the Virginia DC Soccer Hall of Fame in February of 2020, changed his mind; he knew he was dealing with one of America's most persuasive soccer Dads. "Steve put the pressure on, saying, 'Well, if you're not going to do it, I'm not doing it.' It's hard to say, 'No' to Steve."

Raising Tomorrow's Champions

Allowing Children to Find Their Own Pace and Path Through Soccer is the Standard Advice, But Not Everyone Listens

NO COURT IN AMERICA WAS GOING TO award Lori Lindsey's mother custody of her two children. Not in 1982, and certainly not in Indiana. So after Carol Lindsey left her husband for a woman, Larry Lindsey was left to his own survival and parenting instincts. That meant building a soccer goal in the back yard. It meant signing Lori up for every sport and team that her brother, Chris — older by 18 months — played for because there was only so much time in the day for a single father running his own collection agency. And it evolved into setting strict, non-negotiable priorities, like polishing the soccer cleats with mink oil prior to every match and at least 20 minutes of daily viewing of Wiel Coerver's innovative new VHS tapes focusing on soccer skills. Daily workouts were considered as essential as brushing teeth, and more so than combing hair. "You get your butt out back and practice soccer!" said Larry to his children. "That homework can wait."

As soon as he was certain Lori and Chris had talent for the game, Larry dove in even harder. He sat for soccer licensing certification tests and signed up to coach their teams. He stuffed more children than might have been legal into the back of his old Toyota van, drove them to games and ice cream stands, and yelled out "Frogs!" anytime his bodily function might have filled the vehicle with loud sounds and less than pleasant odors. If anyone on the one-girl team wasn't playing well, the man known as "Crazy Larry" in Indianapolis soccer circles let the boys hear about it in colorful terms that could be discerned by the parents three fields away. "He had no problem whatsoever telling the

players exactly what they were doing wrong, and it was the definition of wrong according to Larry," said his second wife, Susan. "He didn't spare anyone."

If Lori and Chris were the offenders? Well, that got its own special treatment back home. During one game in particular, when Lori was 8, her father noticed she was getting into the common children's habit of turning her back to the ball to protect herself when opponents kicked toward her in close proximity. Never mind that the boys

Lori Lindsey, with her Mom, Carol, and her Stepmom Susan Ferrer

were two or three years older, typically far larger, and the ball would sting like heck. "Lori! Stop turning!" yelled Larry. When Lori did it again, he fumed. At home later that evening, he began punting ball after ball at his daughter from less than 10 feet away, insisting each time that she not turn her head or body. It was a drill he forced her to practice repeatedly thereafter. "He thought it was his way of contributing to my success," said Lori, laughing at the story 30 years later. "From an early age he would say, 'You have something special, you have a talent. So I'm going to do all I can to push you as far as you can go.'"

At age 12, Lori began pushing back. She shaved lines in her eyebrows and bombed through the neighborhood on her BMX bicycle, revolting every time her father tried to remind her it was time to practice soccer. She enjoyed basketball, and thought for a while about skateboarding as her sporting future. "I just wanted to play, to be outside, to run around," said Lori. "My dad wasn't having it. He'd say, 'You're gonna crush soccer, you're gonna practice.'" Openly defiant by then, she skipped soccer practice, won a small role as Miep Gies in the seventh-grade production of "The Diary of Anne Frank" — and declared she was done with soccer for good. "I was like, 'Watch this, Dad. You're not going to get your way. I'm going to quit.'"

SEVERAL ORGANIZATIONS EXIST NATIONALLY to address how parents should, and should not, behave when it comes to their children's youth sports experience (see Page 72 and 252). The facts — half of all children quit organized sports by age 11, and more than

Abby Wambach, right, with her wife, Glennon Doyle, and their children

70 percent of girls quit sports including soccer by age 13 — are considered a national epidemic by campaigns like the Aspen Institute's "Don't Retire Kid" initiative. The blame, according to most of the experts, lies mostly at the feet of coaches and parents, who are too often turning the pressure of playing a game into anything but fun. The car ride home from games, in particular, is often cited as a miserable experience by children, who would rather travel with the grandparents if the option is available. When parents grill their children about everything from goals not scored and games not won, to minutes sitting on the bench, or what a coach may or may not have said, it can burn negative feelings into young psyches.

"Parents should say three things after the game," said soccer Hall of Famer Abby Wambach, who inherited three stepchildren in May of 2017 as a part of a package deal that included her new wife, Glennon Doyle. "One: Say, 'I love watching you play.' Two: Pick out a specific positive moment from the game that really showed their character. And three: Ask one question about how the game went. That's it. Those are the only things we say. I don't critique them; the kids just want to know that you're watching. They want to know that you *like* watching. They don't want you to break the game down and they don't want you to tell them what they should have been doing."

Abby comes from a background where her own father was heavily invested in her sporting escapades. Pete Wambach would slip his daughter as much as $25 for a goal scored, and sometimes ask her why she did didn't try harder to score the fourth goal after already netting three. She and Glennon offer no such incentives. On the sidelines

Letting Go is Parents' Greatest Form of Support

WHEN I WAS GROWING UP, I COMPETED WITH MY BROTHER in everything from basketball and football, to street hockey, swimming and running. It didn't matter that I was three years younger and significantly smaller; I always wanted to beat him and, older and wiser, he knew exactly how to push my buttons. To this day, we laugh about the song he used to sing to me, "I am the best, you are the worst!" We laugh even harder thinking about the time we were jumping on the bed, him pushing me off, and me crashing into the wall and breaking my arm. As crazy as that might sound, I have nothing but fond memories of our close bond and realize he was a huge part of making me the athlete I became.

I am sure my parents struggled to watch the competitive fire between the two of us, but I think they understood, even subconsciously, that I was always up for the fight. If they were ever tempted to intervene on my behalf, with my brother or anyone else, they resisted. Their support was always present — with coaches, teammates and opponents — but always from appropriate distance. Shortly after I retired from professional soccer, my mother and I were walking in her neighborhood. She turned to me and said, "Jo, I want to tell you a story. I think you are at a point now where you will fully understand."

We had been at our neighborhood pool and tennis courts, she said, and I was playing my brother in tennis when I was 7. I lost to him that day (as I would for so many days after). As my mother watched from a hill next to the court, I was enraged at my defeat. As we all walked home together, with me still fuming, Mom said she knew no words would cheer me up — so she simply squeezed my hand that was interlocked with hers. We walked farther from the courts and further from the pain, silently step by step, until a smile broke out on my face. I said out loud to her, unprovoked, "I love you, too." I then ran off ahead to catch up with my brother.

COURTESY OF JOANNA LOHMAN

Joanna, with her mother and Abby Wambach

When my Mom finished the story I was quite emotional. That she would remember that detail, a hand squeeze from 30 years earlier, told me how intimately connected she had been with my journey — even as she had the wisdom to let me live my own life from such a young age. I went on to be successful not because my parents made me do it, or willed me to do it, but rather because they were walking supportively beside or behind me the whole time. I thanked my Mom and said out loud, "I hope, if and when I ever have kids, I can be a Mom like you one day." — J.L.

A Parent-Player-Coach Contract

THE NATIONAL TEAM WAS ALL OF 8 YEARS OLD when All-American goaltender Skye Eddy Bruce was a senior in college and still dreaming of joining **Mia Hamm** on the international field. The problem is she had to face Mia first in the 1993 NCAA final and hope to impress Anson Dorrance, the North Carolina coach, who was still leading the National Team. Though she would be named defensive MVP of the tournament that year, her George Mason team lost 6-0 and Skye figured that ended her playing dream before it started. She has remained in the game, however, with a new goal: help parents understand what it takes to raise well-adjusted children on, and off, the field. "The trick for us as parents is to let children lead the way in their own lives," said Skye, who founded the Soccer Parenting Association. Here is the universal contract to which she encourages all parents, coaches and youth clubs to adhere:

ACTIVE HEALTH — We acknowledge the importance of long-term athlete development and we understand that youth soccer participation supports an active lifestyle; the longer children continue to play sports, the more likely they are to be healthy and active adults. **COACH INTEGRITY** — We acknowledge the positive impact a coach can make on a child's life, and we commit to holding coaches to a high standard of integrity, professionalism and compassion so our children feel optimistic about their potential, even in the face of defeat. **LIFE LESSONS** — We support our children's youth soccer participation because we want them to develop grit, determination, and resiliency while learning the empathy, compassion and solidarity that will make them caring and committed adults. **SOCCER KNOWLEDGE** — We foster our children's love of soccer by seeking to educate ourselves about the rules, nuances and intricacies of the game.

Coach Skye Eddy Bruce, with her Richmond Strikers

COURTESY OF SKYE EDDY BRUCE

LOVE OF THE GAME — We acknowledge that every child has varying levels of athletic potential and we seek to establish an environment where ALL children can play youth soccer because they LOVE TO PLAY, not because they want a college scholarship or a professional contract. **BALANCED OUTLOOK** — We seek to use a clear perspective when making soccer choices for our children, ensuring the decisions are in the best interest of the child's long-term happiness, contentment and positive attitude.
— www.soccerparenting.com

now watching her stepdaughters, Abby said she often needs to walk away from what she's seeing and hearing from the parents all around her who are convinced their own daughters will one day follow in her footsteps. It makes her own father seem mellow by comparison. "The thing that makes me sad the most is how different the sidelines are for my kids than when I was going through it at their ages," said Abby, considered one of the most dominant youth soccer players in American history. "You had a random father or mother who would yell, but for the most part growing up, it was just go out and play and then go home. Now, the sidelines are covered with parents who are filming the games, and parents who are yelling at other parents, and parents who are yelling at referees and coaches. Parents yell at each other and their own children — because the parents think that they have the kid that's going to make it to the National Team. We all know the statistics; it's a very, very, very slim chance that your one specific kid is going to actually make it."

HORACE PUGH WAS THAT FATHER, THE GUY HIS FRIENDS call the lottery winner with the can't-miss kid. His oldest daughter, Brianna, earned a soccer scholarship to the University of Oregon just about the time he was offering full-throated sideline critiques of his youngest child, Mallory, then age 12. "Go, go, go!" he yelled. Her talent could be spellbinding at times. Watching his daughter, blessed with almost unprecedented speed while dribbling the ball through and around helpless young defenders, Horace felt he was only offering encouragement: "Come on, pick it up! Faster! Come on! Get the ball!" Little

Mallory Pugh, holding the national Player of the Year trophy, with her father, Horace, and mother, Karen

more than halfway through a game early in the season, the prodigy, who was just four years away from her first National Team appearance, made it clear she wasn't enjoying the non-stop pep talk. Mallory stopped cold in the middle of the field, turned toward her father, and said loudly enough for everyone to hear: "Dad! Shut up!" Horace tried to hold his head high when he felt every eyeball on the sidelines staring his way, but inside he was instantly bruised. "Well, that's disrespectful," he thought to himself, while resolving to remain quiet for the remainder of the game.

A decade later, Horace sees that confrontation as a critical moment, both in Mal's career and in their relationship. "At that point, she had had a ball at her feet her whole life," he said. "She had such a passion for the game and, as a Dad, you want to share in that. You mean well, right? So in that moment, I was a little hurt. But I tried it her way in her next game. I said, 'You know what? I'm just gonna sit here and let her play.' And she literally

Alex Morgan, right, with Havana Solaun

PAUL TUKEY

shredded this team. It might have been four or five goals scored. I think it was because she just didn't have that pressure from the sideline. That was eye-opening for me, to just keep the game fun for her."

That was Pamela Morgan's focus, too, when she began carting her third daughter to recreational soccer at age 5. She coordinated the orange slices for halftime and all the post-game treats while her husband, Mike, focused his energies on other sports like basketball and volleyball and, especially, coaching softball. He was a baseball guy at heart, amazed at how well his daughter, Alex, could throw, catch and hit. In the blink of a 9-year-old's mood swing, however, Alex crushed her father's field of dreams and told him she preferred kicking the ball instead. "But you're so good!" he said in a mild protest. He wasn't quite Crazy Larry Lindsey, but Mike Morgan soon grabbed soccer by the throat in his own way

Negative Sideline Commentary Never Wins

DON'T RECALL THE NAME OF THE FIELD OR THE SCORE OF THE GAME. I do know we were in McLean, Va., on a Sunday morning and the 8-year-old girls were doing what 8-year-olds will do on a soccer field if the referee lets them — which is to run around without regard to the rules. I was mad when the first player was pushed to the ground with no whistle. When it happened a fourth time, I couldn't keep my mouth shut. "Call the game the right way, ref! Someone's going to get hurt!" I said, loudly enough to get his attention. "Consider this a warning!" he said, pointing to the corner where I often preferred to stand in those days. Off by myself, I was less likely to hear complaints from my wife about my commentary that I thought was going to make my daughter play better.

Sure enough, another girl went down, this time close enough for the ref to hear my softly spoken comment: "That's a foul." He stopped the game again. "They're kids!" he said, steaming. "Yes, kids who are never going to learn if you don't call the game!" I said, now mad as hell. "Leave my field. Now!" he demanded. "You're a pathetic excuse for a referee," I replied, making it a point to land one more blow before I exited stage right and watched from the parking lot. I left there defiantly insisting to my wife that I was in the right. That lasted until I re-told the

Our co-author . . . keeping it positive

story to my friend, Allen, who abruptly put me in my place. "Don't be THAT Dad," he said. "You're better than that." A few years, and many interviews with National Team soccer parents later, I now realize not only that Allen was right, I had also been wrong to be so vocal — on the field and off — throughout the first few years of my daughter's soccer life. That ref was wrong, too. I could have filed a straight-forward complaint, through my club, to the league. That would have had a far greater chance of curing his misguided notion that young girls don't deserve to learn the game from thoughtful, rule-abiding referees.

As for my daughter, I have since learned to just tell her I love watching her play — even if I have to bite my tongue hard on some days. It made me feel better to know that even Hall of Famer Brandi Chastain, like so many of us soccer parents, still struggles with the same issues of misplaced passion. "I see my son on the basketball court, or playing flag football, or swimming and I desperately want to say out loud, 'Dig down! Try harder! If you just give it that one extra ounce of effort, you're going to see a massive benefit,'" she said. "I always need to remind myself that the experience is his, and not mine, and if I'm always in his face, he's going to reject it." — P.T.

— signing up for coaching lessons, borrowing the VHS tapes from the local library, and rising at 4 a.m. on practice days to get his masonry business up and running early so he could be finished in time to drive all over Diamond Bar, Calif., and collect players for Alex's team. "He needed players to win, so if that meant he had to get out of bed early to make it work, he was going to do it," said Pamela. "Mike is like Alex, or Alex is like Mike; they both hate to lose."

Future National Team coach Jill Ellis would endearingly call Alex a soccer "predator" with an insatiable desire to win. When Alex was breaking into the professional ranks, one of her childhood idols, Mia Hamm, told *Sports Illustrated* she enjoyed seeing Alex "getting a little pissed off when she doesn't score" near the goal. "It's fantastic," Mia said. "She wants to be a factor every time she steps out there." It was an edge forged back

home in Diamond Bar, where two sisters, three and six years older, never let Alex win without earning it first. By age 10, according to her mother, Alex would study her sisters' movements for hours on end, strategize silently in a corner about Monopoly just so she could compete in family games, and track her squats, crunches and lunges in a journal. When the family instituted an incentive-based system to earn points — for things like good grades, extracurricular activities, helping around the house, and goals scored — that the daughters could one day convert into cash toward a first teenage car, Alex turned it into her personal Wheel of Fortune and wound up with a Lexus. "She almost sent me into bankruptcy," Mike joked to *Sports Illustrated*.

Still, the Morgans took an unusually slow, methodical approach to their daughter's ascent into soccer. Alex was 13 when she tried out for her first club travel team hoping to compete for a California state cup championship. To

Alex Morgan, off the field

this day, said her mother, getting cut remains one of the most difficult, yet important experiences of Alex's life. "We asked the coach, 'Please let us know if she's going to make it, because we need time to find another team,' and he said, 'No doubt, she's definitely in,'" said Pamela. "Well, then he cut her right before the tournament, so she didn't end up playing. She was just devastated." For the first time in her life, Alex doubted her own ability. "Maybe I'm not that good after all," she said. "Maybe I don't have what it takes."

Her parents could see Alex was better than the majority of the girls on the team, but opted to let the disappointment be a life lesson rather than try to intervene with the coach. "She should have made it," said Pamela. "But I just told Alex that she needed to prove it on the field beyond the shadow of a doubt every single time she stepped out there. I said, 'Coaches are people, too, and they make mistakes just like everyone else.' And my husband backed me up." Nearly two decades later, that coach is still around town lamenting a missed opportunity to have had one of America's most famous athletes on his resume. "He has apologized about a million times," said Pamela. "He said he was in a bind because he was going to have to cut another kid to give Alex a spot — and those parents would have gone crazy on him. That's just not the way we chose to handle it."

GLORIA AVERBUCH KNOWS A THING OR TWO about how parents ought to behave in regard to their children's sporting lives. "Do not push your child, or engage her in inappropriate competition, such as serious play at a young age," is one of the bits of advice she offers in the 1999 book titled "Goal! The Ultimate Guide for Soccer Moms and Dads." "What is true of all the soccer superstars I know is that these were their dreams, not their parents' dreams," she wrote in 2002's "The Vision of a Champion," co-authored with Anson Dorrance, who coached Gloria's oldest daughter, Yael, at the University of North Carolina. An accomplished distance runner, Gloria is the author of more than a dozen sports-related books, including five on soccer. Yet even with all that wisdom flowing to the keypad from her fingertips, Gloria admits it only masked the sometimes extreme ebb and flow of parental emotions that began the day that Ashley Michael Hammond — her co-author for "Goal: The Ultimate Guide" — brought Yael to a local field in Montclair, N.J., in 1995 when she was 9. It was

just an hour, with some kicking, passing and dribbling, yet at the end of the session Ashley changed the family's life forever with one declaration: "This is the best young player this town has ever produced."

Gloria nearly fell over backward. "Whoa!" she said, reliving the memory nearly a quarter century later. "That was the moment that blew my socks off and began the process of

Yael Averbuch, with her mother, Gloria

me understanding who Yael was and where she wanted to go." It was also the instant, according to Gloria, when she started to understand that the outcome of her daughter's journey was going to impact her maternal instincts and self-image in ways she had never expected. She recalls one game in particular that still leaves her breathless. When Courtney Jones, daughter of NFL All-Pro tight end Brent Jones, scored a goal to tie a game at North Carolina, the burly football player swooped up Gloria in the Fetzer Field stands and spun her in the air in celebration. "The big NFL guy is gorgeous and he's wonderful and he's nice and he picks me up," said Gloria. "Oh . . . My God! That moment! Everything about it was wonderful. My daughter has given me so many great moments, great, great, great moments."

Yael's single-minded approach to soccer landed her on every youth national team that U.S. Soccer had to offer beginning when she was 14 — and ultimately the National Team by age 21 — but in a subjective team sport like soccer, her success was never a given, nor a linear path upward. During Thanksgiving in 2000, with Yael off trying to make one of her first youth national teams, she phoned her uncle's home in Lexington, Mass., to share some bad news: She had just been cut by a coach who told her she lacked the athleticism to advance further in the game. The instant she hung up the phone, with the rest of her extended family in the next room, Gloria sat on the bed and bawled uncontrollably. "I felt something deeply painful, and I'll be honest, this was all about me," she admitted. "Whether I was living vicariously as an athlete or I was having a midlife crisis, I'm still not sure. I just know I took some of the lowest points so hard. I tried to show wisdom face to face with my children, but boy oh boy." Gloria stands by all the advice in all her books; parents really do need to step back and allow their children to own their own soccer experience — even if she was often feeling internal turmoil as a mother. "For all these years, until the moment Yael stopped playing professionally, I've had a tremendous struggle to separate my personal issues from her ups and downs. She was more mature and resilient than I ever was. I know parents get a bad name when they yell and they get hysterical — and some of them annoy me, too. But I do have empathy."

IF A REVIEW OF NATIONAL TEAM FAMILY HISTORIES taught us anything, it's that no single style of upbringing is a predictor of success. While most parents of these hugely successful women seem to tend toward the attitudes of the Pughs and Morgans, who learn to take a supportive, but hands-off approach to their children, National Teamers have collectively overcome several instances of overbearing mothers and fathers, as well as divorces, abandonments, estrangements, and walking away from the game — at least for a while. If the women ever had a poster parent for how not to behave through the whole process, from forced practices at age 5, to punting punishments at age 8, and father-daughter power struggles at age 12, Larry Lindsey realizes he's probably the prime candidate. "I'm not sure there is one right answer," said Larry, a little less crazy during his retirement in Florida. "You do what you feel is the best for your children and go from there."

Lori Lindsey, with her father, Larry, and brother, Chris

Lori Lindsey exited her would-be acting career after her seventh-grade turn as Anne Frank's savior and soon came back to soccer — this time on her own terms. She was no longer turning her back on the ball, or on any other soccer challenge that her father could devise to make her better. "What I found out by quitting is that, actually, I do love this game," said Lori, a member of the 2011 World Cup team. "I missed it. When I returned,

Lori Lindsey, left, with National Teamer Mary Harvey as State Department envoys

it was honestly like a switch going off." Instead of leaving the Coerver tapes sticking out of the VHS machine to fake her father into believing she had watched, she tried to absorb every minute. At her father's urging, she began lifting weights in the garage years before it became common practice for young athletes. She even shoveled the snow out of the family's Indiana yard in winter so she could have space to get in soccer workouts and wind sprints.

Lori learned to work out her life off the field, too. Larry and his wife, Susan, maintained a functional relationship with Lori's non-traditional mother, which helped ensure a support system when Lori began to explore issues related to her own sexual orientation during her teen years. Larry had maintained a don't-ask-don't-tell position on that topic with his daughter for many years, until a post-game dinner at an Applebee's restaurant in Washington, D.C., during Lori's rookie professional season in 2002. Halfway through dinner, years of bottled-up emotion spilled out when Larry blurted, "Do you like boys, or girls?" Lori cried instantly and moved over to hold tightly to the man who raised her. "Girls," she said. Larry cried, too. Years later, though, that story — coming out to Dad at Applebee's — is just one in a mass collection of treasured Lindsey family memories that make themselves and everyone around them laugh out loud. "My Dad was kind of the opposite of just about every other Dad, and being with Crazy Larry was tough, really tough," said Lori, who became a professional television announcer after her soccer retirement. "But at the same time, I really felt the love underneath it all. That's what I carry forward with me in life."

7 : COACHING

The King of Santa Clara

One Long-Time Mentor Sets a Standard for How to Practice the Profession of Impacting Women's Lives

TIED 0-0, MIRED IN A SECOND-HALF RUT against Connecticut in the quarterfinals of the NCAA tournament in 1999, head coach Jerry Smith had seen enough. He turned and readied a substitute for the woman who would become the most decorated player in Santa Clara University history. When the ball rolled out of bounds and the referee waved the replacement player into the game, sophomore Aly Wagner didn't even bother to turn toward the bench. Jerry raised his dry, deep voice. "Aly." He said it again, this time louder: "Aly! Out!" Aly finally turned toward her coach, bewildered, and pointed to herself. "Me?" With precious seconds clicking away during the playoff game, the 2002 winner of the Hermann Trophy — awarded to the consensus pick as the best player in the country — began walking slowly, reluctantly toward the sideline. As she approached him, with her pace shortening, the stoic coach fumed. When she finally reached the sideline and turned to walk toward the water cooler, Jerry had other ideas.

"You come here," he said in a quiet tone that stopped her cold in front of her other sidelined teammates as the game played on. "Don't you ever give me the slow walk off the field. I love you. You're an awesome player, but you were playing poorly and you're coming off this field. Don't think that YOU can't make mistakes or YOU can't play poorly. And don't EVER think about giving me

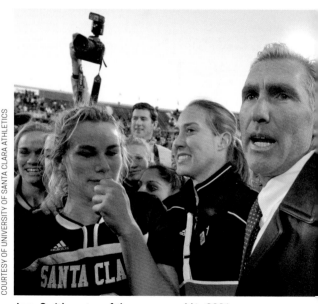

Jerry Smith, on top of the soccer world in 2001

the slow walk off the field again. I won't disrespect you in public. You don't disrespect me in public." With her team seemingly energized by the move, Santa Clara would take a 1-0 lead while the future soccer voice of Fox Sports pouted, literally squatting on the water cooler beyond the end of the bench. When her team scored again, Aly stood up, walked past her teammates, and took the seat next to her coach. "What are you doing?" asked Jerry. "Are you going to put me back in?" she responded. "I took you out and we scored two goals; why would I put you back in?" said Jerry, seemingly settling the issue. Aly, though, was nothing if not persistent. "Come on!" she begged repeatedly. Jerry Smith relented. "If you play better," he said, "I'll put you back in." Aly Wagner didn't miss a beat: "If you were coaching better, I'd be back in the game already."

COACHES ARE QUEEN OR KING OF THE GAME. Whereas individual sports are ruled objectively by results, the team sports, at any level, are controlled by the women and men who dole out the players' most valued currency: playing time. In the pay-to-play world of club soccer, the coach can make the difference between a girl getting better and building a future through the sport, or riding the bench, bursting the thin bubble of a dream, changing teams, or all too often quitting the game entirely. Marian Dalmy Dougherty was on her own Rocky Mountain high when her personal narrative was knocked back down to earth. "You're soft," Jerry calmly told Marian, a four-time MVP of the annual State Cup tournaments for her club team in Colorado. The high school sophomore had just finished playing for Jerry in an Under-19 National Team tournament in Houston. "For being so tall, you can't head the ball. You can't play with your back facing the goal. There are so many things you need to work on if you truly

COURTESY OF SANTA CLARA UNIVERSITY ATHLETICS

Marian Dalmy Dougherty, wearing the captain's arm band

want to make the National Team someday." Stunned, Marian returned to Colorado vowing to never speak to the verbal assailant ever again. "I hated Jerry Smith," said Marian Dalmy Dougherty, now an executive at Nike. "I genuinely hated him. I vividly remember leaving Houston saying, 'I'll never play for Jerry Smith ever again.'"

Marian would be even more stunned, a year later, when one of the first college recruiting letters in her Lakewood, Colo., mailbox was addressed from the small Jesuit school named for its locale on the southern tip of the San Francisco Bay. Santa Clara had just dethroned North Carolina for the National Championship in 2001 and now the team wanted Adam and Diane Dalmy to bring their daughter for the weekend when the community would

Owning Your Own Narrative: Anson's Five-Point Scale

NORTH CAROLINA UNIVERSITY WOMEN'S COACH Anson Dorrance shared the five-point grading scale he uses, with 5 being the highest possible ranking, when he meets with his players three times each year to formally assess their personal progress. He asks players to grade themselves honestly, then he and the other UNC coaches offer their assessments. "A 5 means you're an Olympic or National Team player in that particular category," he said. "A 4.5 is a professional level player; a 4.0 is a UNC starter. Then, a 3.5 is a kid that plays in every half, and we believe in subbing — because I believe in trying to play the kids I recruit. A 3 is someone who travels, but doesn't play. And underneath 3 is a kid who doesn't make the travel team, and obviously doesn't play unless we're winning by three or more goals." He applies the scale, which he said helps build a player's "personal narrative," to these eight categories:

SELF-DISCIPLINE — UNC ties this score to a player's performance on a physical endurance trial known as the "Beep Test," a series of 20-yard runs.

COMPETITIVE FIRE — "How much does a player want to win the one-on-one drills?" said Anson. "That shows a lot."

SELF-BELIEF — "This rating belongs exclusively to the player," he said. "I will never interfere with a person's self-belief. If they think they're God's gift to the game, I will never try to deconstruct that. Even if it's delusional, I still won't touch it — because one of the hardest things to construct in a young woman, and actually women in general, is confidence."

LOVE OF THE BALL — "Lots of players say they love the ball," he said. "But let me tell you about **Tobin Heath** (USWNT 2008-present). She juggled a ball to class; she put her foot on the ball during class. Then she nutmegged people on the sidewalk on the way back to her dorm. That's love of the ball."

LOVE OF PLAYING THE GAME — "Some kids play sports for different reasons," he said. "The ones who love it the most are the ones who will go the furthest."

PA IMAGES/JOHN WALTON/ALAMY STOCK PHOTO

Tobin Heath, always juggling

LOVE OF WATCHING THE GAME — "Do players spend Friday nights hanging out with their friends, or viewing game film?" he asked.

GRIT — "Talent is common," said Anson. "But grit — which is a combination of courage, firmness of mind, strength of character, and resolve — is what matters. Go read Angela Duckworth's book (*Grit: The Power of Passion and Perseverance*) on the subject."

COACHABILITY — Anson doesn't allow players to grade themselves in this category: "This is my evaluation of whether or not they're responding to anything I'm telling them."

celebrate its first-ever national championship in any sport. The Dalmys were thrilled; Marian was instantly defiant. "I am NOT going to Santa Clara! No way! No chance!" she said. A battle — in the normally calm household — would ensue. "I dug in. Hard," said Marian. "I said, 'You can't force me to go to college where I don't want to go!' But my Mom dug in, too. It was an unofficial visit, so she pointed out that I wasn't making a commitment . . . And she's an attorney who has a way of getting what she wants."

In the meantime, more letters arrived from a Who's Who of women's college soccer powerhouses. Notre Dame, Virginia, UCLA and Texas offered formal visits, with promises of instant currency. "I had schools telling me they would give me anything I wanted, including playing right away," said Marian. "I was offered scholarships. Some of the schools were having their football coaches writing me letters telling me they needed me at their schools." Rather than shower her with praise, however, Jerry Smith simply placed the Dalmys at a table with National Teamers Leslie Osborne and Danielle Slaton and their families and let Marian listen to the stories of how a championship atmosphere was borne from a vision that began when Jerry Smith became head coach in 1987. Santa Clara has become one of only two Division I schools (along with the University of Portland) in the country where women's soccer is arguably the most prestigious sport on campus and, by the time the dinner plates were cleared from tables that night, Marian had changed her mind and was ready to commit. Jerry told her he would think about it.

"IF I COULD USE ONE WORD TO DESCRIBE my program, or I could pick one word to use for advice to other coaches out there, it would be authentic — as in always be authentic," Jerry Smith told us in the summer of 2020 as he approached his 34th season in the same job. "I'm not a coach who tells you what you want to hear. I always try to be very honest and authentic. I do remember saying, 'Marian, you are so soft. You're such a soft kid; I just don't know if you're going to make it.' I remember emphasizing that she was really going to struggle trying to play at the next level."

As much as Marian would try to prove her coach wrong for the next four years, Jerry might have seemed hell-bent on proving he was right; from his perspective, she often had more to give. She would start 14 games as a freshman and score

Marian Dalmy Dougherty, center, with Angela Hucles representing the State Department in Morocco

six goals, earning the Coach's Award from her teammates. She then proceeded to start 23 of 25 games as a sophomore, be named all-conference, and even earned designation as captain heading into her junior year. Early that season with the team struggling, however, he called Marian and her two co-captains into his office after a particularly bad practice. "Look guys, things are not going well for us this year, and it's my fault," said the coach

Marian Dalmy Dougherty, foreground, second from left, with the Colorado high school all-state team in 2002

matter-of-factly. Marian squirmed, as if he were talking directly to her. No one said a word. "Don't you want to know why it's my fault," he asked, calmly breaking the silence. "Yeah, coach. Why?" she said. "You know why it's my fault?" he asked again for emphasis. "My most important decision that I make all year for this program is who the captains are. I chose the wrong frickin' captains. I chose you three and I knew I shouldn't have done it. Our team is soft because we have soft leadership and I wish I could find a way out of the situation."

One year, after a particularly bad loss to Notre Dame on a Sunday, Jerry steamed in his office Monday morning before abruptly calling Marian on the team's off day. "Get your team together and be on the field, in your gear, in 30 minutes," he said. She tried to protest, reminding him that her teammates were nursing injuries, icing sore muscles, attending classes, or resting. "Listen to what I just told you," he said without raising his voice and then hung up the phone. As players arrived on the field, still pulling on jerseys and stuffing shin guards into their socks, there were no soccer balls to be found. That meant just one thing. "We ran. And ran," said Marian, ironically now a senior product manager in the running shoes division for Nike. "I have never been beaten to the ground so much in my entire life. Girls were dropping out; we were crying, saying, 'I can't make it.' He kept telling us to run another 120-yard sprint because we didn't make the time he set. We ran about 50 of these 120-yarders. Sixty minutes straight we ran. At one point I remember putting one girl on my back just to get her across the line — because he kept saying, 'If the whole team doesn't make it, you're going to run it again.'"

When Jerry finally blew the whistle, he ordered the team inside the video room, where Marian felt scorched by every minute of the coach's ire from the two-hour session of pointing out poor play and even worse leadership. "The one thing I'm not going to stand for is hypocritical ideas," he told the players. "Don't talk to me about going deep into the tournament and playing for an NCAA championship. You can't say this is your goal when

Mr. Right: Attitude Means Everything in a Coach

BY 2010 WHEN I WAS — IN THE PARLANCE OF PROFESSIONAL SPORTS — a journeywoman, I had already experienced just about every kind of coach. There were yellers, even screamers. There were authoritarians and flakes. There was Jerry Smith (see Page 80), who emboldened me as a captain of my U-21 team, and even took all of us skydiving as part of a team-building experience I'll never forget. And there are some coaches I don't even care to remember.

As a free agent coming off one of my more disappointing seasons with my hometown Washington Freedom in the Women's Professional Soccer League, the door seemed closed on my National Team career. Not ready to quit the game, however, I spent the offseason training with the best team in Japan and simultaneously rejuvenated my body and love for soccer. That spring, I was just hoping that some guy named Paul Riley would even give me a chance as a walk-on. Yes, that Paul

Riley. If you know soccer, you're likely aware that the native of England has since won two National Women's Soccer League championships and is considered one of the most innovative coaches in the world. But, back then, he was basically like me, a soccer vagabond with a varied coaching resume featuring colleges, youth teams, and from 2006-2009 a minor-league team known as the Long Island Fury. The Philadelphia Independence, a new expansion team in the WPS, would be a fresh start for both of us.

Paul innately understood the importance of team chemistry. One of his first moves was pushing ownership to build us a players' lounge, a by-no-means glamorous sanctuary painted in team colors of yellow, blue and gray where the fridge was stocked, the snack bowls were full and the couches were comfortable. The door was always open in Paul's office, located right in the lounge, where players could talk about anything and everything. I'll never forget bringing in my own lounge chair and spending hours in this room, laughing, crushing in ping pong and reading

Joanna, with Paul Riley

COURTESY OF JOANNA LOHMAN

the newspaper while elevating my ever-sore legs. I credit our title run as much to the brain-testing, intensely competitive training as I do to the moments shared eating goldfish in our oasis.

Many times that season I asked myself, "Where has this guy been all my life?" He ran a master class in what Dr. Colleen Hacker, the long-time psychologist for the National Team, calls "catch them being good." Rather than drone on about mistakes, he accentuated the positive in every player. "Look how Joanna cuts out passing lanes, baits the player into the space, and picks off the ball," he said. "It is that key defensive play that allows us to attack in dangerous spaces." Wow! No coach in my career had ever offered such a nuanced observation. By helping everyone on that team feel better about themselves, he was able to take a team of misfits and castaways into the championship game in its first season — and he even helped me get called into another National Team camp. The game of life needs more Paul Rileys. — J.L.

these are your actions on the field; that just is not going to work. You want to back down on your goals? You want to say, 'I'm soft; we're soft? We want to be a .500 team?' Or are you better than that?"

"JERRY IS BRILLIANT WHEN IT COMES TO MOTIVATING PEOPLE," said Brandi Chastain, the soccer Hall of Famer who infamously tore off her jersey after the clinching penalty kick in the 1999 World Cup. She had transferred to Santa Clara from the University of California in 1989 and proceeded to fall in love with her coach. Jerry and Brandi were married in June of 1996, sneaking in a wedding only a few weeks from the start of the Atlanta Olympics that introduced Brandi and the National Team to the American public with a gold medal victory in front of 76,000 fans at the University of Georgia's football stadium. When Jerry states, "I love badass women," he's the most animated version of himself. "That's what I look for in kids I recruit. I want ass kickers on my team; I want badass women on my team. My wife is badass. The world needs more badass women!"

Marian Dalmy Dougherty, with Joe Elsmore at the Nike campus in 2020

When it came time to pick the team for the 2007 World Cup, Jerry made a phone call to then U.S. coach Greg Ryan with a message: Marian Dalmy is a badass and you need to give her a shot. Greg, facing his first international tournament, said he already had too many players, not too few. Jerry doubled down for the player who had withstood everything he knew he could throw at her. "I'm telling you, Greg, this kid just tore it up for me in her last year at Santa Clara. You won't be disappointed." Later that spring, with Jerry waiting anxiously to hear the results of his recommendation, Marian called him. She spoke slowly at first, in a somber tone: "Well, thanks coach . . . Thanks for all your help . . . I gave it my best shot . . ." Then she paused one last time. "And I made the team!" When Jerry abruptly hung up, she called back. "Hey, coach, did you hear what I said?" she asked. The coach continued his ruse. "I've always told you our thing at Santa Clara is honesty," he said, trying to feign a stern tone. "You're gonna frickin' lie to me like that? Marian, you're the softest kid I've ever coached. There's no way you're playing in the World Cup for the National Team." Jerry hung up again.

"Jerry is one of my favorite human beings, but our road together has been so funny," said Marian, speaking both literally and figuratively. The player and coach still get together for dinner whenever Santa Clara visits its northern rivals, the University of Portland. Marian tours Jerry's current generation of players through the Mia Hamm building and the Nike offices, both to inspire them about what soccer can help build, but also to share the life lessons she carries forward from a man who, at times, pushed her almost beyond the edge of what she thought she could bear. "Santa Clara was the best decision I've ever made in my entire life," said Marian, who retired from professional soccer in 2013 just prior to joining Nike. "Don't get me wrong; he was tough. But the experience I had there as a player, as a student, and as a person, helped me grow so much. Jerry is an incredible soccer coach, but he is even a more incredible human being. He cares so much about your success off the pitch that, when I think of the time he invested in me as an individual, I'll be grateful to him for the rest of my life."

The key word from that compliment, according to Jerry, is "individual." Too often, he said, coaches from all levels of sports spend way too much time addressing the entire team, but scarcely any time addressing individual players and their families. No two players are alike, nor should coaches treat them as such. "The real task in coaching is taking the time to get to know everyone; that's why the biggest part of my job is 30 half-hour weekly meetings with every player on my team," said Jerry, who founded the Coaching For Life Academy several years ago to bring the lessons of soccer to other coaches, businesses and community leaders across the country. "It would be simpler to treat every player the same way, but that's not how life works, nor is it how leadership and potential is revealed. By spending the time with people, you begin to learn what they can handle, and how far you can push them. You begin to build trust so that when you push them, they are more likely to respond favorably."

COURTESY OF SANTA CLARA UNIVERSITY ATHLETICS

Julie Johnston Ertz, at Santa Clara

The hallmark of the Santa Clara teams of which he is most proud, according to Jerry, is how personal accountability and freedom of expression have gone hand in hand through three and a half decades. His adherence to rules is legendary. Jerry once simultaneously forced and helped a promising sophomore to transfer to another soccer school because her father broke one of his cardinal directives: parents are never allowed to ask him about their daughter's playing time or position on the field. Yet he said he never minds when a player questions his moves and motives, provided the discussion is handled properly and out of the public eye. One of his favorite stories involves calling current National Team superstar Julie Johnston Ertz down to a hotel lobby in Oregon one Sunday morning during her sophomore season. He said he had an epiphany on Saturday night that she should move from her customary center midfielder position back to the center defensive position on the field to make the team more competitive. "No!" she said in an immediate protest. "That's not going to work! We won't score any goals; we won't be as good a team." Julie refutes her coach's recollection that she shoved her chair in anger on the way back to the elevator, yet she turned out to be correct in her assessment when Santa Clara tied Oregon 0-0 in a game the visitors should have won. "I let her talk and vent and argue," said Jerry. "I've surrounded myself with ass kickers. These are people that have opinions and they're strong willed, the way I have encouraged them to be. I'm not trying to suppress it at all. But at some point, as a coach and a leader, you've got to make a decision. We can't have anarchy."

ANOTHER HALLMARK OF SANTA CLARA is how its teams deploy creativity and finesse as they move the ball up the field. Rather than focus most practices on predictable moves and repetitions in a small area of the field, which is a near constant of modern soccer coaching, Jerry prefers to practice in full-squad formation, 11 vs. 11, on the entire field and teach his players to focus on the various options that exist within each play. Avoiding the temptation of "joystick" coaching, in which he would attempt to direct player movements or bark constant commands from the sidelines, Jerry typically stands quietly regardless of the score or situation. Few players have appreciated that freedom more than Danielle Slaton, who was lightning fast and a 4.0 honor student from nearby San Jose, Calif., getting the full-court recruiting press from Stanford. "I remember thinking at the time that Jerry

COURTESY OF UNIVERSITY OF SANTA CLARA ATHLETICS

would teach me how to see the game and understand the game and not just use my physicality to run over players," said Danielle, who like other future Santa Clara National Teamers from that era, Aly Wagner, Leslie Osborne, Nikki Serlenga and Kylie Bivens, would have a bevy of other high-level college suitors. "He would always be giving me tactical options to consider. He would say, 'Where are we in the game? Are we winning or losing? What is the time? How many fouls has the referee called and is it a tight game or a loose game? How well do you know your teammates? Are they facing this way so you can play the ball to their lead foot, or should you play it to their back foot? How close is the defender?' He would teach you to consider all of those scenarios in a split second and then give you the freedom to make a decision."

Danielle handled the pressure so well, on and off the field, that Jerry called the team together at midfield at the end of her freshman season. With the players eagerly awaiting the announcement of who would be named captain, the coach was secretly nervous about the potential reaction. "Everyone was kind of on pins and needles when you say aloud, 'I want to let you guys

Danielle Slaton, tracking the ball

know the captains for next year at Santa Clara.' That's a big deal in our culture. I thought, 'I'm going to get some pushback on this kid. She's a freshman.' But then everyone — everyone — said, 'Yeah! Awesome!' And I thought to myself, 'Oh, my God, how did that go so easy?'" Santa Clara would steamroll the competition in Danielle's sophomore year, never trailing in a single regular-season game in 1999, and then winning its first three games of the NCAA tournament by a combined score of 13-0 against Brigham Young, UCLA, and the aforementioned game against Connecticut when Aly Wagner spent a good portion of

Open Communication Essential for Players and Coaches

T HE HOBBY AND PROFESSION OF COACHING COULD LEARN a lot from Becky Burleigh, soccer's winningest female coach, according to my soccer daughter. "Becky understands the importance of the person behind the player," said Havana Solaun. "If you aren't in a good mental space, it doesn't matter what kind of player you are, you're not going to perform well." When Havana joined my wife, daughters and me as her host family in the late winter of 2017, she was just two soccer seasons removed from the University of Florida, where she had been a career top-10 player in both goals (30) and assists (32). She had also played 10 games for various coaches on youth national teams, and a handful of games after recovering from injuries with the Seattle Reign in the National Women's Soccer League, but it was clear she was almost wistful about her coach who, in 1998, had become the first woman to lead a Division 1 championship soccer team.

Becky's office door and mind, said Havana, were always open. Coming off a torn anterior cruciate ligament in her knee heading into her senior year, Havana visited her coach to voice displeasure about Florida's workout regimen. "I said, 'Look, the way we're training doesn't work for me. I had a non-contact ACL tear, which should be preventable with proper strength and conditioning.'" Instead of admonishing or benching Havana, Becky listened and, remarkably, agreed with her suggested changes. "Who was I, a senior in college?" said Havana. "But as a coach, she always wants to grow. She always wants to learn, and it doesn't matter who the ideas come from."

Coach Becky Burleigh, with Savannah Jordan and Havana Solaun

More than 500 wins into her career when I spoke to her in 2020, Becky said she "took some heat" for acquiescing to Havana's suggestions. "In the end, I do think you need to listen to the players. I'm not saying the players are experts at everything. But, by the time they're seniors, they're probably experts on their own bodies." Becky said she schedules weekly check-ins with all players. Even before that, she asks parents to sign off on expectations for their daughters' college experience and won't ever agree to talk to a parent without the player involved. To inform her approach to each personality, she also administers a DISC personality test — that groups people's behavior into four categories of D) Dominance; I) Influence; S) Steadiness; and C) Conscientiousness. Havana, said Becky, was a "high C," just like the houseguest we knew her to be: "reserved, private, and highly analytical." She thrived in an environment where information from coaches was shared freely and struggled when it wasn't.

The women, now close friends, agree that everyone benefits from healthy player and coach communication at all age levels. "When coaches just give us the information, we can get better," said Havana, the player. "When players truly listen to what the coaches want, and learn to play that way, chances are, they'll get on the field more," said Becky, the coach. Sounds easy . . . right? — P.T the second half pouting on the bench. Lining up as massive favorites against its perennial nemesis, Notre Dame, in the semifinals, Aly, Nikki, Kylie, Danielle and their teammates thoroughly dominated in a controlled fury that resulted in 17 shots on goal, to just three for the opponents. As it so often goes in soccer, though, the best team didn't win.

"Jerry constantly used to tell us to 'shoot less, but score more. Take one more touch with the ball, make one more pass, and get the higher percentage shot.' I know coaches who would argue it just the opposite, but not Jerry," said Danielle, who found herself having to console her older teammates after the 1-0 shock. That 1999 team holds the NCAA Division 1 record for scoring differential in a single season, outscoring opponents by 98 goals. "I wish

I could have done more for our seniors. They had been in the Final Four for four straight years, and helped take our program to a higher, nationally-ranked level, but never got to hoist the trophy. I remember giving lots of hugs and shedding a few tears, thinking that it was the least I could do for the group who paved the way for us." The stupor from the loss would continue well into the next season, when Santa Clara would be barely a .500 team and struggle to make the playoffs for the first time in years. "When I try to explain what a great leader Danielle was, and why leadership is so important to a team, I tell that story," said Jerry. "In 1999 we're the best team in the nation, and the next year we barely get into the tournament. What the heck happened? It was Danielle Slaton being away with the National Team at the Sydney Olympics. And it wasn't so much that we missed Danielle's play — we did — but what we really missed was her leadership."

The autumn of 2001 was ominous across the U.S., and particularly in Santa Clara. On Sept. 7, Lark Chastain, Jerry's mother-in-law, died unexpectedly of an aneurism at age 56. Four days later, the nation huddled in the horror of Sept. 11. Nikki Serlenga had graduated and it would be the last year that Danielle and Aly Wagner, teammates since childhood, would be together for a final chance at Santa Clara's first national title. Jerry had, however, been doing some 11th-hour recruiting work that required a bit of divine intervention. A transcript technicality originally left Leslie Osborne ineligible, but when a priest from her Wisconsin high school talked to the priest in charge of admissions at Santa Clara, the best youth player in the Chicago area was soon on a plane headed west. The first player to welcome her, with no nudging required from the coach, was the team leader. "My parents got divorced right when I went to school that September," said Leslie, who scored 13 goals with 17 assists as a freshman. "From day one, Danielle always made sure that I was OK. She would take me to San Francisco to introduce me to the city. She would take me to lunch. She was like a motherly sister figure, on and off the field. She knew I could be part of that group and make a difference and I think she really cared about me."

Aly Wagner, with Danielle Slaton and the national championship trophy

COURTESY OF SANTA CLARA UNIVERSITY ATHLETICS

THE FINAL EPITAPH OF ANY GREAT COACH, according to most National Teamers, has little to do with wins and losses — though the 2001 national championship at Santa Clara certainly helped Jerry Smith bring the likes of Marian Dalmy Dougherty and Julie Johnston Ertz to the California coast thereafter. The legacy of a coach, from youth, club, college and the pros, rests more in the collection of people who carry a positive feeling forward in their own lives and then share the goodwill with others. Two decades later, it's probably no coincidence that three of the women Jerry Smith most inspired — Aly Wagner, Leslie Osborne and Danielle Slaton — are now successful broadcasters who earn part of their livelihoods analyzing and simplifying the myriad options of a complicated game. "He was the only coach in my life who ever truly let me be me," said Aly, who made history in 2018 as the first woman to be hired as a play-by-play announcer for a men's World Cup game. She played 131 times for the National Team, winning two Olympic

gold medals and two World Cup bronze medals, yet still counts her game-winning goal against North Carolina in the 2001 college finals as the crowning achievement of her career. "Jerry didn't feel threatened by the fact that I felt confident, and he allowed me to have a personality and express dissatisfaction. What a gift."

The coach, with his wife, Brandi Chastain, left, Aly Wagner, Danielle Slaton and Leslie Osborne

By the time you become a National Teamer, a soccer life will have thrown a spectrum of so-called leaders in your path. "Your youth team coach and your club team coach, then Olympic Development coaches for state and regional and then National Team coaches; it goes on and on," said Leslie, who now serves as the assistant athletic director at her alma mater in addition to her work on camera at Fox Sports. "I've been coached by all types: male, female, or vocal screamers and the borderline verbal abusers who can knock down your confidence in an instant if you let them. The best coach I've ever had was Jerry Smith — and I'll say that until the day I die. He was always cool, calm and collected. I always remember looking at Jerry on the sideline and you wouldn't know if we were up by three or we're losing. Just looking at him gave me confidence, this feeling like everything's going to be OK."

Once upon a time, on a day when Aly was the offensive MVP and Danielle was the defensive MVP in the game that printed the Santa Clara legacy in indelible ink, a writer from *Sports Illustrated* asked the coach for a quote about how two girls from a small Catholic high school can go to a small Catholic college and set the world of soccer on fire. For Aly, he said, the ball was an extension of her body. "She doesn't have to think about the soccer ball," Jerry told the reporter. "That frees her eyes and mind to play the game." Then he paused and offered the best compliment a coach could probably ever offer a badass player. "Danielle Slaton . . . She is the person I want to be when I grow up someday."

NATIONAL TEAMERS FEATURED IN THIS SECTION

Yael Averbuch

Shannon Boxx

Brandi Chastain

Crystal Dunn

Stacey Enos

Lorrie Fair

Lauren Gregg

Lauren Orlandos Hanson

Emily Pickering Harner

Sara Whalen Hess

Angela Hucles

Debbie Keller

Tracey Bates Leone

Kristine Lilly

Carli Lloyd

Jessica McDonald

Carla Overbeck

Ronnie Fair Sullins

Janine Szpara

Rachel Buehler Van Hollebeke

Abby Wambach

Cat Reddick Whitehill

She Really Loves This Game?

Here are the five considerations everyone faces

How Badly do You Want It?

The Personal Effort Required to Reach Lofty Goals Will Likely Mean a Mountain of Challenges

HER FIRST SECRET WAS REALLY NO SECRET AT ALL. Shannon Boxx — arguably the greatest defensive midfielder in soccer history — wanted desperately to be as good, if not better, than her big sister at everything. When Gillian Boxx scored four touchdowns in the football game with the boys in their Torrance, Calif., neighborhood, little Shannon would be silently steaming inside with jealousy. When Gillian, four years older, got all As on her report card, Shannon was quietly devastated with four As and a single B. And when Gillian started to focus her athletic pursuits on softball, becoming one of the most sought-after college prospects in the nation, Shannon was overwhelmed with the pressure of keeping up after her sister received a full scholarship at the University of California. "If you want to go to college, you need to get a scholarship, too — unless you want to go to the local junior college," said her single mother.

For a long while, Shannon would try to take her mother's advice and follow her sister into softball, except that she not-so-secretly liked soccer more. By the time Gillian went off to California and became one of the best hard-hitting catchers in America, Shannon and her mother would shuttle to two club team practices daily, one for softball and one for soccer. Tournament weekends were often a blur of frantic southern California traffic. Shannon would play a soccer match in the early morning, change

Shannon Boxx, circa age 8

COURTESY OF SHANNON BOXX

uniforms in the car on the way to a softball game late morning, followed by one more of each in the afternoon or evening — then four more games the next day. At the peak of it all, still almost maniacally focused on her college goal, Shannon took it upon herself to start visiting her best friend's mother, a psychotherapist, to help her manage a growing feeling of depression. Shannon never let her friend know about the sessions, but she did come away with a decision she struggled to share with her mother: "I'm picking soccer; I'm going to try to go for this," said Shannon. "OK," said Julie Boxx. "But just remember, you either get a full ride or you pay your own way."

Chris Petrucelli, then a young coach of a fledgling women's soccer team at Notre Dame, came through with what most of the outsiders in Shannon Boxx's world saw as a happy ending. When she initially declined his offer of a partial scholarship during her recruiting visit to South Bend in 1993, politely explaining that her family circumstances dictated that she needed all expenses paid, Chris was impressed with Shannon's outward poise and candor and gave her everything she asked for. Just a year later, however, he would be mortified when he saw his star recruit show up at a national club championship tournament in Minnesota with another secret too obvious to ignore. Shannon was rail thin; Chris figured she was battling an eating disorder and sent her a letter the instant he landed back in Indiana. "You

COURTESY OF SHANNON BOXX

Shannon, with her sister, Gillian, and mother, Julie

need to get your situation figured out," he wrote. "Otherwise, we can't guarantee your scholarship." The day she received the letter, she stepped out of the shower, looked into the mirror, and began crying uncontrollably. "Oh, my God, I'm a stick," she thought. "My scholarship! What about my scholarship?" She wrapped herself in a towel and ran down to the kitchen. "Mom, we need to go to Souplantation for the all-you-can-eat!" Julie had warned her daughter before, too many times to count. "Shannon," she said. "You do know it's going to take more than one day of eating food to fix what you've done to yourself." A quarter century later, Julie still agonizes about those days. "It was such a difficult road," she said. "Shannon just had this ideal. Anything I said wasn't going to do any good. The more you hammer on something like that as a parent, especially with my kid, she'd dig in harder . . . But maybe I could have done better."

THERE IS — ACCORDING TO CHRIS PETRUCELLI and numerous others who have been around the National Team for its 35 years — a common denominator among the women who have ascended to those heights. "They're a little cra . . . cra . . . " said Chris, chuckling and catching himself mid-sentence after more than three decades on the sidelines as a coach of some of the nation's best players. "Well, I don't know if crazy is exactly the right word. First of all, it's the love of the game. This is a big piece of it, but there's this internal drive that all the best players have. And the best players have got to be so compulsive and obsessive and just driven. There's nothing else that's going to get in the way of them being a great player. There are plenty of players out there that have been really talented, but didn't have that drive. And there are plenty of players out there who have the drive, but didn't have the talent. You do need a certain level of talent."

Chris loves talking about Kate Sobrero Markgraf, who he called "a pretty average" high school player from Michigan, who desperately wanted to get into Notre Dame. When he told the future National Team legend she wasn't good enough as a sophomore, he figured he'd never hear from her again. "Then she shows up the next year and says, 'How 'bout now?'" said Chris. "Then she keeps working, shows up the year after that, and says again, 'How 'bout now?' This is a woman who might have been the best defender in the world for a very long time. She put in the work." He's also honest about some of the best college players who didn't make it as professionals, including Jen Renola, a diminutive goalie who guided Kate and Shannon Boxx to Notre Dame's first national soccer championship in 1995: "Great college goalie, but

Chris Petrucelli, with his Southern Methodist University players in 2018 after winning his 400th college game

she just didn't have the physical stature required to project as a National Team player." And Chris still laments that one of the most talented members of that team, Cindy Daws Mosley, only played two games with the National Team before a chronically bad foot injury ended her career. "Cindy would play the fall season for Notre Dame every year and then have a screw inserted into her foot and have to skip the spring season," said Chris. "This happened after every season."

Chris knows his encounter with soccer superstar Carli Lloyd, when he infamously cut her from the Under-21 youth National Team for being unfit and unmotivated, will be among the headlines of his coaching epitaph forever. But if he's comfortable with himself for that accurate, life-changing assessment, he's most proud that Carli ultimately listened. "You often have this conversation with a player where you say, 'What you're doing isn't good enough. You're going to have to change or you're not going to get to where you want to go,'" said Chris. "And I would say that 99 percent of players take that conversation and blame it on the coach. They don't ever take a real responsibility for themselves. To Carli's credit, at some point she heard the message and made the changes she needed to make."

For all of the accolades that have come with a career that has placed her forever within the pantheon of women's soccer, Carli's own story has left her scores of followers wondering if her own drive to succeed has been worth it. She acknowledges her detractors: "When I came onto the National Team in 2005, I was a chip-on-the-shoulder Jersey girl who didn't give a shit about what anyone thought of me. I was there to compete." Along the

Love of the Game Kept Me Coming Back

DID I TELL YOU I ONCE DID A TEDX TALK? It was October of 2014, and after some nervous banter with the audience, I launched into my story: "I make $18,000 a year doing what I love. That's not a joke, but feel free to laugh. I laugh at myself all the time because of it. It's definitely a niche sport with absolutely no job security, and stability doesn't exist. Forget the Tom Bradys, and the Peyton Mannings. I do not have a luxury house and I definitely don't have the Ferrari. We're more like players living in your basement, because we can't afford our own apartment. But the funny thing is, I feel like I have the life of a millionaire. To me, I have everything. I am rich beyond measure. I have players coming to my games, who want my autograph, who asked for my picture, and shockingly these players aspire to be me. Yes, me. To me, that is priceless. So, as I stand here today talking to you guys, I want to let you know how I became one of the professional athletes that you've probably never heard of. It starts quite uncomfortable and quite awkward, but it's a story

Joanna, at her TEDx talk in Boston

COURTESY OF JOANNA LOHMAN

I definitely, definitely need to share today."

If you've got a spare 15 minutes, you can still watch the rest of the talk on YouTube. Even if you could jump inside all of my thirtysomething years, you may still come away wondering why anyone, in their right mind, would put themselves through the life of a professional women's soccer player not named Mia Hamm, Alex Morgan or Megan Rapinoe. "How badly did I want it?" That was a question I always answered with a question: "How much do I love it?" I asked it in high school, when all of my friends were at the dance and I was home resting. I asked it every year at Penn State in the NCAA championship when we always made it to at least the "Elite-Eight," which meant I missed Thanksgiving. That meant no turkey, stuffing and pecan pie with the ones I loved the most. And let me tell you, my Mom makes the BEST pecan pie. I asked the question when American leagues folded and I was forced to play and live in foreign countries, and I asked it again after surgeries and the emotional splinters that came from sitting on the bench for game after game.

I can also save you the 15 minutes of watching. My conclusion in the TEDx talk was the same then as it is now, and the same as it will always be: "The amazing thing is that it's not about the money. It's not about the fame or the fortune; it's really about what you get from your sport. I've been the star player, the player that everyone loves and adores. I've been the bench player who struggles to get just one minute on the field. And while I've enjoyed all of my successes, it's the periods of struggle that I'm really proud of — the periods where I've been knocked down . . . That's what I'm really proud of: all the scrapes, bumps, bruises and scars. They've truly defined who I am. It's absolutely been a truly uncomfortable roller coaster ride to the top. It's been unpredictable. It's been unstable. It's been really hard at times — but it's been a ride that I don't ever want to get off of. Finally, I've earned my PhD. And now, this is the only way I know how to live." — J.L.

has told family members, including her parents and husband, to stay home from major tournaments so she could concentrate on training, games and recovery. She was estranged from family members, including her parents and brother, for more than a decade — at least partly due to her focused and dogged determination to live life and play the game in her own manner. In the mid-summer of 2020, with the world still reeling from the COVID-19 pandemic and months removed from her last soccer game, Carli was in the midst of the longest period of self-reflection of her life. She had reconciled with family and paid homage to her husband for his patience through it all. "For the first time ever, I've been able to put my husband first," she told us with her characteristic bluntness. "Brian has been a rock and so supportive of me throughout my career; we started dating

The Buck Stops With You

We asked all the National Teamers about the level of personal accountability and responsibility required to reach their level in sports and life. Here are 10 of their thoughts:

STAY FOCUSED — "You'll notice when you're an athlete that you become so hyper-focused on what you're doing," said **Abby Wambach** (USWNT, 2001-2015). "It's almost like this very selfish inclination. And that's what it takes to achieve high levels of success at something. You have to be completely committed, sometimes to the detriment of the rest of your life — your friends, your family, all of it."

BE FEARLESS — "I remember Anson Dorrance at camps, when somebody would like trip over a ball, he would celebrate. 'You're playing on the edge!' You always have to play on the edge," said **Danielle Garrett Fotopoulos** (USWNT 1996-2005). "That's something I still try and reinforce with our college team — just not being afraid. Don't play with the fear of making a mistake because you're always going to be limited. You're never going to reach your potential."

DEMONSTRATE INDEPENDENCE — "I don't know that people really fully understand what the early pioneers on the National Team had to go through. It was mind-blowing," **Sam Baggett-Bohon** (USWNT 1998-1999). "There was no

COURTESY OF SAM BAGGETT-BOHON

Sam Baggett-Bohon, with her husband and family

money. There was no infrastructure. No training environment. I mean, I remember **Carla (Overbeck)** running sprints up and down the stairs of our hotel at Duke. I remember I was looking outside my window and she was doing suicide sprints in the parking lot. Today's young players could take a lot from that."

in high school, but I finally feel like I've been able to put him number one during this time right now. We've gotten to connect like we've never connected before and I told my husband, 'I feel guilty that I've had to put you second, and I've had to put my friends and my family and vacations — everything — second.'"

Plenty of National Team players have found a level of balance that allows them to excel on the field, yet otherwise maintain healthy relationships inside and outside the game. Carli, however, said being a superior athlete, with the extraordinary levels of fitness and focus required at the National Team level, has never come naturally for her. She said her husband understands: "When I start talking about feeling guilty, he says, 'You wouldn't have done all the work and accomplished all you did if you had behaved any differently.'

DISCOVER PERSISTENCE — "If someone tells you 'No,' it's really up to you whether it's really a 'No,' or not, at least as far as sports goes," said **Kylie Bivens Hopper** (USWNT 2002-2004). "If you listen to the haters and the naysayers, then it's not gonna happen for you. But if you can just remember why you're good and what makes you like stand out — and focus on those things — then 'No' is not a word that's going to happen."

UNLEASH TENACITY — "If you're age 10 or 11, there will be some days you can bring it and some days you can't," said **Tish Venturini** (USWNT 1992-2000). "After that, you should bring your 'A' game most days. That's life. That's how I'm built. If you go out there and give half your effort, then you're letting your team down; they're relying on you. That's how I see it. That's what I tell my own daughter."

EXHIBIT CONSISTENCY — "It's pretty simple. I tried to be the best player at every training session. Every day," said **Heather O'Reilly** (USWNT 2002-2016).

EXUDE SUPPORTIVENESS — "I definitely wasn't the starting goalkeeper, but there was always some kind of shooting activity going on and would give my best in all those situations," said **Nicole Barnhart** (USWNT 2004-2013). "I remember I just kept saving **Abby Wambach**'s shots and at one point, Abby just kind of threw her hands up in the air and said, 'Barney, just let it go in!' And I basically said, 'If I let it go in, then I'm not doing my job and helping you prepare. So, sorry.'"

REMAIN UNSATISFIED — "So many players I ask: 'Who wants to be a professional?' They all raise their hands. I say, 'Do you guys even know what that means?'" said **Yael Averbuch** (USWNT 2007-2013). "That means you're distancing yourself from the rest of this group. You are striving to be the best at what you do. It's addicting. It's like some kind of drug and where all the players who play pro and keep coming back for more always want to do better than they did last time. That's what keeps us in the game."

EMBRACE PREPARATION — "I like to say, 'Luck is where preparation meets opportunity,'" said **Whitney Engen** (USWNT 2011-2016). "I've really tried hard to make sure that no matter what happens, I was always ready. I can think of so many instances in my life where I just kept working with my head down when things weren't going my way. All of a sudden, I get a phone call."

ACT RESOLUTE — "If you really sat down with every National Team player individually, every single one of them from those currently on the team to when I was playing, you'd find no one had it easy all the way through," said **Shannon MacMillan** (USWNT 1993-2005). "Granted, some have had tougher lives than others. But at the end of the day, you have a choice to feel sorry for yourself and use it as an excuse — or you can learn from it, grow from it, and help others learn and grow too."

Carli Lloyd, second from right, reunited with her siblings and parents on Thanksgiving Day 2020

And he's right. I wouldn't do anything differently. I never wanted to just be a good player, or a rich player. I want to be the absolute best that I can be. And so there's different levels and there's different choices and I'm all in 100 percent with being dedicated. There's no in between. There's no, 'Oh, I guess I'll just take this day off and go out with my friends and have some drinks and have a good time.' It's a lifestyle. You finish training on the field. You have choices to go back to your hotel room and hydrate and stretch, and do

some abs; do some pushups. Get your mind thinking about the next game. Or you can go back, walk around the mall, shop, tire your legs out, have some wine or beer at dinner. I chose not to do that. Every single person in this world has a choice on how dedicated they want to be. And I've been all in my entire career."

CHRIS PETRUCELLI'S LONGTIME COACHING RIVAL, Anson Dorrance, keeps Carli Lloyd's autobiography at arm's reach in his North Carolina office. He can cite passages of Chapter 3 — titled "Smackdown" — from memory. "Carli Lloyd is not a popular figure; most of the people that play with her don't like her, but she wrote an extraordinary book," said Anson in reverential tones he reserves for a chosen few. "That book is a wonderful testament about people owning their own narrative and the truth before they could truly progress to their potential. There's a cliché that comes from every player conference with the kids that I've talked to through the years: Average players want to be left alone; good players want to be coached; great players want the truth. The greatest players I've ever coached . . . I didn't really have to coach them. All I had to do really was to tell them the truth. And then, I would watch them make the adjustment to achieve whatever they needed to achieve."

If there is a common denominator for many younger athletes who wind up missing out on high-level success, according to Anson, Chris and so many other coaches, it's the parents who try to impose their own will on their children. For years, the behavior of the prototypical overzealous mother and father, who tried desperately to make all the right moves on behalf of their would-be champions, was captured in the phrase "helicopter" parent. "It was almost an umbilical cord between the parent and the child where the parent was sort of hovering over them and trying to protect them from everything," said Anson. The situation, in his view, has only gotten worse. "The modern parent is a snowplow," he said. "Parents now try to push every obstacle out of the way of their children to protect

COURTESY OF HIGHLINE COLLEGE

them from pain and responsibility. The evolution of parenthood is going right down the tubes. The ideal parents should make the kid responsible for everything in their athletic lives — and one of the most important things that you can absorb in your athletic life is pain and failure."

By 2020, Chris Petrucelli was talking about another special player who could be the latest protégée on his long resume. Jewel Boland's parents often attended her games as she was growing up in Portland, Ore. Her mother was known to be vocal on the sidelines and occasionally butted heads with her daughter about lack of effort. As she aged, however, Jewel's parents stepped back and let her find her

Jewel Boland, at Highline College

own way to acceptance at Highline, a junior college in Des Moines, Wash., prior to her transfer to Southern Methodist University where Chris began coaching in 2011. "It didn't occur to my parents that it was their job to help me get into a college," said Jewel. "It just wasn't a priority where I grew up." Playing soccer at Highline, in an environment where no one was on scholarship or wearing National Team dreams on their sleeves, would come to be her savior when the pain and suffering off the field might have sent her home. On July 26, just prior to their freshman year in 2017, Jewel and another player were hiking with their teammate, Haylei Hughes, at Wallace Falls State Park in Gold Bar, about 60 miles from campus. Jewel, walking just ahead of Haylei, heard a scream and then a splash at the base of a waterfall 80-feet below. The young women tried desperately to save her, but Haylei died from her injuries. Just two months later, Jewel's cousin also died in an automobile accident and, about that same time, Jewel's brother was sent off to prison for seven years. "It was one thing after the other," said Jewel, who scored a school record 36 goals in the midst of all that personal tragedy. "Soccer was all I had. That period of time just really opened my eyes to realize that life is precious and you can't take a single thing for granted. You've got to take advantage of every opportunity, no matter how big or small it is."

The maturity borne from those struggles, both the independence conveyed by her parents and the grief of losing a friend and family member, was obvious to Chris — who made Jewel the first junior college player he had ever recruited. While it was too soon to make National Team predictions, he saw her future in soccer beyond college. "Just a great, great person," he said. "And she's a phenomenal athlete, a super, super athlete. She is a kid who wants to play at the next level and if she doesn't make it, it won't be because she didn't try hard enough." For Jewel, though, playing Division I soccer, as compared to her two seasons at the junior college level, revealed unexpected truths: the players were more talented at SMU, but the effort among the players was actually greater at Highline when scholarships weren't involved. "I've actually had players tell me at SMU that they didn't even want to be there," said Jewel, who served as a captain her senior year. "I'll ask them, 'Then why are you torturing yourself and wasting your time?' Time is precious. I think, for some girls, they've been playing soccer for all their lives, but they don't really know anything else, and their parents' expectations have such an influence."

BY THE TIME JULIE BOXX SENT SHANNON off to Notre Dame in the summer of 1995, she thought her daughter's eating disorder had been solved. When the Fighting Irish started off the season with eight consecutive shutout victories, Chris Petrucelli thought everything was fine, too, until he witnessed Shannon eating nothing but a piece of bread for dinner

during an away game at Cincinnati. "It's nothing, coach, I'm just not hungry," she said, once again trying to keep a secret. That weekend launched the team into a mid-season slump, losing two games and tying two others in a six-game span — and it also quietly pressed Chris into action off the field in the middle of his most storied season. He watched Shannon closely, observing two more occasions of nothing but nibbles at mealtime, before leading her to the student

Shannon Boxx, left, with Marta of Brazil and Birgit Prinz of Germany at the World Player of the Year ceremony in 2005

health clinic where he made sure the medical staff monitored Shannon's food intake for breakfast, lunch and dinner each day. A quarter century later, she's still touched by the gesture. "Chris was always there for me," she said. "I think that's what I appreciated the most about him. It wasn't just about me as a soccer player; he made me feel like someone cared."

When she left the college ranks, still challenged by food, battling her self-confidence, and a body that would go through inexplicably increasing periods of pain and fatigue, she wanted to believe every other coach would be as compassionate. She had played well for the San Diego Spirit in the inaugural season for the Women's United Soccer Association in 2001, but decided to share a new diagnosis with the team's general manager and interim coach for the 2002 season. Her condition was called Sjögren's syndrome, an incurable autoimmune disorder that sporadically damages the body's ability to produce mucus and saliva and also causes arthritis-like joint pain in addition to exhaustion. Given a name for what was wrong, she felt she could work with doctors and trainers and continue to play through pain just as she had always done since high school; the coach, however, benched her without explanation for the remainder of the season and traded her to the New York Power by year end. A label, that of an unfit player, hurt as much as the pain of the disease. "I went from starting to not playing to then being traded, and I thought, 'He really hates me. He doesn't want me on the field; he doesn't even want me on the team.'"

Behind the scenes, ironically, Shannon had already been addressing the whispers about her stamina that followed her to two failed National Team tryouts. She happened to meet an athletic trainer, Craig Bennett, through a mutual acquaintance and started secretly working with him at El Camino Park and Chapman University in Orange, Calif., more than an hour's drive north of San Diego. He suspected an underlying condition made it harder for Shannon to train on some days than others — she never divulged the diagnosis to him — but overall Craig said he's never had an athlete dedicate themselves to a higher degree. "I want you to push me," she told him. "I want you to make me work." The secret sessions continued, even after the trade to New York often limited their training session to Craig devising ever tougher challenges by phone that she would complete by herself 3,000 miles away. "She had this level of drive that I had never seen," said Craig.

Heading into the final World Cup preparation camp of 2003, coach April Heinrichs needed practice bodies to get her regulars ready. Shannon recalls that April told her she had no shot whatsoever of making the team, but that maybe she'd be invited to try out for the 2004 Olympics. Shannon had already bought her own tickets to a few matches so she could watch as a fan, and pre-enrolled for graduate classes at Pepperdine University. April remembered the story slightly differently: "I would never tell a player they had no chance at all, but I do know that within three days of that camp opening I started to wonder about how to tell the veterans that Shannon was going to be on the team. There was definitely a difference in Shannon's physiological capabilities and freedom of expression on the field. With Shannon Boxx, there had always been flashes of some fantastic defending and winning the ball in midfield. Now she could do it from one day to the next." That freedom, according to Shannon, was a direct result of her commitment to Craig Bennett's workout plans. "I figured I had absolutely nothing to lose," she said. "I thought, 'Fuck this. I'm going to prove to everybody, and to myself, that I am good enough.' I put everything out there and, if I still didn't make it? Well, then at least I know that I did everything possible." Among the oldest players ever to make their debut for the National Team, at age 26, Shannon scored a goal in her first game, Sept. 1, 2003, against Costa Rica. Goals in subsequent games thereafter, including the World Cup opener, made her the only player in National Team history to score in her first three appearances.

BY 2005, SHANNON BOXX WAS CONSIDERED probably the most essential National Team player, one of three finalists in international voting for best player in the world, yet just as mired as ever in secrecy. Periods of pain from what she thought was just Sjögren's syndrome seemed to be increasing, even as her role on the team expanded. She shared the truth of her illness with team captain Christie Pearce Rampone, but otherwise kept the information to herself. "I had to tell someone; I couldn't go it completely alone," she said. "But I also felt I couldn't share it with everyone without risking losing my position." In 2007, a round of blood tests for the entire National Team threatened to expose a new revelation that Shannon's diagnosis had been upgraded to lupus, a more serious autoimmune disorder characterized by sudden bouts of intense pain — called flares — to the skin, joints and internal organs. When she begged the doctors to retake the test, she considered it somewhat miraculous that her blood sample came back normal and she was allowed to play.

Shannon Boxx, with her sister, Gillian

The closest she came to being outed to coaches against her wishes would come in Cancun, Mexico, in late October of 2010 during a World Cup qualifying tournament. Shannon could recognize the impending flares in an instant by then; at dinner the pain began in her feet and legs, and then begin to creep up her body. When she could no longer hold her fork without pain, she excused herself from the team, limped her way to the elevator and struggled inside her hotel room to pull on compression pants that sometimes helped to relieve symptoms. When her teammate, Heather Mitts, arrived at the door, Shannon was naked and helpless, crying on the floor. "Oh, my God, you're white as a ghost! What's wrong?" said Heather, who was intending to call the team coaches and trainers. "No!" Shannon begged. "Please. Please don't ask any questions. Please, can you just help get my

Don't Make the Same Mistakes I Did

MY SON'S ATHLETIC CAREER IS ALWAYS A TOUGH SUBJECT for the two of us, even now, more than a decade later. So many moments come to mind for me, probably none more than the Little League game when he was 12 and I was head coach aiming for the best record in the league — which meant I would achieve *my* goal of being named coach of the local all-star team in the state tournament. My son was playing catcher and I could see he was cranky. I called timeout and walked toward the plate. "What's up with you?" I asked. "I want to go play shortstop," he said. "You're our catcher," I replied. He wouldn't relent. "I'm sick of catching," he said. "But you give us the best chance of winning," I said. Then he nailed me. "You're the only one who cares about winning, Dad. Everyone knows that." I kicked him out of the game and told him to leave the field.

The co-author, with his son, Duke, and his daughters, from left, Christina, Angie and Aimee

I've been determined, ever since, to avoid those confrontations with Angie, my daughter who tried out for her first club soccer team the week after she turned 7. We even chose a small club, Potomac, instead of the regional powerhouse, Bethesda, because it seemed *less* competitive. But then the games started. Angie played with the 7-year-olds on Saturdays, and was soon invited to play with older girls on Sundays, even the best "blue" team. When she scored the blue team's first two goals of the season, after about eight straight losses, I was back in and overly invested. Angie loved it all at first. A minimum of three games a weekend, with more on tournament days, seemed great. Soon enough there were Olympic Development Program tryouts, Development Academy invitations, and endless spousal debates about whether Angie was trying hard enough on any given day.

Then my son reminded me: "Dad, you're doing it all over again." About that same time, the president of the Potomac club invited me to listen to a presentation by John O'Sullivan, who founded the Changing the Game Project in 2012, in part, to address parents like me. He said a lot of things that night, but the two I remember most are: "No parent in the world can will their child to be great at something" and "the most important thing to say to your children is that you really just love to watch them play."

How much soccer is too much is now the constant conversation with Angie. She's still ferocious on the field, but she reminded me once again that a child's body, and mind, have limits. She still seems to love the games and practices. But does she go out back and practice by herself with the ball the way I not-so-secretly wish she would? Sometimes, but not always. "Soccer is your choice," I tell her. And I mean it. I have to, because I know all too well from experience that the most important outcome when soccer ends, at whatever level, is that Angie is happy, healthy, and we are friends. It's been such a long road back for my son and me. He says he forgives me for being such a jerk, but I wish I never had to apologize in the first place. — P.T.

pants on and help put me in bed? Just, just please don't ask. I can't tell you. I'm so sorry."

Shannon, remarkably, would recover to start in all five games of that tournament — and in dozens of games across the next five years until her retirement after the 2015 World Cup victory at age 38. In 2012, fully entrenched as an all-time great player, she had finally divulged the secret she'd been keeping from coaches ever since that benching back in San Diego and openly wonders to this day if she should have been forthcoming about her lupus much sooner. The support, from National Team coaches and teammates, was 100 percent positive. "I don't know the answer," she said. "Right now I mentor a lot of younger people that have come to me and said they have lupus. They love soccer, they're playing, and asking me, 'Do I tell my coach, or not?'" The answer, she said, is individual for everyone. If you have a coach you can trust, like Chris Petrucelli was for her, she said she'd tell him. If not, however, she understands and supports the desire for privacy. Injuries and illnesses keep players off the field, or employees out of the office, and sometimes bosses and coaches, like teammates and friends, assign a stigma — consciously or otherwise.

COURTESY OF SHANNON BOXX

Shannon Boxx, with her mother, Julie

"Early on in my career, I think it was really smart that I stayed quiet with my diagnosis, because it could have been the one thing that told them that it's OK to cut me," said Shannon. "Fear is a very normal thing for anybody that has lupus or something similar. Patients in any jobs will have brain fog to the point where they can't really work on a given day, but no one understands what extreme fatigue feels like unless you've lived through it yourself. People will say, 'You look fine; you look normal. You must be just lazy.' That stings. When you have people questioning your effort, it's so tough." Ultimately, Shannon said, anyone facing a larger-than-life goal like making the National Team, or someone facing a debilitating illness that makes life feel like an unfair challenge, should take a page out of her mother's playbook. Love your children and encourage them to keep working for what they want. Julie Boxx, who told both of her children they would need to earn scholarships if they wanted to attend a four-year university, is the only woman in American history with daughters who earned Olympic gold medals in different sports — Gillian in softball (1996) and Shannon in soccer (2004, 2008 and 2012). "I've never ever forgotten Mom's comment, that I wasn't going to be able to eat my way out of my problems in just one day," she said. "And she couldn't fix it for me. My mom never handed me anything except for rides to practice. She did it right. I think that mentality, to keep fighting, keep pushing, carried me fairly well."

Who's Your Go-To Voice?

*Navigating the Journey Through the Soccer
Landscape is Best Led by Someone Who's Been There*

THERE'S AN UNMISTAKABLE SOUND, call it a heavy thump, when a soccer ball is struck well. In the fall of 2000, Les Armstrong recognized the power echoing from far off in the distance during one of his legendarily intense practices. Once. Twice. Then dozens of times. By then fully distracted and curious, he stopped practice and told the boys, including future Major League Soccer player Brandon McDonald, to get a drink. Les, a salty, stout professional Irish footballer who came to America in 1986, moved in with his uncle, and soon helped make the Sereno Club of Arizona one of the go-to travel soccer organizations in his new country, stood and stared — then waved a group of parents onto the field. "Who the hell is that?" he asked. One of the parents recognized the ball's assailant as Brandon's 12-year-old little sister, Jessica, who was often dropped off at the practice field to fend for herself because no mother or father was ever at home.

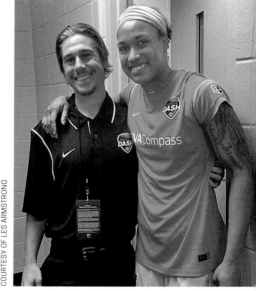

COURTESY OF LES ARMSTRONG

Jessica McDonald, with her mentor's son, Matt Armstrong

"We scour the earth for players, but with Jessica it was as if she fell out of the sky," said Les, who retains his thick brogue after 35 years in Tempe. "We watched this kid smashing balls into the net from about 30 yards out. So I encouraged one of the parents to go over and ask her if she was playing on a soccer team. It turns out she had played some soccer, but not for a competitive club. We offered her a spot right then and there . . . And I'd like to be able to say the rest is history." In their version of the player-mentor relationship that remains strong to this day, Les needed to first find donated funding from families in the local community to keep Jessica traveling with the club. With a distant father in and out of jail and an abusive mother dealing with significant substance abuse issues, Brandon and Jessica were cared for by a collection of aunts and uncles and a single grandmother, who was raising even more of her grandchildren in a crowded apartment. Even as she progressed through the years, with state championship level skills in soccer, basketball and especially track and field, Jessica would turn to her mentor when her biggest challenge of all — academics — threatened to derail her dreams of playing soccer for Anson Dorrance at the University of North Carolina.

IF LES AND JESSICA HAVE ONE OF MOST HIGH-PROFILE soccer examples of the importance of the player-mentor relationship, both on the field and off, many other National Teamers' patron saints have proven to make the difference between realizing dreams or wasting potential. As soon as a girl starts scoring goals, the opinions about what she should do next — from elite travel clubs, to private trainers, to the Olympic Development Program and Girls Academy — will surely follow. Knowing who to trust in making those decisions is essential. "I think it's vital to have a mentor, actually," said Lauren Orlandos Hanson, who garnered a single 28-minute appearance with the Women's National Team in China in 2001 prior to winning a college national championship at the University of Portland in 2002. Though injuries and the lack of a women's professional league at the time cut her playing career short, she's now the head coach at San Jose State University in California and knows how much the minds of young players — and dreams of their parents — need clear guidance. "Ideally, the mentor is someone that knows you from when you were younger, all the way through when you're an adult. I think a mentor is somebody who

Les Armstrong, with two of his professional protégées, McKenzie Berryhill and Cali Farquharson

COURTESY OF LES ARMSTRONG

can lead you in the right direction when you're having a challenging time, or even in a positive frame of life. A lot of the players on my team have a really close relationship with their club coach. Some of them have a good relationship with their junior college coach, too. As their college coach, I develop relationships with those people because it helps me coach my players better."

Making that special connection can come from references; if parents can find a successful community and club soccer program, chances are the organization will possess or know of coaches and other individuals who will be ideally suited for the mentor role. Just be sure the motives are purely about the player and not just the parent's pocketbook. Often times finding the right person comes only from trial and error; expect to have to work with several potential mentors before the truly best option comes along with the demeanor to connect with any particular young player. In the case of Jewel Boland and National Teamer Janine Szpara, their relationship evolved through the years, from an on-the-field youth coach at age 12, to grief counselor at age 18 and coffee shop confidant by age 22.

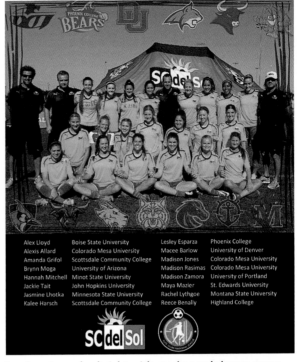

Alex Lloyd	Boise State University	Lesley Esparza	Phoenix College
Alexis Allard	Colorado Mesa University	Macee Barlow	University of Denver
Amanda Grifol	Scottsdale Community College	Madison Jones	Colorado Mesa University
Brynn Moga	University of Arizona	Madison Rasimas	Colorado Mesa University
Hannah Mitchell	Minot State University	Madison Zamora	University of Portland
Jackie Tait	John Hopkins University	Maya Mazier	St. Edwards University
Jasmine Lhotka	Minnesota State University	Rachel Lythgoe	Montana State University
Kalee Harsch	Scottsdale Community College	Reece Benally	Highland College

Les Armstrong, back right, with coaches and players, many of whom parlayed their club soccer careers into college scholarships

"In my mind, in terms of talent, Jewel has always been head-and-shoulders above the average player since she was a young girl," said Janine, who played six games in goal for the National Team in 1986-87 in the midst of four years at Colorado College where she set a record than can never be broken: four consecutive years as a first-team All-American. In 2019, EverybodySoccer.com named her the greatest goalie in college soccer history. "Jewel's issue has always been recognizing that from confidence flows commitment, and vice versa."

Janine could see early on that Jewel, who was in her senior year at Southern Methodist University in 2020 after two years at Highline junior college, often seemed to "play down" to the level of teammates or opponents during her teenage years. At a Portland Thorns Youth Academy game in 2015, Janine angrily pulled Jewel off the field, even though the Thorns were ahead in the

Janine Szpara, doling out advice

game. "What are you doing out there?" Janine asked, only to have Jewel push back: "No one else is playing hard, why should I?" Five years later, Janine's not-so-subtle message stands out. "Janine could have come at any of the players on the field in that moment, but she came at me first, because she expected more from me, more than I expected from myself," said Jewel. Two years later, when Jewel's teammate died tragically (see Page 101), and her cousin was killed soon after, Janine was standing by with warm hugs and softer, more encouraging words. "You are special, you are strong, and you still have soccer," Janine told her. "I am here for you if you need me."

Having watched Jewel devote herself fully to soccer, from record-setting goal totals in junior college, to joining Chris Petrucelli at SMU, Janine believes she was witnessing a lasting change — one cup of coffee at a time. "An old coach of mine used to have a saying about 'Coca-Cola' players," she said. "That's someone who does something great and then celebrates it in their mind, like they're having a Coca-Cola. Jewel would do something good

(see Page 101)

WHY GET A MENTOR?

A parent's job is to parent, and that can't help but be biased even in the best of circumstances. A coach's job is to coach, not just one player on a team, but all of them into a cohesive unit. While both parents and coaches can play a mentoring role, a personal mentor is ideally someone uniquely and objectively focused on a single individual for her personal betterment. "By age 10, I was playing up two to three years and my parents knew something was going on," said **Carin Jennings Gabarra** (USWNT 1987-1996). "They looked for opportunities that weren't necessarily obvious and I had some critical mentors that helped me play and do things that other girls at that age couldn't do."

Essentials of a Good Mentor

HONESTY — "First of all, find someone you trust, in other words someone that doesn't blow smoke. Once you can find that person, then you've got to basically own whatever they're telling you." — Anson Dorrance, University of North Carolina coach

EXPERIENCE — "I'd say my biggest mentor has been **Brandi (Chastain)**. She has been there, she has seen it all, and I've been able to just soak up everything she says. She's just such a diehard workhorse, a tactician, a student of the game and anything she does is so heartfelt. She just makes everything so much more fun and, through that association, it brings the best out in me." — **Leslie Osborne** (USWNT 2004-2009)

PERSPECTIVE — "The mentor relationship is not just about training them to be to be good players, because a lot of my players have gone on from the game and I have continued to communicate with them. They're good people; they're good citizens who take care of people. They're nurses, and in some cases they're doctors. It doesn't really matter what they do, as long as they have strong core values they took from the game." — Les Armstrong, director SC del Sol Development Academy for a couple of minutes here and there. We used to talk about me wanting to see her do that all the time, for a whole game, so that, ideally, she gets to the place where she wants to do it for herself all the time. I want to see that competitive will, that fire that my teammate April Heinrichs brought to the game, or the fight and the consistency that Michelle Akers showed every single minute of every single game. It's a champion's type of mentality. When we meet now, I think Jewel is starting to understand what that means. I do think she wants it for herself."

LIKE IRISHMAN LES ARMSTRONG, AN AUSTRALIAN COACH and mentor named James Galanis never sugarcoats a single word to a player, boy or girl. It's a lesson he learned south of the Outback, when a bunch of good-intentioned fathers were in over their heads as coaches. Though James played for South Melbourne in Australia's National Soccer League, and later with Northcote City in the Victorian State League, he carries a hint of regret about what might have been. "I know for a fact that me and my friends underachieved in terms of

COURTESY OF LESLIE OSBORNE

Rose Lavelle, Andi Sullivan, Leslie Osborne, Kelley O'Hara and Emily Sonnett

INSPIRATION — "Rose's mentor, his name was Neil Bradford, was just truly gifted, especially with the little ones. Everything was a game; everything was fun while they were learning. He just really reeled her in. He would always instill confidence, saying things like, 'It doesn't matter that those girls are bigger. You are smarter. You have more skill.' He'd say, 'She's got the fastest feet in the business!'" — Janet Lavelle, **Rose Lavelle**'s mother

MOTIVATION — "If you can find somebody in your life who fits you, helps motivate you and increase your drive, it can make all the difference. Mine knew how to push my buttons. He'd say, 'You know, **Mia Hamm** can juggle more than 500 times in a row.' I didn't really need help with drive, but — of course — I had to go out and try to beat Mia in juggling." — **Lauren Orlandos Hanson**, USWNT 2001

Where to Find the Best Mentor?

START AT THE TOP — Find out if there's a former USWNT player in your area and figure out a way to connect with her. If she is too busy to talk, or take on a new project, she will likely have suggestions for who to call. Former and current men's professional players can also be excellent options as mentors.

SEEK OUT COLLEGE PLAYERS — Some of these young ladies will be happy to become "big sisters" and share insight about their experiences. Almost all of them are living in the dignified poverty known as undergraduate life and will be happy to make a few extra bucks sharing life and soccer lessons for a fee.

NETWORK — In the same way you ask around about the best doctors, lawyers and accountants, ask folks on the local club teams for leads on the best trainers and mentors. Your state youth soccer association can also be a good resource.

Alexis George, with her family

soccer because we didn't have a mentor," said James, who has previously worked with National Teamers Carli Lloyd, Heather Mitts Feeley, Julie Johnston Ertz and several others in addition to becoming a coach with the Atlanta Beat in the Women's Professional Soccer league. "We would have listened to anyone, but the people we had around us were Dads who hadn't played. If a person had been there, had walked down that road that I was looking to go down, and I respected them? I guarantee I would have done whatever they told me to do. But you need somebody who's been there because they know the pitfalls; they know what's coming and how to handle adverse situations. They know how to deal with injuries and how to deal with coaching situations. You need someone who's straight up going to tell you the truth."

Even before the advent of women's professional leagues and the 1999 World Cup elevated the U.S. National Team in the American consciousness, Alexis George heard an almost daily earful from the mentor she called "Cannon Foot." Alexis' parents didn't want to leave anything to chance with their daughter's college soccer aspirations. Approaching her junior year in high school with the height of the recruiting season at hand, they asked James to accompany Alexis from New Jersey to the Quantico military base in Virginia to the annual Washington Area Girls Soccer League tournament where hundreds of coaches would be swarming. Still a couple years away from opening his own soccer school and a decade away from assuming his first professional coaching position, James was taking any soccer gig that paid. On the defensive end of the field, the mentor watched Alexis kick, catch or deflect every ball that that came in the direction of the Medford Strikers' goal crease. Her talent, in fact, would catch the eye of a bevy of suitors, including Georgetown University, where Alexis would become a two-year starting goaltender.

"James shot so freakin' hard the ball felt like a rocket coming at my face," said Alexis, a mother of two, who is now a Washington D.C. financial analyst. Though the George family never needed to worry about a college scholarship — Alexis' father, Jim, is both an attorney and physician — her parents insisted she never miss one of James's grueling workouts.

James Galanis, words of wisdom

The Lean, Mean Machine

SCOTT WINSTON WAS A CONSTANT AT OUR PRACTICES for the Bethesda Scorpions, but not in the way of most parents who sat in their cars or lined the field when I was growing up. Mr. Winston, the father of my teammate, Jen, ran. And ran. And then ran some more. He would push himself around the track at Walter Johnson High School through intervals, faster and slower progressions, for the two-hour duration of our workouts and still be going, rain or shine, when the rest of us were leaving. I would watch in awe of his thin, muscular body seemingly floating a foot above the ground; I remember that, even in the dead of winter, he wore just plain white socks to shield his hands.

Scott Winston, retired, but still running

When he wasn't running at some sort of unstoppable pace, he would always wish us good luck with a broad smile on his face.

I realized early on in my youth career that I wasn't the biggest and most talented player. If I wanted to take my game to the next level, I would have to be the fittest and grittiest player on the field. While many players' parents paid for expensive trainers at gyms, all I had to do was look at the man who wouldn't stop running laps. "Will you turn me into a lean, mean running machine?" I asked. For years, Mr. Winston did exactly that and then some. I would show up to Walter Johnson, or any public space we could find, and Mr. Winston would train me in ball work, push me through grueling track workouts, and without a doubt, run me up some sort of nearby hill. More times than not, Mr. Winston would be running next to me. Pacing me, pushing me.

It was in those workouts, hands on my knees, gasping for air, legs aching, where I built my endurance, inner strength and, most importantly, self-belief. I knew if I could complete a Mr. Winston workout in the humidity and 100-degree heat of July, I could do anything. The pain was transforming into power. In our down moments, Mr. Winston and I spoke about life, my family, and how I was doing in school. He never accepted a penny for all the energy, wisdom and care he showed me and it was because of him that I began to rise through the ranks — from the Maryland State Olympic Development team to the Region 1 team, and then as the captain of the U-21 Women's National Team. I was a 90-plus minute central midfielder who would run her opponents, almost literally, into the ground. I was known as the engine of the team, a constant and consistent source of positive energy that drove my team to victory. I was my own version of Mr. Winston.

Just prior to my camps with the National Team, my ultimate goal, he would intensify my workouts. Invariably, on the last day before I headed out, he would say, "Jo, you are ready." Those four simple words thrust me into camp with confidence. I was what I wanted to become: a lean, mean, running machine with the drive of a woman determined to get up that hill, one last time. Fast forward to 2016, long after Mr. Winston's workouts. At age 34, when most of my peers had since retired, I receive a call from the Washington Spirit speed and conditioning coach. He said, "Jo, we've been looking at your GPS data in preseason training. You are actually running twice as much as most of your teammates in practice." At the same time our team doctor would marvel at my low heart rate. "You must be very fit," he would say. "That's probably why you've played so long." I may be retired now, but, thanks to my mentor, I'll never stop running, either. When it's cold, I'll have socks on my hands. — J.L.

"My Dad believed in me becoming the very best version of myself, no matter what it was," she said. By the summer of 1998, the family even paid James and his wife, Colleen, to join them for their annual two-week summer vacation to the Grand Cayman Islands so James could lead Alexis through two-a-day workouts that began on the beach at 6 a.m. For the morning sessions, she dove again and again in the sand until the skin on her knees was virtually raw. In the afternoons, James moved the sessions to a local park with ramshackle goals where his 17-year-old student learned to pop up quickly after dives — to avoid her body getting attacked by red fire ants.

"I'd be lying if I said there isn't a little PTSD associated with my soccer life," said Alexis, seemingly only half joking. "But I'll also tell you I'd do it again in a heartbeat. James . . . James just knew how to push the right buttons. He taught me I could always dig deeper, always

How Rolly Moved Us

"DAMMIT, ROLLY," I MUTTERED UNDER MY BREATH as I pulled my car into the parking lot of the Bells Mill Elementary School in Potomac, Md., on Oct. 26, 2018. With temperatures in the 30s and rain blowing sideways, these were harsh practice conditions, even for the standards of my daughter's somewhat maniacal private trainer. I had hired Rolly Magallanes as a soccer mentor for my daughter almost a year earlier on the advice of Mark Cantor, president of the board of directors of the Maryland Youth Soccer Association. Rolly had worked closely with Mark's daughter, Jenna, from pre-teens club soccer through her admission to Cornell University. "Rolly is an acquired taste, not for everyone," said Mark. "But if your daughter is really serious about soccer, I can't think of anyone better. He will definitely tell her the truth."

Angie was barely 8 years old when Rolly reluctantly accepted her for a tryout. "She better come to play," he said over the phone before beginning a long rant about the pay-to-play soccer culture that he believed rewarded mediocrity. At that first trial session that included two 12-year-old boys and a 15-year-old girl, Rolly never gave any indication about what he thought of my daughter's performance — except for chastising me sharply when I retrieved an errant ball and kicked it back toward the players. "That's the players' job!" he shouted. "We don't baby our children here, Dad."

After 60 minutes of darting, spinning, sprinting and kicking, I could see Angie was exhausted and still beyond nervous as she and the other three players dragged Rolly's tattered equipment bags of goals, cones and balls across the field toward his old beige Corolla. I walked ahead to collect $50, Rolly's fee, from my glove box. After handing him the cash, I took my daughter's hand and turned to leave. "Next time," said Rolly, "I want you to kick the ball a little harder, Angie. Do you understand?" She lifted her head ever so subtlety as a grin washed over her face. "Yes," she said quietly, then she pulled me down toward her. "He said 'Next time,'" she whispered in my ear.

I then turned to find Rolly trailing just behind me. "I can't have Angie dragging down the older players," he said. "If you can bring me two or three other players her age of the same caliber, I'll train her. If not, we'll have to wait until she grows." With fair warning to the parents, I invited about 10 different girls, ages 8 or 9, for Rolly's often brutal assessments and workouts, the intensity of which none of them had ever experienced. Some made the cut; a few left in tears, never to return. For that year, though, the man who was equal parts warm nurturer and Army drill sergeant became a constant in Angie's life, coming to her games to offer encouragement and frequently calling on the iPhone to try harder, and always deliver under pressure. I learned to handle criticism and hecklers — the ones in West Virginia were the worst — and to always be on time. James just hated it if you were late. And I'll tell you it was never about making it pro, or the National Team. Those weren't even options as far as we knew. It was simply about being the best version of myself that I could be. Those are lessons that I still pull from every single day of my life."

SEATED NEXT TO ONE OF HIS STAR SOCCER PUPILS on a flight back from a tournament during her senior year in high school, Les Armstrong was startled during a conversation about college plans. He noticed Jessica McDonald's reading material of choice for a crucial book report for English class, about the Brazilian soccer superstar Pelé, was filled with illustrations and large print intended for grade-school readers. Reacting just as he would

Rolly Magallanes, RIP

COURTESY OF THE MARYLAND STATE SOCCER ASSOCIATION

talk about everything from nutrition, to proper sleep, finishing schoolwork, and recovery from injuries. From January to early autumn, the girls happily played weekly in snow, rain, and the simmering Maryland sun with their trainer loudly barking commands: "A little harder! More hustle! We need full concentration!"

Still, the weather on Oct. 26 seemed over the top. Even Rolly should have canceled practice — if only he could have. I noticed his car was not in the lot when I parked in the usual spot next to the soccer field. Just then Jason Travis' number popped up on my iPhone; he is Angie's club soccer coach, so I hit the speaker button for Angie to listen. "Did you hear the news?" he asked. "No," I said. "Rolly is dead," said Jason. "He apparently had a heart attack on the field last night while he was reffing a high school game." I instantly turned off the speaker phone and quickly ended the call to tend to my daughter. "What does that mean? Rolly is dead?" she asked softly.

"Does that mean we're not going to have practice?"

While Angie didn't want to talk about Rolly for days, and clearly didn't understand the full ramifications, I felt I'd lost an extended member of our family who I assumed would be helping to guide my daughter's soccer and life goals for at least the next decade. Nearly two years later, however, I realize that he still does. Every time she spins away from a defender to get open on a throw-in, she's deploying a "Rolly move" he taught her over and over again. When she stands confident and poised over a penalty kick, or organizes her equipment on her own, I know it's partly because of someone who left an indelible impression. "I still miss Rolly," my daughter told me recently. "Me too . . ." I said. "Me too." — P.T.

on the soccer field, Les didn't mince words: "That's the freakin' book you're reading? That's for a 12-year-old!" As Jessica's tears flowed with the depth of her struggle exposed, her mentor quickly softened: "You'll get it," said Les. "It may take a while, but your talent and perseverance will take you to the apex of where you want to be."

Working cross country with Anson Dorrance, Les helped Jessica enroll for two years at a local community school, Phoenix College, where she became national junior college soccer player of the year in 2006, while most importantly raising her academic achievement to allow admission at UNC. Another national championship, one of the 22 Anson has won in his more than four-decade career, followed as soon as Jessica arrived in North Carolina. Thirteen years later, she would be a World Cup champion, who still recognized the role of the man who plucked her out of obscurity.

"It wasn't an easy thing to play under (Les)," said Jessica, herself a mother of a young boy, Jeremiah. "He was a very tough-minded person and he instilled that in us, and especially in me. I mean, you should have seen the fitness that we used to do in club soccer. It was insane. Looking back, I don't even think we would do that today at the National Team level — but that's what helped us succeed." Having also coached and mentored two other National Teamers, Sydney Leroux Dyer and Julie Johnston Ertz, as well as several other high profile female and male players from the U.S. and Mexico, Les' reputation for developing talent is indisputable. The intensity of his workouts and the flavor of his language, however, have occasionally come under fire from parents, fellow coaches and administrators through the years; in 2008, Les was asked to step down from Sereno, the club he founded, and he soon joined a competing organization, SC del Sol. He was defiant that year when a reporter for the *Phoenix New Times* questioned him about the intensity of his club's workout regimen: "Take your boots, get the hell out of here," he is quoted as saying. "We don't want players who are going to decide when they're going to train and not. This is a special environment. If you want to be here and prosper, then you'll play by my rules."

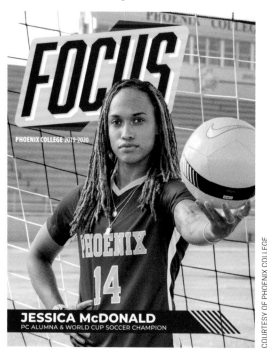

COURTESY OF PHOENIX COLLEGE

Jessica McDonald, doing Phoenix College proud

A dozen years after the Sereno revolt, Les was a grandfather, confounded by the Gameboys and iPhones in the hands of his children's children. He wished they were outside playing, he said, but was recognizing that — for most people — times were changing. "I can't imagine how difficult that must be, as a parent, to know to motivate a kid who says, 'You know what, Mom and Dad, I'd rather be home with my iPhone today than go practice,'" he said. He also told us he has recurring nightmares about being too harsh on his own son, Matt, and wishes he could do a few things over in that regard. These days, at SC del Sol, the kinder and gentler man has devised a program whereby the youngest players

Jessica McDonald, celebrating her Arizona heritage

come in and play kicking games that bear only a scant resemblance to soccer. "It's got a fancy name, 'unconscious development,' so that the kids think they are games, but what we see is that they're actually improving their skills and technical ability and fostering the love of the ball and the game." Every once in a while, when a child with potential comes along, he'll still think to himself, "Who the hell is that?" If the girl, or boy, is really special, he might even take the player under his personal wing. And, yes, the language will still be salty from time to time.

Jessica McDonald laughs when she hears complaints about her friend's vocabulary. Yes, she said, parents should seek out the right fit for their young player. If a child is highly sensitive, someone like Les might not be the best choice — and there's nothing wrong with that. "In my case, though, with trying to balance multiple sports and then focusing on school and crazy things happening at home, I'm just so happy that Les found me and gave me a chance," she said. "I was very privileged to have someone like Les Armstrong to tell

Jessica McDonald, with Anson Dorrance

me the importance of education, to guide me in the right direction. Maybe the language was colorful; it was. But it wasn't like I would go home at night crying if he hurt my feelings. It was never to that point — it was just being tough on us and not letting us slack. So, to me? I'm obviously very thankful for those people in my life like Les, who have helped shaped me into the person that I am today."

Doctors' Advice: Have Plan B Ready

Three National Teamers Demonstrate that Fulfilling Challenges May Only be Beginning When Playing Soccer Ends

SOCCER, FOR YOUNG SARA WHALEN HESS, was only ever about fun. As a child on Long Island, she resisted the temptation to join one of New York's elite travel teams, and spent virtually her entire youth enjoying the same group of friends from her hometown in Greenlawn. After an all-state career at Harborfields High School in soccer, basketball and track, which earned her at least as much attention from college coaches as kicking a ball, she stayed close to home at the University of Connecticut because the northeastern out-

post of soccer didn't seem like a pressure situation. When a call reached Storrs, Conn., from Tony DiCicco, who had just been named the head coach of the National Team in 1994, the college freshman laughed it off. He had seen her play against North Carolina that season, but "I knew he was making a huge mistake," said Sara, who traveled to the U.S. team's training camp in Sanford, Fla., and proved it. "In no way was I ready."

After being cut, she shrugged her

Sara Whalen Hess, back row, third from left, after winning the 1999 World Cup

COURTESY OF MICHELLE AKERS

shoulders and headed back to Connecticut to focus the next three years, so she thought, on her psychology degree. "I honestly didn't even know if I wanted to play college soccer at first," said Sara. "That call, that opportunity, really was stunning to me. I had always just planned on finishing school and going to grad school and living near my parents, something kind of basic like that." That taste, the feeling of matching her speed against Mia Hamm and her toughness against Michelle Akers, would keep her awake at night — and on the soccer field by day. She honed her skills, carried UConn on her back to the

upper echelon of the soccer world, and built a resume that included three-time All-American and national player of the year as a senior. "I knew I wanted to be invited back to the National Team. By the time I got out of college, I was ready."

Her timing in those days, she said, was impeccable. Sara was called to the National Team camp again in 1997. By 1999, with America hosting the third women's World Cup tournament in our biggest stadiums, Sara was typically either starting, or among the first players off the bench. When Michelle suffered a concussion in the final in front of more than 90,000 fans in the Rose Bowl in California, Sara subbed in for the remainder of the game and rode the winning wave of excitement from the cover of *Time Magazine,* to a starring role and a silver medal in the 2000 Olympics

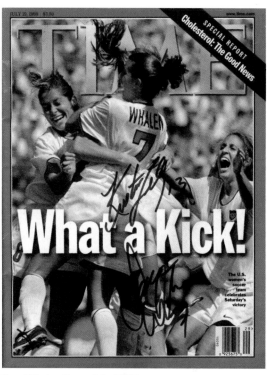

Sara Whalen Hess, July 1999

in Australia, to a founding position as one of the top players selected by the New York Power in the WUSA, the first women's professional league. Home games were played just a few minutes from her parents' house and, on the off nights, New York's society pages even covered her groove. "Everybody knows Say is a dancing fool," said her teammate Tiffeny Milbrett, revealing Sara's nickname to the *New York Times* on March 11, 2001. Little more than 15 months later, however, a catastrophic knee injury ended all of that in an instant. "I was just always so, so lucky in life, until I wasn't," said Sara. "Soccer wasn't supposed to work out for me, but when it did, I really came to love it. I loved my life. My teammates. The game. And, just like that, the thing that was never supposed to work out in the first place had stopped working out altogether."

PLAYING HIGH-LEVEL SOCCER ENDS FOR EVERYONE. For some, it's injuries, or because the college scholarship dollars they envision never materialize. For others, maybe the scholarship ends with a degree in hand, but no one is willing to pay anyone except the very best players for their performance thereafter. The financial reality, to this day, is that no one — even the most elite female players in the world — make enough money during their on-field careers to sustain them for life. Abby Wambach, who stepped onto the National Team just as Sara stepped off, would score more goals than any American player in history, but left the game initially wondering how she'd put food on the table after retirement. Her speech on that subject to the Barnard College class of 2018 went viral and, a year later, would serve as the basis for her best-selling book titled *Wolfpack*:

> *"I received my (ESPY) award along with two other incredible athletes: basketball's Kobe Bryant and football's Peyton Manning. We all stood on stage together and watched highlights of our careers with the cameras rolling and the fans cheering — and I looked around and had a moment of awe. I felt so grateful to be there — included in the company of Kobe and Peyton. I had a momentary feeling of having arrived: like we women had finally made it. Then the applause ended and it was time for the three of us to exit stage left. And as I watched those men walk off the stage, it dawned on me that the three of us were stepping away into very different futures. Each of us, Kobe, Peyton and I — we made the same sacrifices, we shed the same amount of blood, sweat and tears, we'd left it all on the field for decades with the same ferocity, talent and commitment — but our retirements wouldn't be the same at all. Because Kobe and Peyton walked away from their careers with something I didn't have: enormous bank accounts. Because of that they had something else I didn't have: freedom. Their hustling days were over; mine were just beginning."*

One of Sara's teammates, Ronnie Fair Sullins, had been hustling all her life. Ronnie had to, just to keep up with her identical twin sister, Lorrie. The Fairs raced to doorknobs, or to the bus stop. They competed at dinner to see who could finish their meals first so they could get outside to see who could score the most touchdowns in their backyard football games with their older brother, Greg. They competed in track, beating all comers in Los Altos, Calif., with regularity — except each other. Sometimes Ronnie would win; other times it would be Lorrie. And some of those times, Ronnie said, she just let her sister win rather than deal with her wrath. "My sister would not talk to me if I won," she said, laughing at the memories. "There were times I remember, in the middle of a race, thinking to myself, 'Do I really want to endure the next several days of being ignored by her?' So I'd just pull up a little at the end and let her have it."

When it came to soccer, her sister's competitiveness would be the most hard to swallow. Both were invited to try out for the Olympic Development Program's western regional team, but only Lorrie made it. Ronnie stayed out late that night, commiserating over bottles of Gatorade with a few other girls who were also cut. Caught

Lorrie Fair, left, with Ronnie Fair Sullins

COURTESY OF ANTHONY DICICCO JR.

THE KEYS TO FINDING LIFE BALANCE

Achieving National Team status in soccer requires immense hours of focused training, yet everyone who has made it has developed strategies to help cope with the game's stress:

LOOK OUTSIDE THE GAME — Many players told us that tying their lives too closely to soccer left them foundering upon retirement. "When my career ended, I was kind of lost; my identity was so wrapped up in being a soccer player and I didn't really know how to figure out what to do next," said **Danielle Slaton** (USWNT 1999-2003). "Don't be afraid to ask for help, and don't be afraid to find new tools in your toolbox that maybe you didn't learn in soccer."

FOCUS ON OTHERS — Being too self-centered can create feelings of isolation. "At some level, you have to be really selfish to become a professional athlete," said **Cindy Parlow Cone** (USWNT 1996-2004). "You have to put yourself first to make sure you're getting good grades, you're eating the right foods, you're training the right amount. But to be a good teammate there also has to be a level of selflessness and that requires a certain level of maturation. I would say I wasn't a good teammate until I joined the National Team and learned to take pride in helping others achieve their goals and be the best they could be, too."

KEEP YOUR MOTIVATION IN PERSPECTIVE — Be honest about why you're playing the game, and maybe why you want to make the National Team. "Ask yourself, 'Do you want to be a star, do you want to be the best?'" said **Staci Wilson** (USWNT 1995-1996). "Do you really want soccer for a career? Do you want to make a lot of money? If the answer is, 'Yes' to all those things, go for it. But understand that all of those outcomes are really, really difficult. So you better love the game first and foremost."

AVOID BURNOUT — Focusing on one singular goal can be suffocating and detrimental to your physical and mental health, so open your mind and body to new experiences. "If somebody is interested in a lot of different things and they're being forced to only do one, they might get burnt out, because they feel it's restricting them," said **Yael Averbuch** (USWNT 2007-2013).

SET EXPECTATIONS OFF THE FIELD — Just like it is important to set goals on the field, it is equally important to aim for milestones off the field. "My kids have goals, whether they want to make a team or get good grades, take care of the dog better, or reach out to their grandfather more." said **Danielle Garrett Fotopoulos** (USWNT 1996-2005). "Even the little goals, like one ones they write up on their mirror, are important on a daily basis."

ADAPT YOUR DREAMS — Priorities change as time goes on. Check in with yourself to make sure you are staying true to who you are. "I hear a lot about girls who get to high school and find other interests — and I just think it's okay to have a dream, and then have that dream change," said **Whitney Engen** (USWNT 2011-2016). "It's OK to say, 'You know what? Maybe this isn't for me.' Don't sacrifice yourself as a person just to try and fit a role."

HOWARD SMITH/ISI PHOTOS

Ronnie Fair Sullins, 17, with Michelle French in 2002

by camp counselors and brought in for breaking curfew, she was humiliated by the questioning. "Are you the sister who made it?" a coach asked Ronnie, who shook her head side to side. "Well, it's better that way," said the coach. Ronnie would need to board the plane home by herself, then sulk for the week alone in the bedroom she had shared with her sister since birth. She was sure she would quit soccer. "I was crying and I was mad, of course, at everybody else at first," said Ronnie. "I made up my mind I was going to take some art classes, and I'd go be an artist. I had all sorts of silly ideas."

That forced introspection, however, would bring an epiphany. "The bottom line was that I had to look deep inside and say, 'Did I really deserve to make the team? Or was it a situation where I should have done more work outside of practice?'" said Ronnie. "Deep down, if I was honest, I just wasn't spending as much time as Lorrie was with the ball." She decided from there, she said, to control what she could, which was schoolwork and more practice time. While Lorrie headed off as one of the top recruits in the country to North Carolina, in the midst of the Tar Heels' near stranglehold on women's college soccer supremacy, Ronnie accepted her own soccer scholarship offer at Stanford. Recognized to this day as one of the best players in the history of a school that's won three national titles of its own in the past decade, she would eventually join Sara Whalen Hess on the New York Power and, for a brief moment, take the field again with her sister. On May 9, 1997, Ronnie subbed into a game against England — with her mother and brother watching on the home state field — to mark the first time in history that sisters would appear together for the National Team.

For Ronnie, though, the most significant moment of her life might have happened back at Stanford. While preparing for the professional soccer draft, she met with her academic advisor. He noticed that, as a biology major, she was just a few physics and organic chemistry classes short of the requirements for medical school. "I'm not *that* crazy!" she said, but then proceeded to heed the advice. While Lorrie was winning World Cup titles and Olympic medals in her 120-game National Team career across 10 years, Ronnie retired after three National Team appearances and three seasons as a professional — then went back to school for more than a decade for one of the most grueling journeys the medical profession can offer. At the ceremony honoring her ascension into pediatric surgery, no one was more proud than her twin.

"If we're talking life lessons, I would argue that her story is almost more important than mine," said Lorrie. "By all accounts, my sister had a really incredible soccer career — but

Dr. Ronnie Fair Sullins, 2019

in some respects, it was kind of eclipsed by mine. We'd have family members at parties who would come up to her and ask, 'Are you the one who plays soccer?' I think that was pretty hurtful. But she responded by going and getting a medical degree, and not just any degree. She goes into pediatric surgery, which is one of the most competitive fields in the country. For her fellowship, there were just three placements in the whole country. When I went to her graduation, it wasn't like any other graduation you would imagine. It was literally *her* graduation — an entire weekend dedicated to one person. The head of the program at Children's Hospital of Wisconsin said, 'I'm probably going to offend some people in this room because some of our fellows have stayed on with us, but Ronnie is the best fellow we've ever had in the history of the program.'"

WHILE DR. RONNIE FAIR SULLINS SAID SHE HAD no thought of becoming a doctor before the Stanford advisor made the suggestion, fellow Stanford alum Rachel Buehler Van Hollebeke said the idea had been on her mind her whole life. Her great grandfather, J.W. Buehler, started a family tradition in medicine by making house calls on horseback at the turn of the 20th century. Her grandfather, Lyle, was a doctor and her father, Donald, recently retired after 40 years as a cardiothoracic surgeon. Whatever soccer threw at her, whether it be the frustration of making youth national teams without much hope of advancing, or the surprise of getting called into the 2008 Olympic team training camp, Rachel always had another goal to keep her grounded. Just a month before the National Team would leave for Beijing, in the midst of intense sometimes two-a-day practice sessions, Abby Wambach held cue cards covered in medical terms while Rachel crammed for the Medical

Rachel Buehler Van Hollebeke, taking on Marta at the 2011 World Cup

College Admission Test, a seven-and-a-half hour exam that typically requires the average would-be doctor to find about 300 hours for focused preparation. She would make the National Team, pass the MCAT, and win the Olympic gold medal all in the same summer.

"I had always lived a double life, from growing up in high school, balancing youth national teams and academics, to college soccer," said Rachel, modestly shrugging off the stunning accomplishment. "I think I liked having another outlet to be able to channel some intensity and focus into something besides soccer." Passing the MCAT gave her a three-year window to make a decision: medicine or soccer, or take the test again in the

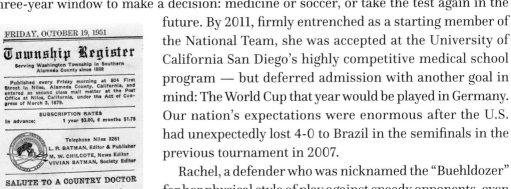

FRIDAY, OCTOBER 19, 1951

Township Register

Serving Washington Township in Southern Alameda County since 1888

Published every Friday morning at 804 First Street in Niles, Alameda County, California, and entered as second class mail matter at the Post Office at Niles, California, under the Act of Congress of March 3, 1879.

SUBSCRIPTION RATES

In advance: 1 year $3.00, 6 months $1.75

Telephone Niles 3261

L. R. BATMAN, Editor & Publisher
M. W. CHILCOTE, News Editor
VIVIAN BATMAN, Society Editor

SALUTE TO A COUNTRY DOCTOR

It is with sincere regret that we learn this week of the temporary retirement of Dr. Lyle Buehler of Niles. Doctor's orders have put him in the position of taking an enforced vacation that will last at least six months or more, depending upon how rapidly he recovers from a condition that undoubtedly came about from overwork.

A long Buehler tradition . . .

future. By 2011, firmly entrenched as a starting member of the National Team, she was accepted at the University of California San Diego's highly competitive medical school program — but deferred admission with another goal in mind: The World Cup that year would be played in Germany. Our nation's expectations were enormous after the U.S. had unexpectedly lost 4-0 to Brazil in the semifinals in the previous tournament in 2007.

Rachel, a defender who was nicknamed the "Buehldozer" for her physical style of play against speedy opponents, even scored a goal against North Korea in the opening game of the tournament. In the quarterfinal rematch against Brazil, however, she suffered a soccer player's second-worst non-injury nightmare. In trying to defend Marta, widely considered the best player in the world at the time — and

Love Soccer, But Keep Your Options Open

THOUGHT FOR SURE I WAS BONA FIDE. With several National Team appearances already on my resume, I was so confident heading into the 2003 Women's United Soccer Association draft that I deferred the spring semester of my senior year to be ready. Then — cue the sound of a record scratching as loudly as you can — I walked through the Penn State "quad" one day in the late fall of 2002. "Did you hear the WUSA folded?" asked the assistant coach of the men's team. He was matter-of-fact; I felt like I was literally spinning, suddenly untethered to an almost life-long dream.

I tried to make it work. Still in the pool of players the National Team would call from time to time, I bounced around teams in the U.S. and abroad, until I heard the real sound of my back breaking in

Joanna, the corporate executive

2006. It was a seemingly simple play: I took a ball off my chest, turned quickly to play it to a teammate and then, "Pop." Just like that, I was in surgery to repair a herniated disk and facing a long recovery with no income. Enter plan B. It came in the form of a godsend from a father, a soccer dad, with an offer I couldn't refuse: I trained his daughter and, in turn, he trained me in commercial real estate — while I continued to rehab my body. Three real estate licenses later (D.C., Maryland and Virginia), I officially became a part of a firm called Studley. I even had my own office while playing a new game that seemed oddly familiar. Hustle, in the form of cold calls to law firms, non-profits, and corporations, was required to encourage these organizations to renegotiate their leases. Strategy and tactics, the art of honing my craft to convince CEOs and presidents, required quick thinking. Hearing "No" was just like having a bad practice; I came back the next day and tried even harder.

I was good, so good I helped create the first "carbon neutral calculator" for office buildings, resulting in an invitation to meet former Vice President Al Gore. I cut some deals and cashed some checks, some that would surpass my entire year's salary as a soccer player. I also saved every penny, knowing that the game was still pulling at my heartstrings. I stayed in shape and was ready when the new Women's Professional Soccer league draft rolled around in 2009, and again in 2012 when the National Women's Soccer League debuted. Thanks to my plan B, I never had to worry about the leagues' futures. I had created my own security blanket. — J.L.

many would say of all-time — Rachel was called for a penalty inside "the box," which is the white-lined 18-by-44 yard area in front of the goal. That meant a penalty kick for Brazil and, in a debated decision that will last as long as soccer fans can still click on YouTube, a "red card" for the offender. Stunned, Rachel lined up with her teammates, only to be reminded by team captain, Heather O'Reilly, that the red card meant she needed to leave the field. When officials then told her to exit the field level of the stadium entirely, she ran crying room to room in the cavernous basement until she found a tiny television in the doping room, where athletes are checked for illegal drugs. Rachel watched, with millions of fans around the world, as Megan Rapinoe's crossing pass found Abby's forehead for the most famous goal in the history of women's soccer. The Marta penalty kick had been equalized in the 122nd minute of play — 32 minutes into overtime — and the U.S. went on to win on a penalty kick shootout. "I felt terrible," said Rachel. "I'm not a red-card kind of player. I was praying the whole time that we'd be able to get through it and get the win. It was so suspenseful and insane. I was literally screaming; when Abby scored, I started sobbing."

After sitting out the next game, as required by rules after a red card, a soccer player's worst nightmare awaited in the World Cup final against Japan when Rachel's defensive miscue in the 81st minute gave up an easy tap-in goal. While the Japanese women — seemingly propelled by the emotion of their nation's fans recovering from one of the

COURTESY OF DR. RACHEL BUEHLER VAN HOLLEBEKE

Dr. Rachel Buehler Van Hollebeke, at home in California in 2020

most destructive tsunamis in world history — celebrated their eventual victory, Rachel said she never felt quite the same way about soccer ever again. "In sports, just like life, there are things that happen that you can't control," she said. "It was hard for me to let go of that play, or the red card. I was definitely being aggressive, but I still don't think I deserved that call. It was hard for me to move on when something difficult like that happened. I'd have these flashbacks, like a form of post-traumatic stress disorder."

With the plan B of medical school waiting any time she was ready, she once again thought long and hard about her future. Instead of leaving the game quite yet, however, she found her way to a sports psychologist. Mental healing, for the future doctor, would come in time to win a gold medal in the 2012 Olympics and spend three more years in the game that she had to learn to love again. "I learned to stop fighting the negative images that came into my head, because that would just make them stronger and more painful," said Dr. Rachel Buehler Van Hollebeke, who finally did start medical school on Monday, Aug. 31, 2015, about 15 hours after she played her last game Sunday evening and retired from the Portland Thorns of the National Women's Soccer League. "Instead of fighting those negative thoughts, my psychologist helped me learn to breathe through the images and visualize rain, as if the bad stuff was being washed away. For me, it worked . . . That, and time, which helps heal a lot of things."

FOR PSYCHOLOGY MAJOR SARA WHALEN, time didn't seem to be healing much of anything as the summer of 2002 stretched into the fall, winter and spring of 2003. When a staph infection nearly killed her after the operation to repair the torn anterior cruciate ligament suffered in the soccer game, doctors needed to start over almost a year later by taking out the metal support material they had originally inserted in her knee. Constant trips to the hospital, with round after round of antibiotics, didn't seem to be working. Rehab, simply trying to walk again, brought constant setbacks. "I was plummeting; my health kept deteriorating and I just couldn't recover," Sara told us. "It was a very, very sad time dealing with the loss of my physical self, then also my job and my friends who were all on the team." Speaking to author Sam Weinman for his 2016 book, "Win at Losing: How Our Biggest Setbacks Can Lead to Our Greatest Gains," Sara was even more dramatic:

Dr. Sara Whalen Hess, with her husband, Jon, and their family

"You can't feel that way indefinitely. Your body can only sustain so much pain. It was like, 'Just fucking end it. I can't deal with this anymore.'"

At one of the lowest points in her life, Sara was reminded of one of her primary remaining assets: her college degree. About two years after the initial soccer injury, with the medical doctors having finally solved some of her health issues, she hobbled — with the aid of knee braces and crutches — to Fordham University and enrolled in its graduate psychology program. She recalls being inspired by a guest lecturer, who told her that the triumphs, the injuries, and even the near-death experiences could have a higher purpose in educating and inspiring others. "That's when I dove back into school," she said. "It was amazing, it put me in a completely new direction where I'm able to use my experiences for something that, potentially, could help other people, and actually myself, feel better."

Dr. Sara Whalen Hess, having since married Jon Hess — the former Princeton lacrosse player who saw her through the depths of all that despair — found herself going, "100 miles an hour again to what I wanted, which was to get my doctorate in that field." She was speaking somewhat metaphorically. In reality, she was taking baby steps each day out on the West Side Highway in New York. On the bad days she could barely crawl, but on the best days she would jog, even for a minute at time, and often in tears from the overwhelming pain. By November of 2004, she had gathered up every ounce of resolve that soccer had ever taught her and stood at the starting line of the New York City marathon. Her goal was finishing in four hours, yet four hours and 19 minutes later she had achieved the biggest triumph in her life — one she shares with young aspiring athletes to this day. "I had that backup plan," she said. "When things were going great in soccer, I thought I'm never going to use it because everything seemed so awesome. When things weren't so great, the backup plan was there for me." And yes, her friends will tell you, 'Say' can still dance. "Of course!" said Sara. "A girl's gotta have fun."

Is Winning Everything?

The College Coach Most Known for Victories Emphasizes all the Good that can be Gained From Defeat

N THE BEGINNING, THE STEADY STREAM of soon-to-be National Team players began to congregate in the same place for same essential reason: because they could. In 1981, Stacey Enos, the standout for the first-ever girls soccer team at her high school in Tampa, Fla., heard about a new male coach at the University of North Carolina who was finally taking a women's sport seriously. That same year, Emily Pickering, a local high school legend on Long Island in New York, liked the idea that someone was actually offering her scholarship dollars to keep knocking people over on her way to the ball. For Lehigh University sophomore Lauren Gregg, the choice was simple. After a one-year sabbatical at Harvard University — in which she scored two goals against North Carolina in an unofficial national women's championship tournament — she had to either return to Pennsylvania and play again with men, the only soccer option on that campus, or accept an offer to transfer schools and play with the women she had just beaten.

Stacey, Emily and Lauren helped win the first official women's NCAA championship in 1982 and, for the next 30 years, Anson Dorrance's teams would win the vast majority of the rest of those, too. Mia Hamm's proclamation: "The person who said winning isn't everything never won anything," became part of the core ethos and outsized aspiration that drew legions of the world's best female players, year after

COURTESY OF EMILY PICKERING HARNER

1986 National Teamers Emily Pickering Harner, left, with Janine Szpara, Marcia McDermott, Stacey Enos, Lori Henry, April Heinrichs, Ann Orrison-Germain and Kim Crabbe. Emily, Marcia, Stacey, Lori and April all played together in college.

Cat Reddick Whitehill, standing back left, with the boys in Alabama

year, to aspire to be in Chapel Hill, where the few second-place trophies that the Tar Heels did acquire were demarcated as dust-covered door stops in Anson's ramshackle office. For Cat Reddick Whitehill, a pastor's daughter from Alabama who grew up with Mia's poster on her wall, that reputation was deeply ingrained in her psyche by the time she became the top high school recruit in the nation in 1999. Cat had started out by competing with, and usually dominating, the young local boys at first. When she switched to playing with girls, Cat's club soccer team won state titles each year. Her high school team, Briarwood Christian School, never lost a single game in her four years in which she scored a national record 211 goals. Phil Reddick, a former Virginia Tech football player, told journalists of the day that he was amazed that his then teenage daughter could give him a run for his money, whether pressing leg weights in the gym, or predicting the winners of college football games during their Thursday morning father-daughter breakfasts at the Birmingham Chick-fil-A. She wanted to win. Period.

Hundreds of colleges offered women's soccer by the time Cat was a senior, but she was nothing if not confident when the recruiters tried to sway her with an underdog appeal. "Wouldn't you rather be the team that beats North Carolina than just be North Carolina? That was a good ploy," Cat told one of Anson Dorrance's many biographers, Tim Crothers, for his 2006 book titled "The Man Watching." "Being the underdog appeals to a lot of girls, but I asked myself, 'Is a team that's never beaten North Carolina going to make me a better player? Do I want to be on the team that tries to beat North Carolina, or do I want to be on the team that wins?'" For most of Cat's Tar Heel career, Tim was watching from close range. To thoroughly research the book, the long-time senior writer for *Sports*

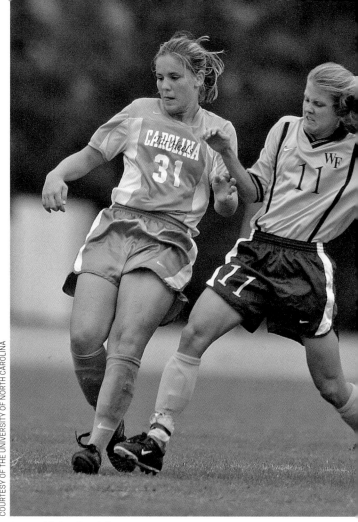

Illustrated magazine embedded himself with the team for more than four years starting in 2001. The result was a detailed, intimate portrait of a college culture that — as much as any women's athletic program in history — has spawned America's pre-occupation with winning, playing time and scholarships. The coach's rhetoric was as grand as the record. "My thrill during our games is the understanding that every team that leaves the field against us knows they were beaten by a greater force. No, not a better team. They ran into a force," said Anson, as quoted by Tim in a pre-game speech against Villanova during Cat's senior year. "They found the center of our chest and it was hard and they couldn't knock us down. So when you're tackling out there today, I want

Cat Reddick Whitehill, at North Carolina

you to throw your body at the girl with such a clattering of bones and gristle that she'll be worried about having a scar from her kneecap to her ankle. I want her wondering, 'If I finish this game, will I ever be able to wear a skirt again?'"

The actual introduction to North Carolina initially left Cat Reddick stinging from a culture shock of her own. More than 70 goals in each of her last two high school seasons, and her first appearance with the National Team, left her thinking that the UNC freshman orientation packet — with instructions on expectations for fitness levels — wasn't even worth opening. In the heat of a North Carolina August of 2000, just six weeks after her first National Team game, she promptly failed Anson's mandatory fitness test. Even worse, Cat found herself at or near the bottom of all 28 categories of performance rankings after each practice in North Carolina's legendarily public "Competitive Cauldron," and she began the season on the bench behind a non-scholarship player. When North Carolina lost at Florida State that fall and Cat only played a few minutes of the game, her grandmother, a Tallahassee resident, was blaming Cat's plight squarely on the coach. "That Anson!" she exclaimed. "He needs to play you, or he's going to hear from me!"

LIKE ANSON DORRANCE, TIM CROTHERS IS A NEAR life-long Tar Heel. A journalism graduate of the school, he made a name for himself with feature stories in *Sports Illustrated* about peculiar personalities, many obsessed with winning — including a 15-year-old golf

What's in a Number?
Plenty, When it's Retired

UNIFORM RETIREMENTS CONJURE UP CERTAIN IMAGES, RIGHT? Championships. Most Valuable Player awards. Lots of trophies and, in soccer, tons of goals and assists. Highlight reels. Insert the drum roll here . . . I scored *six* times in my four seasons as a defensive midfielder for the Washington Spirit, with one assist. Total. By the time I retired, I had — at least on the stat sheet — an entirely unremarkable 51-game career with my hometown team, whose best season on my watch ended with me watching from the bench. See Page 195, if you'd like to re-live those gory details. My time with the Spirit, in fact, wasn't so different from the other 12 years of my professional soccer life. I joke that my lowlights actually EXCEED my highlights. Let's see: My professional teams lost all three of the championship games in which I had played; I saw

COURTESY OF JOANNA LOHMAN

Joanna, the last Spirit player to ever wear jersey No. 15

two professional leagues crash and burn around me in bankruptcy; I was one of the last players cut from the National Team prior to the 2007 World Cup. And did I tell you I still have splinters in my butt from all the time sitting during some of my pro seasons?

But did I also tell you that I, Joanna Lohman, became the first player in the history of the Washington Spirit to have her jersey retired? No one will wear the number 15 ever again. I'll admit that even I was pleasantly shocked when I heard the news. "How?" I wondered. "Why did a player like me, a player who seemed to lose sometimes more than she won, deserve an honor such as this?" But then the calls started coming in from my peers and the Instagram messages arrived from fans, who reminded me there are different ways of keeping score. "Thanks for being a great role model and person!" said one mother.

"My daughter and I have enjoyed watching you over the years. Good luck with the exciting second phase of your career." Then another fan: "Congrats on an amazing career. You're such a positive person and amazing role model!!! Can't wait to see what you do next." Then a friend . . . "What an incredible human being you are! It is a true honor to have been able to film you and get to know you! Thanks for everything, Jo!"

Those hundreds and hundreds of messages made me realize that my character was equally, if not more, important than my game. I wasn't known for unbridled success, but rather the opposite: resilience, strength, compassion and re-invention. My legacy was about humanity and who a person can become if they use failure, rejection and change as fuel to rise from the ashes. It is exactly why I write this book now telling you about many ways to define greatness and that we all struggle — and it's within the strife where we discover true beauty. The Spirit didn't retire the jersey of a "winner" in the traditional sense that so many of us strive for when we lace on those first pairs of cleats. They did retire the number of a fighter, a self-professed Rainbow Warrior and noted failure expert who lives a relatable, real life. Warriors fall. We get up. And we do it again and again. Now that is #winning. — J.L.

phenomenon named Tiger Woods in March of 1991. "I don't want to be the best *black* golfer on the Tour," Tiger told Tim. "I want to be the best golfer on the Tour." A decade later, Tim was a professor at his alma mater, fulfilling an idea for a book about the school's already legendary soccer coach that had long been festering. Anson was 22 years into his women's soccer experiment by then and, right away, the writer began to recognize a gross misperception. "People thought, maybe some still do, that Anson is all about winning," Tim told us. "And there was a time when he saw his players as nothing more than chess pieces on a board. There was no real emotional connection. It was really just a bit strict: 'I'm the coach here and you're the players, and there will not be a lot of bonding involved. I'm going to kind of order you all around and tell you what to do, and hopefully we'll make this work.'"

Tim was allowed into every team meeting, and to listen in on player-coach conversations. He sat on the bench during games and rode the bus and planes to games, including the

Lilly's Winning Formula: Set Realistic Goals

RATHER THAN FOCUSING ON WINNING GAMES at a young age, National Teamers recommend focusing on individual improvement instead. **Kristine Lilly** holds one of the American sports records least likely to be broken, having played 354 games with the U.S. Women's National Team including five World Cups. In 2019, she co-authored a book "Powerhouse" (Greenleaf Press) with Dr. John Gillis and Dr. Lynette Gillis focused on business and life lessons from her 23-year career. In Chapter 3, the authors talk about the importance of setting goals and writing them down. We asked Kristine to adapt that chapter for today's young athletes:

Why Goal Setting is Important — "You need goals that give you the motivation to perform in whatever craft you're doing. Goals help you strive to get better. If we don't have goals, we're kind of just sitting in the comfort zone where nothing's really happening and we're just kind of cruising through life."

Set Specific Goals — "People can say, 'This month I'm going to work out.' But that's just kind of way out there. Define what that means: Once a day? Once a week? Once a month? The more specific you can be, believe it or not, the easier it will be to achieve your goals."

Be Clear — "Beyond being specific with your goals, also be clear. For example, running on Monday can mean so many different things, so clarify that. Say Monday is going to be running hills for 10 minutes. Wednesday can be running for 20 to 30 minutes. Fridays can be running for an hour. That way, no interpretation is needed; you know exactly what you're going to do."

Define Priorities — "List what is really important to you, because if something is not important, you're less likely to do it. Get things that really matter to you at the beginning of the national championship won during Cat's senior year. Tim talked to the earliest players like Stacey Enos, who adored her coach's uncanny ability to unlock the complexities of the game, even as she bristled at his sometimes scathing, often sarcastic rebukes of players' fitness and physiques. Tim ruffled Emily Pickering Harner, who told us she objected to Tim's depiction of North Carolina's freewheeling party culture in the early '80s, in which the young coach looked the other way as long as the women didn't let their hangovers slow them down on the field. "Anson was not our friend," said Emily, who holds the distinction of assisting Michelle Akers on the National Team's first-ever goal, then scoring its second goal, in 1985. "During our era, Anson was very robotic. He was so robotic, it was hard to think of him as being human. It was his Dad and brothers that humanized him. All the players knew Jack and Peter and his Dad, because they were the only three people in the stands back in those days."

The more Anson won, the more the North Carolina mystique grew. After he discovered

Kristine Lilly, with her daughter and first book

list; then toward the end put ones that are less important."

Distinguish Individual vs. Team Goals — "As much as you have your own personal goals, you can't get caught up in those individual goals, because if you get caught up too much, you could even hurt the team. Make sure these individual goals are going to help the team. One of the easiest things for me to prioritize is fitness. That's one thing you can control and if every player on your team is fit, it is going to help your team. If your goal is to say, 'I'm scoring five goals every game,' that becomes more self-serving because there will be situations where passing is a better option for the team than trying to score yourself."

Track Goal Achievement — "You can't manage what you don't measure. So, for instance, I'm a left mid-fielder and I want to cross the ball as my goal. I need to be specific and track that during the game to see how I'm doing. I would say, 'I want to have four crosses into the box that create goal-scoring opportunities.' And then someone would track that for me so we could review it later."

Set Stretch Goals — "As much as we need those goals that you can accomplish in a day, a week, or a month, we need our longer goals to become World Cup champions and win gold medals, or even simpler things like losing 30 pounds by the end of the summer or the year. Have something out there that all these small goals are leading to. Having a stretch goal out there keeps you motivated and keeps you accomplishing these smaller goals."

Recalibrate as Needed — "In soccer and life things happen. We have a goal in mind and something alters that, whether it's an injury or a setback. I think we need time for dealing with it, to actually pout or be sad or angry, and then reevaluate. Say, 'OK, now this is my situation.' That's where you have to start to have different goals."

April Heinrichs in that basketball gym in Littleton, Colo., the Tar Heels lost her first collegiate game 3-1 to Connecticut, but then went undefeated for the rest of 1983 — and 1984 — and some thought Anson might never lose again. In the 12-year span from 1982 to 1994, the only national championship North Carolina didn't win came on a fluke play against George Mason University in 1985 when Stacey was playing injured. She is still haunted by the instant that led to the loss that she partially blames on herself. "I had hurt my knee in the semifinals against Colorado College and I probably shouldn't have played, but it was the last game in my career and I wanted to be out there," said Stacey. "When they crossed the ball in, I just hesitated . . . I didn't deal with it well." When Stacey mistakenly deflected the ball with her head to a George Mason forward, her National Team teammate

Stacey Enos, comforted by her coach

FROM "THE MAN WATCHING" BY TIM CROTHERS

Pam Baughman-Cornell, the goal sent shockwaves through college soccer.

A photograph of that game's conclusion, included in Tim's book, stands out both for its content and its caption. Stacey appears inconsolable — with Anson's right arm around his player and his left hand in his pocket as he looks off into the distance. "The moment captures a crossroads for the program, illustrating that the Tar Heels were no longer invincible, just as Dorrance was realizing that he needed to be more emotionally supportive of his players," Tim wrote. Thirty-five years later, Stacey figured "that might have been the first hug Anson ever gave anyone on the team. That was a tough day for the both of us. Anson wanted to kick the living shit out of everybody and I thrived in that environment. I mean, I loved it. I thought he was a brilliant coach and not the kind of coach that I, or probably any other woman, had ever had any exposure to previously. Losing wasn't an option. So when we did lose, maybe we both learned a lot that day. There's more to life than winning."

THIS WAS NOT A MOMENT ATOP MOUNT CRUMPIT, where the Grinch's heart grew three sizes in an instant, but rather the beginning of a slow-but-sure evolution. Stacey, who joined Lori Henry as the two Tar Heels to play in the first National Team game in 1985, felt that Anson's demeanor began to change in earnest in 1987 when he found his own version of Tiger Woods. Mia Hamm was just 15 when Anson recruited her to the National Team, and only 17 when her parents dropped her off in Chapel Hill and signed the paperwork to make the coach her legal guardian. "He started to take control of the team, the whole team environment, by then," said Stacey. "He had Mia to take care of and I think he took that responsibility very seriously."

National Teamer Tracey Bates Leone said her coach's softer side had really been there all along, even before she entered UNC in 1985. Anson had previously been her youth coach, including at a regional camp in Michigan in 1984 when all the players were awakened

Tracey Bates Leone, escorted down the aisle by her coach, Anson Dorrance

for a surprise pre-dawn meeting. Anson's father, Nathan "Big Pete" Dorrance, had died suddenly of a heart attack. "Anson stood in front of us and told us the story about how his Dad really had wanted him to go to law school, and how he was literally hours away from being a lawyer," said Tracey, whose own father had died years earlier. "He told us how he started coaching the women's team and put the lawyer dream aside. In the beginning, his Dad didn't quite understand that. But then when his Dad saw him with his team, he said, 'I get it now, I understand why you changed your dream.'" When Anson left the meeting, wiping tears from his eyes, Tracey and a teammate found him in his hotel room packing his suitcase. Their goodbye hug was sustained and heartfelt. "I've always thought it amazing that he did that, that he took the time to really tell us how he felt," said Tracey, who would ask Anson to walk her down the aisle a few years later when she married her husband, the long-time soccer coach Ray Leone. "Anson was like my Dad; I viewed him as my Dad."

That morning in Michigan, according to Tracey, was perhaps the most poignant example of a lesson Anson helped her and so many others learn through the years: winning can be the goal, but adversity is always a better teacher. Anson was as disarming as he was unequivocal when we spoke with him about life lessons from the game in February of 2020. He had coached more than a thousand victorious soccer games by then, more than anyone else ever has or likely ever will, but wanted to be sure today's parents heard him loudly and clearly: "One of the most important things that you can absorb in life, especially your athletic life, is pain and failure. What a wonderful environment to fail in — because it really doesn't matter. Even in this environment, winning doesn't really matter. Your education matters; your character matters.

Cat Reddick Whitehill, with Tony DiCicco, left, and J.P. Dellacamera

Winning Comes in Many Forms

ANGIE HAD JUST TURNED 9 WHEN THE FALL SOCCER SEASON started with her Potomac club's new rule: no one was allowed to play "up" with older girls any longer. That meant my daughter was separated from virtually all the girls with whom she had played since she joined the club two years earlier, but she'd be playing for a heralded new coach, Jonah Schuman. He had just earned his "A" license from U.S. Soccer — the highest level of certification a youth coach can achieve. Right away, Jonah let the team know he defined winning differently than Angie's previous coach. The final score of games didn't matter as long as the players, all 12 of them, were having fun and developing their skills.

When Jonah pulled her out of a preseason tournament game with about four minutes to go, Angie watched from the bench as her team gave up two goals and lost 5-4. I don't recall another time in life when she was more upset, or cried any harder, on the ride home. "Coach feels like all the girls deserve to play equally," I told Angie. "You already had your turn." I was doing my best to back Jonah, but the truth is I had a really hard time with the decision. I'm old school, which means any sports team I had ever been on put its best players on the court or field at the end of a close game.

Angie, standing far left, with her teammates and coach Jonah

The following weekend, Angie was invited to play as a guest with the older girls. They lost every game, too, but Angie enjoyed the weekend far more in an environment with her friends where the coach clearly tried to win on the scoreboard. For the next two months, I honored my daughter's wishes by bringing her to the older team's practices and games and, near the end of the season, Jonah said he would reluctantly agree to make a club exception and formally allow Angie to switch teams for the winter and spring. Proving there were no hard feelings a few months later, he invited Angie to rejoin his team for an end-of-season tournament. Before posing with the girls and their championship medals, Jonah let it be known he would be moving on to coach a high-level Girls Academy team the following year. "Maybe I'll see you again, Angie," he said. "Let's keep in touch."

In the small world that is soccer, Angie was soon back playing part time with Jonah. At age 11 on an Under-13 team of the some of the better players in the area of Washington, D.C., Angie was not anywhere near the best player out there — but I appreciated that Jonah and the other coaches put her in games and gave her a chance to improve. That's winning, no matter what the score. Meanwhile, Angie also played full-time for her Potomac club team with her buddies, some of whom she'd been playing with for more than half her young life. With three minutes to go in a close game, her coach wouldn't think of taking her out. She had some game-winning goals, and some tough losses. All of it, the winning, the losing, and the fight for playing time against better competition, will help her in the long run. I'm thankful Jonah made that opportunity possible. — P.T.

But whether or not you succeed, win or lose in sport? Or whether or not you're in pain from a decision a coach made about playing time, or from losing a game? These are wonderful things to experience as a kid, because you then get to make a decision: If you want to win all the time, invest in it. Invest in your development. And if you don't like the feeling of getting your rear end kicked in, then do something about it."

Cat Reddick Whitehill said she took that message to heart just about time she held her grandmother back from accosting her coach about playing time. The fitness training on the field might have been miserable, but it was nowhere near as bad as the feeling she suffered in her gut when she finished near last in a sprint or a two-mile run. "I was so mad at myself for thinking that I could come into UNC and not listen to Anson or read his packet," said Cat, now a soccer analyst on television. "I was mad because I thought that I was better than that. My ego got into it. I think it was great for me to kind of get dropped a couple of notches so I could really look inside myself and say, 'Do I want to be the best, and how can I get to be the best?'" By the time of the 2000 NCAA championship game against UCLA, Cat was in the starting lineup for the first time all season, scored the winning goal, and was named defensive MVP of the tournament. A month later, after the holiday break, Anson called his future National Team star into his office to express a concern. "He had heard rumors that I was going to transfer," said Cat. "I said, 'No, Anson. I'm staying.' As hard as that fall season was for me, I became — not just a better soccer player — I became a better person because of it."

TIM CROTHERS AND ANSON DORRANCE, WRITER AND COACH, have stayed in touch around campus ever since the book revealed the good, bad and occasionally even ugly inner-workings of a dynasty. Since then, the facilities are newer; Anson's office no longer looks like a shack in a trailer, and the bright new playing field bears his name. The NCAA championships don't happen anymore with timeclock regularity — the most recent, 22nd of all time, came in 2012 — but Tim thinks his old friend is more content with what he's accomplishing in his fifth decade in the job than he was in his first. "Over the years, I have watched him evolve to the point where I think he clearly cares more about his relationship with the team than he does with the success of the team," said Tim. "I saw that change occurring even during the five years that I researched the book where he tries to build the players off the field as much as he builds them on the field. Their character, different character issues, that is his passion."

COURTESY OF CRYSTAL DUNN

Crystal Dunn, a proud Tar Heel

When Crystal Dunn hears from Anson these days, she wells up with pride when he talks about her accomplishments, and not the fact that she's become a bona fide National Team

COURTESY OF THE UNIVERSITY OF NORTH CAROLINA

North Carolina, a dynasty represented in the 2019 World Cup

superstar since leading the Tar Heels to that 2012 title as college player of the year. "He talks about me as being a great person," said Crystal. "For me, that is exactly what I've always wanted — to be remembered always for being a good person, being a good teammate. Of course, being a talented soccer player matters, but what I truly enjoyed about playing for Anson was his incredible care in investing in you as a person." She said his primary trait, directness, might have been her best preparation for life. "Anson is a very tough, tough guy. He definitely did not hold back if you weren't playing well; he had no issue telling you to your face. And I think that's actually what drove people to be even better; that's what drove our culture, knowing that if I'm not playing well, there is no beating around the bush."

Lauren Gregg has watched her mentor's progress from close range — she was a National Team player in 1986, then a National Team assistant to Anson and Tony DiCicco for years thereafter — and then from afar as the first-ever coach at the University of Virginia. Also working as a physician and psychiatrist since her playing days with the men of Lehigh, and the women of Harvard and UNC, she is considered one of America's greatest soccer minds and historians. In the summer of 2020, she was thrilled to announce that her own daughter, Meilin, accepted Anson Dorrance's offer to play at North Carolina. The decision, she said, had nothing to do with a thousand wins and counting. "What Anson tapped into for me, actually touched my soul, was the idea that, 'Wow, somebody actually believes in me that way that I want to believe in myself,'" said Lauren. "He treats me the way I want to be treated and challenges me no differently than he would a guy. He also taught all of us in women's soccer

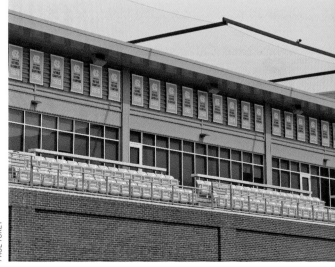

PAUL TUKEY

The 22 banners hanging over Anson Dorrance Field in Chapel Hill

Crystal Dunn and Lauren Gregg, with Lauren's younger daughter, Meili

that the sky's the limit. You want to play in a World Cup? He was the one who said, 'We're going to figure out how to do that,' and he did. It just resonated so deeply. It's impossible to describe."

Lauren sees the newfound parity in women's college soccer and knows that Meilin could have pursued her National Team dreams at any of 20 other schools. Lauren rejects the notion, however, that anyone will ever truly catch up with North Carolina, where the modern players recite the team's 13 core values from memory and the coach now rotates about 20 players on the roster freely — even if that doesn't always give his team the best chance of scoring the most goals on any given day. The evaluation of what winning truly means, said Lauren, takes a longer view; today's parents and youth coaches have taken Mia Hamm's old quote about winning out of context. "When Mia said, 'The person who said winning isn't everything never won anything,' she wasn't referring to 10-year-olds, or 14-year-olds, or even college players," said Lauren. "And maybe Anson didn't understand that quite as well in 1982, but he knows it in his soul now."

Anson Dorrance, with his legacy recruit, Meilin Gregg

Is Seeing Believing?

*Visualizing Outcomes and Setting Aside Mistakes
are Keys to Any Successful Endeavor*

AUTHOR GLORIA AVERBUCH STUDIES PEOPLE. As a writer of numerous books in collaboration with champion female distance runners, including Norwegian Grete Waitz and American Joan Benoit Samuelson, it had always been Gloria's job to examine the intersection of sports, personality and performance. By 1999, though still a marathoner herself, Gloria had refocused professionally on soccer, her daughter's obsession. When Gloria got word, in the frantic media build-up to that summer's World Cup, that the National Team was sending some players out to the Meadowlands in New Jersey for a feel-good news clip with the local weatherman, she jumped at the chance to expose 12-year-old Yael to the pros. The cameras rolled. With her daughter among a bevy of girls hanging on the National Teamers' every word, Gloria stood off to the side and pointed to one of the players, who was kneeling down to meet the girls at their level and asking them their names. "That one right there? She's special," she whispered to Aaron Heifetz, who was still the National Team's lead press officer more than 20 years later. "They're all great," said Aaron. "Maybe," said Gloria. "But that one, she has the 'it' factor. She has really got it."

Fast forward to two weeks later, just days prior to June 19 when the National Team would begin its collective barnstorm into the hearts and minds of the nation with a sold-out 3-0 victory against Denmark at Giants Stadium. On this

COURTESY OF JOANNA LOHMAN

Brandi Chastain, stepping off the National Team bus in 1999

morning, the players were stepping off the bus, one-by-one. Mia Hamm. Julie Foudy. Then Saskia Webber, Briana Scurry and others. Brandi Chastain was waving to the throngs of girls, and a few boys, as soon as she exited the door — before pausing for brief instant. "Hi, Yael!" said Brandi, as if she were cheerfully calling out an old friend. Yael's mouth fell open and her face reddened. "My daughter had this look I had never seen before, or since," said Gloria. "First of all, the fact that woman saw Yael in the crowd, and remembered Yael's name after that brief encounter on camera. Who does that? I'll never forget; I can still see Yael's braces gleaming in the sun. Her face, her smile, is the moment that showed me the awesome power of role-modeling."

FOR DAYS AND WEEKS AFTERWARD, YAEL PLAYED and re-wound her VHS tape recording of National Team highlights of her new favorite player and it wasn't long, according to her mother, that Yael began imagining she was Brandi Chastain and using the moves herself in her own youth games. Yael didn't know it at the time, of course, but psychologists, like Angela Hucles' mother, Janis, have long deployed the term "guided visualization" for the conscious act of copying — then imagining — good outcomes. Boys had been doing this in sports for decades, whether emulating the iconic batting stance of Babe Ruth or the side-armed throwing motion of Mia Hamm's husband,

Old-school VHS of the first World Cup

Nomar Garciaparra; for most girls without access to as many athletic role models, though, it was a newer phenomenon. "I remember, before the games, my mother would always try to get me to see myself running down the field and kicking the ball and scoring a goal.

Angela Hucles, with her parents, Michael and Janis

And I would always roll my eyes," said Angela. "When you're a pre-teen, or a teen, you just don't get those things." When Angela's father, Michael, somehow found a copy of a VHS tape of the 1991 women's World Cup tournament, however, she wore it out. Focusing on Michelle Akers — whose 10 goals in that tournament is a World Cup record that still stands — made Angela believe a future in soccer was possible. "I thought, 'Who are these people, these women, who actually enjoy the sport as much as I do? I had been playing on all boys teams at the time, so just to see other females competing at that level and having the same feelings as I did about soccer. That was really life-changing."

By the time Angela made it to the National Team herself in 2002, she realized her mother's thoughts on guided visualization were already deeply embedded into the culture thanks to a long-time consultant. Brought into the team by coach Tony DiCicco prior to the 1996 Olympics in Atlanta, a field hockey and soccer coach-turned-psychologist named Colleen

Hacker had long believed that the mind — and how it processed and predicted success and failure — was often the difference between winning and losing. The PhD believed in goal-setting, and daring to dream big. And she also felt that a mind comforted and supported by others, achieved through the act of team bonding, was likely to respond far better in moments of stress. Most times, Dr. Hacker told us, she liked to keep her activities fun. At one of her first training camps with the team, she drove everyone out to the top of a cliff in Portland, Ore., told half of them to put on a blindfold, and then set them off down the narrow ledge. The catch is that they were paired off and guided, with no touching allowed, by another teammate with no blindfold who could still see her way to the bottom. "It was all about building trust," said Brandi. "The message was that the only thing keeping you from falling off the cliff was your teammates."

Diane DiCicco, the widow of coach Tony DiCicco, left, with Dr. Colleen Hacker and Lauren Gregg during a 2019 tribute to the 1999 World Cup champions

As the 1996 Olympics grew closer and stress levels grew higher that summer, Dr. Hacker figured the Americans needed a way to train for a victory, yet blow off steam. Taking them to one of the large concrete buildings at the University of Georgia, at the site of the soccer games in Athens, she encouraged each player to repeatedly dance, jump and spin their way to the top of the steps — while the rest of the team belted out the theme song from the movie "Rocky." Never mind the bemusement of all the students on campus witnessing the spectacle, the championship imagery was clear to the team. "Initially, I think some people might have wondered, 'Who is she, and what's this about?'" said Dr. Hacker. "But my idea was that if I can help make a 3 to 5 percent difference in their performance, that might make the difference in a game. I didn't go in there with illusions of having some magic potion. It really was still about hard work, practice, building skills and strategies. But if I could help the team deal with the weight of the Olympic Games being in the United States, and being a gold medal favorite, then it was worth it."

Beyond the team-building exercises, Dr. Hacker also implemented new National Team policies, many of which are intact to this day, that were designed to free the players to become the best versions of themselves. She anointed Brandi's mother, Lark, and Carla Overbeck's mother, Sandra, as "parent captains" — not to provide orange slices at halftime, but rather to keep track of seating arrangements, transportation and all the other needs of families and friends. If a National Team parent lost their ticket, they were not allowed to call their daughter and stress her out about it. "What Dr. Hacker brought to our group was this awareness of the things around us, the things that really mattered," said Brandi. "She taught us how to be in the moment, how to understand what you needed, and what you didn't need."

The 99ers Made It All Seem Possible

MY CAREER DREAM GROWING UP WAS IMAGINARY AT BEST. When my elementary school teachers would ask me what I wanted to be when I grew up, I was as consistent and unequivocal in my responses as they were perplexed in their reactions. "A professional soccer player!" I declared proudly, even though there was no such thing. At least not for women in America. But I played anyway, not because I ever expected a paycheck, or really even dreamed of "making it." It was the sport, the experience, that set my heart on fire.

Then, seemingly out of nowhere — at least from the outside looking in — the 1999 World Cup happened and women's soccer hit rock star status. A sold out Rose Bowl victory for the National Team scored them magazine covers, television appearances and even an invitation to the White House to meet President Clinton and a group of youth players aspiring to be just like them. One of them, believe it or not, was me. My entire Bethesda Scorpion team gazed adoringly as Mia Hamm, Julie Foudy, Brandi Chastain, Briana Scurry and the rest of the team walked off the bus and onto the White House lawn right next to us. I was in awe of the way they carried themselves, and how Julie spoke so eloquently before the other team captain, Carla Overbeck, gifted Al and Tipper Gore with a

COURTESY OF JOANNA LOHMAN

Joanna, foreground, with her teammates at the White House in 1999

signed ball and then Mrs. Clinton and the President with a crystal soccer figurine and a team shirt emblazoned with "99" on the back.

Having just turned 17, I'll never forget the way I blushed when my Scorpion teammates shouted out to Brandi Chastain: "Joanna's going to be on the National Team one day!" Sure, I'd dreamed it forever, but my teammates' boldness instantly tied my stomach in knots. I was nervous. I was fangirling. More than anything, though, I was excited to truly believe I could one day be in their cleats. The moment felt life-changing; I know I charged home that day so inspired to get back out on the field and get to work.

Fast forward to 2015 and I was back at the White House watching the World Cup as a member of my professional soccer team, the Washington Spirit. My team asked me to stand up and say a few words to a group of young players who might as well have been me and my teammates 16 years earlier. I was struck, again, by the magnitude of the moment. Here I was, a professional soccer player — a woman who literally achieved her dream — having the chance to inspire those who walk behind me just like the 99ers did for me. Feeling every bit the proud elder statesman, I stood in front of a crowded room: "Let me tell you about the time *I* went to the White House. It was 1999 . . ." — J.L.

Dr. Hacker also believed in the power of music to trigger positive feelings — and in a life philosophy that she captured in the title of the book, "Catch Them Being Good," that she co-authored with head coach Tony DiCicco and Charles Salzberg in 2002. She asked

SPORTSWOMEN *of the* YEAR
World Cup Champion
U.S. Soccer Team

each player to submit two of their favorite songs as background music for individual highlight videos that she, Tony and assistant coach Lauren Gregg would edit together. These were required viewing prior to every game to help National Teamers visualize their goals, both literally and figuratively. "I never knew these were going to be as important as they were," said Dr. Sara Whalen Hess, now a psychologist herself. "Sometimes, in an intense environment like a soccer field, your confidence can get shattered pretty quickly when you make a mistake. She talked a lot with the coaches about 'catch them being good,' to the point where Tony would call out a strong play or a good pass. Most coaches don't do that. Colleen had us ready to conquer the world when we came out on the field."

SARA WAS FROM THE 1999 TEAM, WHICH, PROBABLY MORE than any other National Team in history, would generate evocative imagery. By then, Mia Hamm was a full-blown superstar, with commercials for Pert shampoo, Gatorade and Nike that made her the first female team sports athlete promoting products — and inspiring young girls — in prime time. Thanks to encouragement from tennis great Billie Jean King, and leadership from Julie Foudy, the women were starting to get paid something incrementally closer to what they deserved. And thanks in large part to Yael Averbuch and David Letterman's favorite "it" player, Brandi Chastain, the National Team was beginning to get attention in ways that sold gobs of tickets, even it sometimes made feminists cringe. Brandi played along when the late-night host referred to the team as "Babe City," and then grimaced and swallowed hard when press officer Aaron Heifetz unwittingly led her into a photo shoot for a new men's magazine called *Gear*. The art director's surprise concept was to have her pose wearing nothing but a soccer ball.

6
SANTA CLARA
BRANDI CHASTAIN '91

"When we were promoting 1999, we did every interview possible," said Brandi, now a mother of a son and a stepson with her husband, Santa Clara University coach Jerry Smith. "We went to every television channel; we did the weather and we did sports. We did anything because we were trying to sell this World Cup. When we got to the magazine office, and were told the idea, I said, 'Hey Aaron, this is not what you told me this was going to be.'" Attempting to visualize the outcome, in the heat of a skyrise Manhattan moment, left her rifling through all possible factors. Without even enough time to discuss the situation with her husband or parents, Brandi considered walking out the door. "The issue became, 'What do I say if I don't do it, and what do I say if I do it? Who am I representing and who am I not representing?' I had to answer those questions pretty quickly . . . Where I landed is that I'm proud of the work that I put in and I've always been highly conservative, and very conscientious, and uncomfortable with my body. Here was an opportunity for me to say, 'This is it; this is what I have — and I should feel good about it.'"

The response to the entire team's promotional efforts led to unprecedented fan appeal. The Averbuchs were among 78,972 spectators for that World Cup opener in East Rutherford,

Mia Hamm, the face of the 1990s for Nike, Gatorade and Pert

N.J., which is more than the New York football Giants ever drew to the same location. More than 65,000 fans showed up in Chicago, with 50,484 in Foxboro, Mass., 54,642 in Landover, Md., and 73,123 in Palo Alto, Calif. A world record for a females' sporting event — 90,185 patrons, many of them impressionable young girls and their fathers — waited breathlessly in the 100-degree sauna that was the Rose Bowl final against China. "It's a sight to see," the director of public relations for the Women's World Cup told the *Los Angeles Times*. "I don't know if it's the Spice Girls or the Backstreet Boys or the Beatles or what."

Behind the scenes, however, the National Team mania might never have happened if not for Colleen Hacker. As the team was preparing for the tournament, Tony DiCicco cut Debbie Keller, a player from the University of North Carolina, who had scored 18 goals in 46 games for the National Team from 1995 to 1998. "I belong on that team," said Debbie, who sued Tony DiCicco and U.S. Soccer to have her position restored. She told *Newsweek* and anyone else who would listen at the time — including some of her teammates — that she felt she was cut because she had recently filed a lawsuit against former National Team coach Anson Dorrance for making romantic advances toward her and otherwise creating a hostile environment at UNC. Anson quietly, but vehemently, denied all the allegations, most of which were later withdrawn by Debbie. Tony was cleared of any wrongdoing by an independent arbiter. In that moment, however, the National Team was comprised of eight former Tar Heels caught between a former college teammate and coaches, Anson and Tony, whom they adored.

"That situation could have completely torn the U.S. Women's National Team apart," said Dr. Hacker in the summer of 2020. "It could have set off an incredibly difficult legal precedent. There were incredible relationships and loyalties and friendships that were tested mightily." At one point, to help the team address the issue, she rolled a portable coat rack, covered in a bedspread, into the middle of a meeting. She walked behind the rack — intended to symbolize the elephant in the room — then in front of it as she talked about the

Guided Visualization: Tools of the Trade

We live in an era of unparalleled opportunity for young people to maximize performance. With a deep understanding of psychological cues, blended with the immense resources of television, Internet and live events, prospective elite athletes can unlock a powerful toolbox to help them achieve their goals:

TOOLS FOR YOUR MIND

MAINTAIN CONFIDENCE — How you feel about your own ability to accomplish a task is the most likely predictor of success. **Rose Lavelle** (USWNT 2017-present) met with a psychologist after a series of hamstring injuries got her down. "I was complaining a lot," she said. "Having someone to talk it through and help me find a different perspective made all the difference. The key was that she never offered the perspective without me getting there myself through a guided conversation."

TRAIN FOR RESOLVE — When a body is optimally conditioned, the mind often follows. "My mentality has been the fuel behind my success," said **Carli Lloyd** (USWNT 2005-present). "I learned the only way I will be able to separate myself is through my mentality. At the top, everyone is skilled, tactically smart and fit, but if you want to be the best you need to have the strongest mind."

SHAKE OFF MISTAKES — Bad stuff happens, in sports and life. You try not to do it again, but often you will anyway. Making a conscious physical reminder to remain mentally in the game, known as a "mistake ritual," has helped members of the National Team, according to **Brandi Chastain** (USWNT 1988-2004): "Mine happened to be pulling on my ponytail. **Julie Foudy** and **Shannon MacMillan** both had a rubber band on their wrists and they would snap the rubber band after a mistake. **Mia (Hamm)**

did a pulling up of the socks."

MAP YOUR OUTCOME — As audacious as it may sound, it's OK, and maybe even essential to keep big-picture dreams in mind. "One of my favorite parts of my book ("The Champion Within") is when **Tiffany Roberts** drew a picture when she was like 7 or 8 of her being in the Olympics," said **Lauren Gregg** (USWNT 1986). "That obviously had nothing to do with whether she was good enough yet, or not. You can allow yourself to dream that way no matter what the dream."

HONE THE FINER POINTS — Once you've determined your long-term goal, put it on a shelf and check back in with it from time to time, but not day to day. "There are so many things that are out of our control in sports and life, whether it's injuries or playing time," said **Lori Chalupny** (USWNT 2001-2015) "It's just so important in the moment to focus on the things you can control, like fitness and effort, and put everything else aside."

KEEP IT SIMPLE WITH A SONG — Dr. Colleen Hacker, long-time team psychologist for the National Team, advises that listening to the same songs, time and time again, can trigger positive thoughts. For **Rachel Buehler Van Hollebeke**'s inspiration, she turned to "Kissed a Girl," from Disney's "Little Mermaid." **Ashlyn Harris** likes "Show Me Love" from Robin S, while **Alex Morgan** plugs in "Mother's Daughter" by Miley Cyrus whenever she needs to psyche herself up.

— At her Hall of Fame induction ceremony, **Julie Foudy** (USWNT 1987-2004) told the attendees how much she had relied on the inspirational power of special quotes. Standing beside fellow inductee **Mia Hamm** in the HOF class of 2007, she called out Canadian author Claude Bissell: "Risk more than others think is safe. Care more than others think is wise. Dream more than others think is practical. Expect more than others think is possible."

TOOLS FOR YOUR EYES

— Boys have been informed and inspired by their sports heroes on television for more than half a century. For a 4-year-old living on the New Mexican border with Colorado, a 13-inch Hello Kitty TV tuned to a Spanish-speaking channel was key to her development. "I was just so desperate to watch soccer that I didn't care what TV it was on, or what language the call was in!" said **Mallory Pugh** (USWNT 2016-present).

— When watching games, focus on an athlete who is most like the one you want to be . . . realistically. "Who I remember the most growing up was definitely **Michelle Akers**," said **Angela Hucles** (USWNT 2002-2009). "She just completely dominated the World Cup; she was just a beast. I was a forward for the majority of my life, so I definitely could relate to that. She stuck out so much and I was in awe of how powerful she was."

— With the average teen spending more than seven hours per day on screen time, smartphones can be the enemy of athletic excellence. Watching videos to perfect technique, however, is considered essential training. When **Mia Hamm** joined the National Team as a 15-year-old and saw **Carin Jennings Gabarra** dribble, she knew she had work to do to keep up. "I was introduced to the Coerver Series," said Mia (USWNT 1987-2004). "When I wasn't in an organized setting or with my team, I could always do this series of dribbling drills. It gave me confidence."

— For the youngest players, taking in a club, high school or college game in person can create a lasting positive impression. Ideally, young players should take in professional games when possible. "When the Washington Spirit was the Washington Freedom back in the day, I would go watch those games," said **Andi Sullivan** (USWNT 2016-present). "I was lucky that my family was able to take me, so I had these role models so close to me. It made my dream seem so real."

— When **Yael Averbuch** (USWNT 2007-2013) began uploading her training videos to YouTube in 2012 while playing in Sweden, she instantly "realized that people do want to see what kind of things I do in my backyard as a pro player." She took it upon herself to develop a revolutionary app that offers video instruction on perfect technique, as well as results tracking, motivational tips and feedback tools. "Techne Futbol is aimed at helping players around the world master skills with the ball," she said, "But also to instilling important character traits, such as work ethic, discipline, consistency and accountability."

Rose Lavelle, in third grade, imagining she's Mia Hamm

COURTESY OF LISA NEUBAUE

importance of the team and unity. "Everybody understood the seriousness of it. It wasn't a petty misunderstanding," said Brandi, who had her own misgivings about Anson after he had once questioned her commitment to fitness and cut her from the National Team. "There were definitely people emotionally involved, but Dr. Hacker showed us we had to put it aside for the good of the team."

BRANDI CHASTAIN SHARES ONE OF THE MORE DUBIOUS World Cup records with an Argentinian and an Ecuadorian, who both scored *against* their own national teams — known in soccer as an "own goal" — while also scoring *for* their teams in the same game. In Brandi's case, the biggest on-field embarrassment of her career would come only five minutes into the game against Germany at Jack Kent Cooke Stadium just outside of Wash-ington, D.C., with President Bill Clinton and his family in the stands. When Brandi attempt-ed what should have been a simple pass backward to Briana Scurry in goal, a miscommuni-cation saw the ball roll slowly, but agonizingly surely, into the net for a 1-0 German lead. For-tunately for her, however, her teammate, Carla Overbeck had absorbed one of Dr. Hacker's most important lessons about guided visualization: "Park it." In other words, when you make a mistake, imagine yourself put-ting it in the parking lot until after the game.

ZUMA PRESS INC./ALAMY STOCK PHOTO

Brandi Chastain: Unveiling a statue in her honor at the Rose Bowl
Opposite: Wheaties, *Newsweek* and *Gear* magazine

That day, on July 1 in front of a global television audience, Carla sprinted to her teammate to be sure to get to her before anyone else. "Forget it. Brandi, like, forget it," she said, pulling her face ever closer to hers so she could hear. "We NEED you in this game. You need to hang in there. We will get the goal back." After each team scored another goal, Brandi would indeed tie the game by scoring off a Mia Hamm corner kick. "It was the perfect implementation of 'park it,'" said Dr. Hacker. "Now, 'park it,' doesn't mean forget about it. We don't want to forget about mistakes; we want to use them and we want to grow from them. We want to use mistakes as fertilizer — but we also don't want to let them ruin the moment."

Brandi would have one more opportunity to put the theory to the test. Nine days later, after 120 scoreless minutes in the World Cup finals that year against China, assistant coach Lauren Gregg began to draw up the list of would-be penalty kickers for the sudden-death soccer ritual that would decide the championship. Each team was allowed five players, and Lauren initially remembered a mistake — Brandi had missed a penalty shot against

China's legendary goalie Gao Hong in a loss three months earlier — and was intending to leave her out of the rotation. Tony DiCicco stepped in, however, and told Lauren to add Brandi back in . . . but with her opposite foot. She was ambidextrous, nearly as adept kicking left-footed. "Brandi wants to have the responsibility on her," Tony told the British tabloid known as *The Guardian* prior to his death in 2017. "Some players are afraid of failure, they don't want the role. Brandi wants it. She wants the spotlight. That's the type of player you want in penalty kicks."

She had learned all of her lessons by then and, fertilized by her every mistake, she could see clearly. Brandi knew Gao Hong would try to psyche her out with a broad, confident, even smug smile — so she kept her head down to avoid eye contact. Brandi knew from her husband's coaching to keep all of her movements to a minimum just prior to taking the kick to reduce any chance of error. She sensed, too, that Yael Averbuch and Angela Hucles and hundreds of future National Teamers were watching and that, in ways both subtle and profound, their soccer futures depended on what happened next: a desperate dive by the Chinese goalie that couldn't stop a perfectly envisioned ball in the back of the net. In that moment, Sara Whalen Hess set off on a mad dash toward Brandi that landed her on the cover of *Time* magazine and other news photos all over the world — in all the publications that were not comfortable showing a woman celebrating in the sports bra Brandi revealed after tearing off her own shirt.

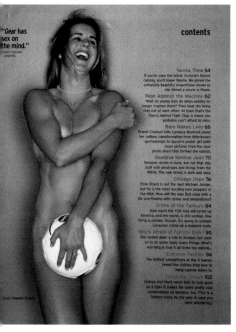

"They call me Hollywood," wrote Brandi in the preface to her 2004 book, "It's Not About the Bra," co-authored with Yael's mom, Gloria. "I guess my friends and teammates feel the name fits. I was part of that historic day for American women's soccer, July 10, 1999, when — after 90 minutes of white-knuckled but scoreless play and two overtimes — the United States defeated a tough and talented Chinese team in penalty kicks to win the women's World Cup. I took the final penalty kick in that game. You've seen the photo of the moment after; I'm the one on my knees, my face a mask of excitement and ecstasy, my arms flexed, my shirt held up in celebration. And yes — I'm wearing a black sports bra. How did I know this moment would be so revered? How could I know that image would make the cover of *Time*, *Newsweek*, *Sports Illustrated*, and countless newspapers across the country . . . that I'd mix it up on "Late Night" with David Letterman, participate on game shows like "Jeopardy," or become a commentator on television sports? Who could have imagined all of this?"

NATIONAL TEAMERS FEATURED IN THIS SECTION

Michelle Akers

Amanda Cromwell

Stacey Enos

Julie Foudy

Carin Jennings Gabarra

Amy Allmann Griffin

Linda Hamilton

Lauren Orlandos Hanson

Ruth Harker

Sara Whalen Hess

Lindsey Horan

Mia Hamm

Rose Lavelle

Carli Lloyd

Shannon MacMillan

Kim Maslin-Kammerdeiner

Tiffeny Milbrett

Mallory Pugh

Tiffany Roberts Sahaydak

Becky Sauerbrunn

Briana Scurry

Hope Solo

Cat Reddick Whitehill

Are You Ready for Elite Status?

That's when the choices get tougher

The Alchemy of Team Chemistry

Soccer's Most Controversial Player is Central to an Ongoing Debate About Individual Expression in a Team Environment

CONFLICT AND TEAM CHEMISTRY were already at odds, and the first game in National Team history hadn't even started. Crammed into the locker room below the stands at Stadio Comunale Armando Picchi on the northern shores of the Adriatic Sea on August 18, 1985, the 16 American players were certain they were being booed lustily by the Italian crowd. Michelle Akers was particularly incensed, not because the natives seemed inhospitable, but because the American coach, a sharp-tongued Irishman named Mike Ryan, had decided to bench her — even though she was the best player on his team and, as time would tell, in the world. He told the media Michelle was injured and, putting the team first, she let that story get repeated in books, magazines and newspapers for decades. In 2020, she revealed that the coach, who passed away in 2012, was simply harboring a hometown Seattle grudge from their days competing with and against each other on the local club circuit. Her ankle was sore, but fine. "It was a power struggle, his way of showing me who was boss," Michelle told us in 2020. "But I wasn't going to make a huge scene."

Meanwhile, the team's most jovial player, Stacey Enos, had taken note of one of the waiters back at the high-rise

Game program, 1985

hotel overlooking the beach in Jesolo, just a short sail down the intercoastal canal from Venice. To Stacey's surprise, he was waiting for her with red, white and blue confetti near the tunnel that led onto the field. "He was smiling, and in that instant I realized everyone else was, too," she said. "I figured out from him that everyone was saying, 'USA, USA, USA' only they were pronouncing it 'Ooooosa, Ooooosa, Ooooosa, AH.'" Moments later, when the players gathered in a circle prior to taking the field, it was Stacey who seized the moment and forged the first link in a verbal chain that has bonded every single National Team together through the generations. "On three!" she exclaimed. "Ooooosa, Ooooosa, Ooooosa, AH!" Ever since that day, three and a half decades later, the National Team members utter the same chant in the opening huddle of every game. "I love that they still say that," said that day's backup goalie, Ruth Harker. "To be part of the tradition that team stands for means a lot. We were able to put our thumbprint into the program so to speak. We didn't know we were essentially starting a sorority that day."

COURTESY OF STACEY ENOS

Stacey Enos, left, with her wife, Annie Jonas, and their son

It's a sisterhood bonded, according to member after member, by one of sports' most coveted enigmas. How to build team chemistry, and how to keep it, has been the subject of countless books, team rallies and pregame speeches of every stripe. "Chemistry is what gets us through so many situations," said Julie Foudy, one of the National Team's most vocal and longest-serving captains. In 2017, the woman nicknamed "Loudy Foudy" by her teammates, published "Choose to Matter," a book with chapter titles including "Team Chemistry is a VERB" and "There is no I in Team, But There is a ME." She credits some of the National Team's greatest successes to the team's cozy, supportive relationship. "We win the 2004 Olympics on chemistry. I think we weren't the better team against Brazil. You can say we win in 1999 because of chemistry, too, when Brandi (Chastain) scores against our own team in the opening minutes of the quarterfinal

First-ever National Team jersey

against a really good German team (see page 148). But we just believed in each other and trusted that we are going to overcome this. Carla (Overbeck) lifts Brandi back up in that moment and says, 'You're fine. We've got this. And, in fact, you're gonna win it for us.'"

Megan Rapinoe, left, with Sam Mewis, Alex Morgan, Meghan Klingenberg and Becky Sauerbrunn in a promotional photo for Julie Foudy's book, "Choose to Matter"

JULIE WAS RETIRED BY THE WORLD CUP TOURNAMENT OF 2007. Michelle Akers, too, along with other icons like Mia Hamm, Joy Fawcett and Brandi Chastain, all of whom had achieved almost mythical soccer status by the turn of the new century. On the face of it, the successive teams were more than adequately re-stocked on the field with familiar faces both newer — including Abby Wambach, Cat Whitehill, Shannon Boxx and Carli Lloyd — and older: Kristine Lilly was still in the midst of her 20th of 23 years on the team. The Americans also had the best goaltending lineup on the planet, with a gifted upstart named Nicole Barnhart backing up the gold medal winning legend of the 1996 and 2004 Olympics and the 1999 World Cup, Briana Scurry, who herself was playing behind a burgeoning new superstar: Hope Solo. She had been a National Teamer since 2000, earning occasional starts whenever Briana was either unhealthy or unfit, but by 2007 Hope was in the midst of starting a record string of 55 games without losing.

Hope had a rough game by her standards in the opener of the World Cup against North Korea that year, allowing what players call a "soft" goal that slipped through her hands on a wet day that ended in a 2-2 tie. From there, though, the American goal crease seemed like an impenetrable force field. With Abby at the height of her career, with three goals and an assist in three games, the National Team steamrolled its way through Sweden, Nigeria and England in an eight-day span by a combined score of 6-0. With a victory against Brazil and its own superstar, Marta, seeming possible — probably even likely — American head coach Greg Ryan (no relation to Mike) made what is almost universally considered to be the biggest coaching blunder in women's soccer history: He announced he was benching Hope in favor of Briana, who hadn't played a game in the three months, ever since Hope had been away at her father's funeral.

Outside the team, the condemnation of Greg's move was swift. Julie Foudy, working the stadium field as an analyst for ESPN, questioned the decision on air with Tony DiCicco, who had been the head coach for the 1996 Olympics and 1999 World Cup with Briana as his goalie. "It's a tough decision going in because you're creating a negative impact, when you really want to be going in focusing only on positives," said Julie. Neither Tony, nor any other National Team coach, had ever changed goalkeepers in the middle of one of the two major tournaments. "This is the wrong decision . . . If there isn't a goalkeeper

The Ties That Bind

We spoke to dozens of National Team players about the importance of building team chemistry in the context of an environment where teammates are often in competition with each other, or expected to have a media presence. Here are some of their comments:

REMEMBER NO ONE'S PERFECT — "I think there are times we have all probably done something as players that wasn't loved by the team, but you're judged by the balance of your contribution and what you do to help your team. How you are, what you say, what you don't say — what you abide by — is all part of being a teammate," said **Kristine Lilly** (USWNT 1987-2010).

DON'T STEP OVER THE LINE — "Team chemistry is a challenge because there are people who are different, who are not going to fit into a mold. And I think it's about understanding how to be inclusive of people who are different from you in the way that you think. But there's also a difference between being different and being destructive," said **Angela Hucles** (USWNT 2002-2009).

TAKE A DEEP BREATH — "I think it's never a good idea to speak to the media, or post something on-line, if you're overly emotional. Once it's out there there's no taking it back, so I think it's just better to be thoughtful about it," said **Shannon MacMillan** (USWNT 1993-2005).

LIKE IT, OR LEAVE IT — "If you're on a team, you're on a team for a reason. If you want it to be all about you, then go play tennis or something else. Sometimes people outperform others, but it's the coach of that team who gets to decide who plays and who doesn't. If you are not into the team thing, go find another profession," said **Carla Overbeck** (USWNT 1988-2000).

ALL ROLES MATTER — "It doesn't matter if you're best friends off the field, but as soon as you step on the field, you're all there for the same purpose, and it should be for the

COURTESY OF NICOLE BARNHART

Nicole Barnhart

betterment of the team. I knew that I was basically the second keeper and Hope (Solo) was the first keeper, so I would go out and do whatever I could to help her prepare and improve and be the best version of herself," said **Nicole Barnhart** (USWNT 2004-2013).

UNDERSTAND NUANCES — "You can't hold players to different standards. They're a part of the DNA of a team. But individual players respond differently to criticism, to feedback, to praise. So I think we do need to take the time to individually know what these players respond to and how to get the best from them. I think you do have to treat some players differently at different times, but it's the understanding that when you get out onto the field, you're always going to have the best focus and the best effort, the best attitude," said **Becky Sauerbrunn** (USWNT 2008-present).

LEARN THE ART OF TACT — "If you don't fit the mold 100 percent to what that National Team is looking for, or even a college team, they're eventually going to find someone else who does fit the team dynamic. I agree with speaking your mind. But I think there's a time and place to keep your opinions to yourself," said **Caroline Putz Leith** (USWNT 2000).

controversy, why make one?" stated Tony, as if he were looking into the now divided locker room. "It's not just those two players. Every player is affected." Inside the team, the move revealed what would be a caustic blow to delicate team psyche. "Up to that point, Hope was my best friend," said Cat Reddick Whitehill, who was one of three players who visited Hope in her room after Greg informed the team. "You had to feel for her in that moment." Abby, who along with fellow team captain Kristine Lilly had lobbied the coach to start Briana in goalie due to her solid history against Brazil, alluded to her own regret years later — though neither woman likes to address the situation directly. "There's probably some things that I would go back and change in hindsight, but because it's 2020, I can't," Abby told us. "I can't go back and change the choices I felt like I made that didn't work on every championship that we didn't win."

Megan Rapinoe, left, with Amy Allmann Griffin and Hope Solo

BY HER OWN REMARKABLE ADMISSION IN her 2012 best-selling autobiography "Solo: A Memoir of Hope," controversy had followed Hope Amelia Solo, virtually since her conception when her mother visited her father inside the Walla Walla State Penitentiary. No one was ever truly sure of the real identity of her father, a con man and grifter, but it eventually became common family knowledge that Jeffrey Solo might not be his given name. Arrested for kidnapping Hope and her brother when she was 7, her father nonetheless taught her the game of soccer — which would prove to be her ticket out of an impoverished life in Richland, Wash. — but he also lived homeless for many years thereafter. Her college coaches at the nearby University of Washington, struck by Hope's fierce love and loyalty to the man who would emerge from the woods unshowered and unshaven and sit in the highest point in the stands during her games, have remained just as dedicated to their most famous player. "She was one of the best, most supportive teammates we've ever had at UW," said Amy Allmann Griffin, who served as Hope's goalie coach in college and remains one of her closest friends.

Amy had appeared in 24 games of her own with the National Team beginning in 1987, but when coach Anson Dorrance brought in a new starting goalie just prior to the 1991 World Cup, the move relegated Amy to third string. Fearing negative repercussions for team chemistry, Anson brought Amy to China anyway after team members spoke out. "For me, it's the best compliment or biggest badge of honor I have ever received from my teammates," said Amy. "I know they went in to see Anson and said, 'If Amy doesn't go, we're not going.' That doesn't happen very often; that's pretty risky. And I'm a 5-foot-4 goalkeeper, so it's not like I'm going to win them games. As far as Xs and Os go, that World Cup goes on just fine without me. But, maybe as far as team chemistry goes, I was still a big part of the team." For the player left stateside to make room for three goalies, however, the decision still stings.

"I would also be good for chemistry; I was a really good reserve," said Amanda Cromwell, now the head women's soccer coach at UCLA. "I had people in my corner, too, who were saying, 'What the absolute f...? We're going to keep three goalies and leave a field player home?' But I get it. I was friends with all the goalkeepers and they're great people. It's a tough decision for a coach."

In her media interview prior to the World Cup semifinal game against Brazil, Hope Solo said she didn't like getting benched, but

HOPE SOLO
3 clean sheets in 4 games played

Hope Solo, on camera after the World Cup loss in 2007

accepted it was a coach's decision and pledged to support her teammates. Once the game began, however, she seemingly cast aside some of the most sacred, albeit unwritten, rules in team sports. Her frustration appeared visible from the bench and to fans worldwide. When her teammates, who appeared tentative from the start, scored on themselves after a miscommunication in front of the net, Hope appeared more angry than supportive. A referee's bad call ejected Shannon Boxx from the game and left the U.S. team down a player and, while Hope steamed, many of her teammates were crying by halftime. At the end of the game, which the National Team unimaginably lost, 4-0, Hope tearfully left her teammates to be with her family at the edge of the stands. Several minutes later, she appeared calm and clear-eyed, but didn't hold back when a Canadian reporter asked her for a comment: "It was the wrong decision, and I think anybody that knows anything about the game knows that. There's no doubt in my mind I would have made those saves. And the fact of the matter is it's not 2004 anymore. It's not 2004. And it's 2007, and I think you have to live in the present. And you can't live by big names. You can't live in the past. It doesn't matter what somebody did in an Olympic gold medal game in the Olympics three years ago. Now is what matters, and that's what I think."

Within minutes, Carli Lloyd learned via text from New Jersey that Hope's comments were blowing up on ESPN, where Julie Foudy, most especially, was shaken to her core. By the time the players turned on their televisions in their rooms a few hours away in

Chemistry Bonded Us Against All Odds

THE 2016 WASHINGTON SPIRIT TEAM WAS STACKED with, count 'em, seven players from National Teams. We had American stars including Crystal Dunn, Ali Krieger and Christine Nairn, along with Estelle Johnson from the Cameroon senior team and Estefanía Banini from Argentina. Then there were Francisca Ordega and me. Talk about a team with personality. And talent. The media wondered, in preseason, how we would make it all work and "if there were enough soccer balls to go around," in reference to all the women who were accustomed to playing a starring role elsewhere. The key was chemistry — and that team had bonding in abundance. My buddy, Franny, and I made sure of it.

I'm not a big shopper, but happily spent a day at the mall with Franny trying on Gucci sunglasses to match her sandals. My lifestyle wasn't even legal where she came from, but Franny never once questioned my choices. From the outside looking in, we were as different as black and white, straight and gay, Nigerian and American. We were two individuals from different backgrounds, religions and continents — Franny was rumored to be from a royal African family — yet she had me at hello. Maybe it was her smile. Or maybe it was her sharing her mastery of the Shaku Shaku, an authentic African dance, that became must-see moments of the "Franny and Jo Show" that

Joanna, with Franny Ordega

COURTESY OF JOANNA LOHMAN

kept things light all season long, both on the field and off. We were literally two peas in a pod, rooming together on the road, teaming up for water gun fights, practical jokes and belly laughs — the kind that last so long they make your abs ache later.

I know for Franny, an international player far from home, it meant the world to her to have a best friend who watched her back. That spilled over to the field, allowing Franny to thrive as an individual and fit comfortably into the Spirit's defensive scheme as we charged into the league finals. We didn't get there just from the Xs and Os on the chalkboard at halftime. And yes, we lost that championship game in devastating fashion (see Page 204), but the team will go down as the greatest I have ever played for — both for the wins and the friendships, especially Franny's. Thanks to her, I even amassed hundreds of fans in Nigeria and received weekly requests to come visit Lagos, the nation's capital. In 2019, I had the pleasure of visiting her country as a sports diplomat with the Department of State. A Nigeria jersey that Franny gifted to me was packed tightly in my suitcase. As I entered the TV studio for a segment on a morning show in Lagos, called "Sunrise," I was donning my "ORDEGA" shirt for her whole country to see. It seemed a fitting tribute to a friendship that defied all odds. — J.L.

Carli Lloyd, with Hope Solo in 2012

Shanghai, Hope had become a full-blown pariah. She thought she was blasting Greg Ryan to the reporter; when her teammates heard the words, though, they interpreted them as a direct slam of Briana instead. Hope's private attempts at apologies to Briana and the team, which immediately suspended her and wouldn't even let her ride on the bus with them to the World Cup consolation game, fell mostly on deaf ears — except, notably, Carli's. "Hope's character, the way that she grew up, you know she's not afraid to speak her mind when she sees something that's not right," Carli told us. "Hope knew that players, not the coach, were making that decision to bench her in 2007. And so, as a player myself, that was really hard to see. And I remember making the decision to stick by her, because I am someone who stands up for what I believe. I did not think that the way that she was being treated was appropriate of any human being. She didn't murder somebody; she simply chose to speak her mind in the media."

IT'S SAFE TO SAY THAT, FOR ALL OF HER NATIONAL TEAM RECORDS in appearances (202), victories (153), shutouts (102) and other various goaltending awards and accolades, Hope Solo also earned the distinction of most complicated legacy in team history. She was in the best form in her career in 2008 in leading the United States to an Olympic gold medal, even when it was later revealed that she had been playing through shoulder pain for years. She made amends with most of her teammates, but was still stirring the pot when she told a blog known as ThePostGame in 2011 that she had been treated unfairly in 2007. "People like to keep everything so positive — like we're the girls next door," she said. "We like to do everything together, and all that. Why are we sugarcoating? Just because

Alex Morgan, with Hope Solo, in 2016, Hope's final season

we're teammates doesn't mean we're all best friends. But that's how women's sports have been portrayed. We're not your girls next door. We have opinions; we have arguments." Fired from the team for good in 2016 for calling the Swedish national team "cowards" in deference to their defensive tactics in beating the U.S. — an abrupt termination that Abby sarcastically referred to as a "lifetime achievement award" — Hope has continued to be outspoken in her lawsuit for equal compensation for National Team players, or in criticizing the U.S. Soccer Federation for failing to equitably support soccer at all levels. She has been especially outspoken about the lack of minority youth involved in pay-to-play club soccer.

More than a decade after the team's most controversial moment, players of every era have opinions about Hope — and most of them are strong, and many of them are divergent. Feelings are still raw for the players on the 2007 World Cup team who lived through the spiraling chain of events, or even more personal moments with their mercurial teammate. "To be honest, Hope did fit the mold of a team-oriented player when we first came up together," said Cat Reddick Whitehill, her roommate in June of 2007. "When her Dad passed away, I was the one who actually had to call up family members and tell them that her Dad had passed, because she couldn't bring herself to do it. That's how close we were. But, when I look back, that's the time when we were starting to see some weird signs coming from her behavior." After Jeffrey Solo's death, Cat arranged for Hope to receive counseling from Cat's mother, then tried to offer advice of her own after the infamous benching. "I was trying to tell her, 'You can't let this whole thing just kind of unravel, because we're a team, and team is just so important.' But I also know that we just got slapped by Brazil; we were completely embarrassed, and then Hope does what she does. And so, did the team make all the right decisions with regard

to Hope? No, I think that there were a lot of emotions that got involved."

For Julie Foudy, the unofficial spokesperson for the pioneering era that began near the beach in Italy in 1985 and symbolically concluded in the 2004 Olympics, the emotions are not as raw, but they are perhaps even more personal. Julie's first teams started out playing for $10 a day in meal money and had to fight, together, for even the most basic of necessities of women's (instead of men's) uniforms, decent travel accommodations, safe playing fields and even a nominal paycheck. Julie's mentor was Billie Jean King, who taught the women's soccer elders to go on strike to gain leverage in the fight for equal pay, and her role model was Mia Hamm, who rarely accepted an interview, photoshoot or

COURTESY OF AMY ALLMANN GRIFFIN

product endorsement deal without pausing to determine if her teammates could also participate and benefit. Even though Julie had not supported the suggestion that Hope be benched, she wholeheartedly backed Kristine Lilly's view that Hope had broken a code of team ethics. "I don't dispute that Hope is a great competitor and a great goalkeeper, and I always have given her that credit," said Julie. "But she would not have survived with our group. We would have said, 'This behavior isn't OK.' And that's just a fact. I've interviewed Hope — back in the days when we used to talk — and she would say stuff like, 'Team chemistry is

Julie Foudy, with Amy Allmann Griffin

bullshit.' Or, 'Men don't care about chemistry. It's just a female thing.' And I'd say, 'I disagree entirely.' Go back over the course of history and look at the team chemistry of different men's sports, and how they were so successful because of it. I don't condone Hope's behavior as a teammate to other teammates. That's where we've chaffed over the years, because I take such a priority on that being an important part of your success as a team. She doesn't."

AMY ALLMANN GRIFFIN TOLD US SHE HAS A MISSION on her life's bucket list, one that may be a fantasy, but she's not giving up. She'd like to get her friends Hope Solo, Julie Foudy and a few others in the same room to broker a truce — and could convene the meeting with a chant that binds them all, whether they like it, or not. "Oooosa, Oooosa, Oooosa, AH! . . . Let's talk." Hope's controversial public persona, insists Amy, is not the private woman she has known for 25 years. "What everyone sees is the 5 percent of Hope and what everyone doesn't see is the big-hearted person who fights for the little guy, because that's who she is and where she came from," said Amy, who doesn't see much distinction in substance between Hope battling with the Players' Association about benefits and equal pay as compared to the work Julie, Kristine and Mia were doing with Billie Jean back in the '90s. "A lot of the things that Hope is fighting for, she'll never reap the benefits of. When she has kind of gone off the rails on commentators, or about how the National Women's Soccer League is treating its players, she's not doing that to help herself. She was trying to help the person that was getting paid $800 a month make a livable wage. I think both of them (Hope and Julie) want the same things. And they both have a platform to do it, but they both have very different ideas because they grew up in different eras. So one of these days that's going to be my job, as the team chemistry person, to bring everyone together."

Amy also doesn't hesitate to hold up Hope as a role model for today's youth, on par with any of the National Teamers who have come before, or after. "I think the legacy of Hope, for young girls and women, is that it isn't your job to be everyone's favorite person, because then you miss out on who you really are," said Amy. "And, as a mother, I think it's important for parents to let their kids know that they can be who they are. Hope would say, 'I've made mistakes, but I can't dwell on them — just like in the game of soccer. I can just be better next time.' In the heat of the moment, sports is emotional. That's a lesson, too. When you say a couple things, it's kind of hard to take them back." Throughout 2020, Hope was either expecting her twins, Vittorio and Lozen, or taking care of the newborns with her husband, former NFL tight end Jerramy Stevens; she didn't respond to requests for interviews for this book. To give us a sampling of her friend's demeanor when the media isn't watching, however, Amy shared a recording of a 90-minute ZOOM presentation that Hope conducted for free for the benefit of members of the Girls Academy soccer club of Washington, Amy's new employer.

Hope Solo, with Amy Allmann Griffin's sons, Nicholas and Benjamin

This version of Hope was warm and funny. She was, even when speaking to the young girls, obviously still a fighter. Hope defended her role in the infamous lawsuit in which the National Team sued U.S. Soccer for equitable compensation, and for never backing down from any conflict. She was also compassionate, remembering the names of young players who had shared their personal highlight reels and requested her feedback. "I saw your training video and it's awesome. I loved it," she told Neeku Purcell, an aspiring National Teamer. "You're training hard, but you were able to laugh at yourself. I saw the tennis ball when it went through your legs and you kind of laughed. I love that, because you can't be too uptight as a goalkeeper." Then Hope Solo, pariah or passionate competitor — depending on your perspective — shared her views on some of the keys to being a good teammate: avoid Tweets, Facebook posts and Instagram stories whenever possible. "It's really not conducive to the team environment," she said. "When you look at social media, people get more endorsements from the more followers they have. People get more attention the more they celebrate goals. So it really becomes this 'me, me, me' environment instead of 'Let's get on the bus and talk about practice,' or 'Let's think about the game that we just won or lost as a team.'" She would be hard-pressed to find anyone who disagreed.

The College Courtship

The University System Has Built U.S. Dominance, But Competition May Soon Dictate Changes

FOR SOME OF THE BEST MEMBERS OF THE high school class of 2016, the recruiting letters started showing up by their freshman year and Kim Maslin-Kammerdeiner's daughter was all business. Kim made 17 appearances for the National Team as a goaltender beginning in 1988 — and still holds the record for the longest streak, 843 consecutive minutes, without allowing a ball to get past her. Determined to follow in those footsteps, hellbent on pursuing a dream shared by millions of little girls nationwide, her daughter, Meghan, couldn't wait to tear open the envelopes from colleges. "I think for most people growing up, playing for the National Team is a really abstract thing to be reaching for," said Meghan, who graduated from Freedom High School in Virginia a year early so she could get to work on her dream as soon as possible. "For me, it felt so tangible because I've grown up with the World Cup gold medal that's hanging in our library. The dream was very real every day. So when I went into the recruiting process, I communicated with the coaches that I wanted a program that would develop me to be able to play professional soccer."

Mallory Pugh, meanwhile, wasn't having any part of the chaos. The more her father, Horace, pleaded with her to sit down and review the solicitations from college suitors, the louder she turned up the volume on her headphones. Then, after she led Mountain Vista High School to the Colorado state championship as a freshman, the family needed a bigger mailbox and more phone lines. "We'll talk about it after the game," Mal would tell her father. But then she'd go

COURTESY OF KIM MASLIN-KAMMERDEINER

Meghan Kammerdeiner, with her National Team mom, Kim, and her father, Roger

to her friend's house afterward to get as far away from college talk as possible. More than 400,000 girls play high school soccer in the U.S., with tens of thousands more girls of that age playing with private clubs, and many of them dream of getting noticed by just one of the 338 colleges that offer Division 1 soccer scholarships. "When every one of them wants your daughter, that creates its own kind of stress," said Horace. "For Mal, that was probably the most stressful time in her entire life."

By the time Meghan had committed to Ohio State and Mallory provided the UCLA head coach, former National Teamer Amanda Cromwell, with the happiest moment of her recruiting career, Carlyn Baldwin was already enrolled at the University of Tennessee. She played half the time in the team's first game, started its second game and most of the season thereafter. But when the year ended, with Carlyn named as an all-conference freshman, she wanted more soccer. Some of her teammates, who were ready for the holiday break, rolled their eyes when she tried to cajole them into training with her in the offseason. "You start to wonder if you're in the right environment to meet your personal goals," said Carlyn, who had considered the option of playing professionally in Europe right out of high school. "If I had to do it all over again — and I don't mean this in a disrespectful way to the University of Tennessee or the coaches — I would have gone abroad sooner because of my long-term goals, just to get in that professional environment at a younger age."

Mallory Pugh, committing to UCLA in high school

COURTESY OF MALLORY PUGH

FROM MODEST BEGINNINGS, when three small Vermont state colleges, Castleton, Johnson and Lyndon, began offering women's college soccer to a handful of students in the early to mid 1960s, a survey of the American landscape now reveals a vast spectrum of soccer choices for females since the legislation known as Title IX mandated equal athletic opportunity for men and women beginning in 1972. With about 29,000 female student-athletes participating, the sport ranks second behind track and field in total numbers within the National Collegiate Athletic Association. With junior colleges and non-NCAA schools factored into the equation, the total of women playing the game collegiately in 2020 has grown to about 42,000 — while the associated pile of scholarship money, about $300 million annually, can portray a uniquely American success story. The U.S., and to some extent Canada, are the only nations in the world that tether sports and college academics so closely and the results in terms of producing players for World Cup and Olympic victories speak for themselves. "A huge driving force for the development of the women's game is the popularity and success of the collegiate game," said Anson Dorrance, whose University of North Carolina team won the first-ever women's college soccer championship in 1981, a year before the NCAA was involved. "The model that's continued to vanquish the world's international game is the collegiate model."

All that scholarship cash, to be sure, has the power to change lives. More than half the National Team players we spoke with told us they could not have attended their college of choice, and some couldn't have afforded college at all, without a scholarship. The lure of the money, however, can change the fundamental nature of why girls and young women play, or why parents sign up their children for rec-reational, and especially club soccer, in the first place. "When you coach at the highest levels of college soccer, the vast majority of the conversations you have with players is about how much money you're going to give them, or not," said Kim Kammerdein-er's National Team center fullback Linda Hamilton, who launched the women's program at Old Dominion University in 1994. Linda began coaching at Division

Linda Hamilton, with Chinese legend Sun Wen

3 Southwestern University in Texas in 2015. According to ScholarshipStats.com, about 60 percent of the scholarship dollars in women's soccer, roughly $180 million, are offered in Division 1, which means players need to be the best of the best to receive significant financial support. Of the approximately 9,500 women playing D1, only about 1,000 receive all their expenses paid. Other team members either receive partial athletic scholarship packages or no money at all. Division 2 schools offer a total of about $60 million in schol-arships to about 7,500 players — about $8,000 apiece on average — while Division 3 only offers academic financial aid.

"College is definitely a wake-up call. This is essentially a job," said Meghan Kammerdeiner. "Right away, it became really real that I was playing so that my coaches had a career and they could put food on the table for their families. I was playing for my teammates. I was playing for my education. It's not like I was playing anymore just because I love soccer, which I fortunately still do." As a senior, she was one of only three of the original eight players still around who had arrived at Ohio State together as freshmen. Some left due to injuries or playing time. Some simply discover that college soccer is a commitment they didn't love. Meghan's own devotion and National Team dream has been both tested

Carin Jennings Gabarra, with her Navy team

and tempered by three knee surgeries and arduous rehabilitation. After serving as team captain as a sophomore, she then struggled to meet the team's fitness thresholds for years afterward and lost her captain's status as a result. "We have a very demanding program and we don't lower our standards for any individual," she said. "We're upholding it for the teams that came before us and the ones that are going to come after us — and there are definitely people that are uncomfortable with that."

Linda Hamilton, like so many other former National Teamers who are now college coaches, encourages all players to do an honest self-evaluation about why they're in the game. The focus, she said, should be on passion, and not a payday. With the possible exception of those chosen few players who are on full scholarship at a premier Division 1 soccer program, every student and family's top priority should be academics — where there are significantly more scholarship dollars in play at all levels of colleges. "There is so much misplaced ego involved when people start choosing colleges," said Linda. "Kids and parents basically see the athletic scholarship, of any amount, as a measure of value. If a coach is giving you $5,000, that means they value you at $5,000, which may not be all that much. But the kids and parents who take that deal feel like they have some status: an athletic scholarship. In reality, even at a Division 3 school like ours, the average student receives about $20,000 in academic aid and there's a 91 percent acceptance rate at medical school or law school. That, to me, is status. Kids ought to be taught to focus on being the best students they can be, but parents get caught up in the hype of the soccer scholarship, or in their daughters making the National Team."

Set Your Priorities Before You Pick a School

MY RISE IN SOCCER ALWAYS FELT ORGANIC and unforced. Starting out in recreational leagues, I then joined the local Bethesda club team and, soon, the Maryland Olympic Development Program. ODP is a pathway still available today, along with the option of the newly formed Girls Academy clubs that generally have strong ties to the U.S. Soccer youth program. In my case, I did make the Region 1 ODP team comprised of players from Northeastern coastal states, and eventually earned my first call into the National Team camp at age 17. At that point, playing Division 1 college soccer wasn't necessarily a direct goal, but rather a fortuitous byproduct of all the work and passion I put into the game. When the recruiting letters started rolling in during my sophomore year of high school, my parents seemed delighted, albeit a bit surprised, that a full scholarship to play college athletics was a real possibility. I'm sure I wasn't in Mal Pugh's stratosphere of interest (see page 164), but just like her, I didn't pay too much attention to the letters at first.

Lohman named as Hermann finalist

By Derek Levarse
COLLEGIAN STAFF WRITER | dml268@psu.edu

Penn State women's soccer was fortunate enough to have had an athlete like Christie Welsh to put a Blue and White stamp on the collegiate game. When she won the prestigious Hermann Trophy as the sport's top player in 2001, it was a landmark for the Nittany Lions.

Now, Joanna Lohman has a chance to add her own name to the history books.

Lohman was named a finalist for the Missouri Athletic Club's Hermann Trophy yesterday for the second straight year. Lohman, a senior midfielder who just finished her last season as a Lion, is one of three players up for collegiate soccer's top award. The winner will be announced at a banquet at the club on

Joanna, one of three finalists for college soccer's top award

COURTESY OF JOANNA LOHMAN

By my junior year, the letters were stacking up. Every day, I would walk to the end of my driveway and collect propositions from Harvard, the University of Illinois, Duke and so many others. The next thing we knew, Becky Burleigh, who in 1998 had been the first female head coach to win a national soccer championship, was sitting in our living room talking about what the Florida Gators had to offer. My mother recalls me chewing my gum loudly as Anson Dorrance preached the North Carolina way, but didn't offer any scholarship money, during my unofficial visit. I have absolutely no recollection of this story, but Mom said she knew, by my behavior, this was not my choice. Being the youngest child in my family, but the first to be heavily recruited, my parents and I didn't know what to make of this pageantry — but we did understand that not having a lot of debt after college seemed like a good idea.

In addition to a scholarship, a respected academic institution was priority number one and I knew my four final choices, Virginia, Michigan, Duke and Penn State, all checked that box. I wrote down my other must-haves: 1) freshman year impact; 2) a connection to the players; 3) good social fit; and 4) a bond to the coach. Penn State aced everything. The gritty, blue-collar work ethic was embodied by Patrick Farmer, who was at once demanding, gregarious and humorous, while wearing shorts 365 days a year regardless of temperature. If you've been to Happy Valley in winter, you know that made him a tad eccentric. It wasn't unusual to hear Pat counting out loud to 10 during practice, "1, 2, 3 ..." so as to not explode at his players. I'm guessing someone had to teach him that somewhere along the line. Pat also left after my freshman year to coach in the newly formed Women's United Soccer Association, our game's first professional league — but I rolled with the changes. I became a team captain, the first four-time First Team All-Big Ten selection in the school's history, and a four-time Academic All-American with a 3.98 GPA. I had decided a school, not a coach, was most important. I'm a proud Nittany Lion, always and forever, and so thankful that I had my priorities aligned. — J.L.

THAT WAS NEVER, IRONICALLY, GOING TO BE AN ISSUE inside the household in Arnold, Md., where Talia Gabarra might have been excused if she had a National Team obsession. Her father, Jim, was a member of the U.S. men's National Team in 1988-89; her mother,

Carin Jennings Gabarra, on a 1991 trading card

Carin, was a National Teamer from 1987-1996. A decade later, Mia Hamm was in the delivery room when Talia was born and Kristine Lilly was soon named her godmother. Shannon Higgins-Cirovski, one of the heroes on the 1991 World Cup team that included Kim Kammerdeiner and Linda Hamilton, was Talia's youth coach. And on the day she played for her first high school state championship, against Leonardtown in November of 2015, her Broadneck High School team received Tweeted shoutouts from Mia, Kristine, Julie Foudy and, for good measure, Abby Wambach, who wrote: "Do something I never did and win a state championship!!! #bebetterthanme." It helped that Carin, who was named the best player at the 1991 World Cup, is considered by trained soccer observers to be among the best scorers in the history of the game. "To a lot of kids, these women may be role models, but to Talia, they're just people. They're her friends," said Carin, who has served as head women's coach at the Naval Academy in Annapolis, Md., since the sport's inception at the school in 1993.

Carin underscores Linda's view that the ideal motivation for any family should be the physical fitness and life lessons their daughter will discover through soccer — and that inspiration for playing should come from within. "One of the reasons I love my job and I've been here for so long is my kids are 100 percent accountable," she said. "I've never had, in 27 years, a parent call me to talk about their kid and their playing time. These kids are extremely driven and want to earn everything themselves." Carin said she realizes she'll probably never win a national championship, and will likely never coach a National Teamer, but neither will the vast majority of coaches anywhere. "We get the best kids, the best people. We want those driven kids that do the extra work, but also have the intangibles to become leaders. They have character; they do the right thing."

TIFFANY ROBERTS

Carin stands by her claim that the topic of her daughter making the National Team herself has never even come up between them, even though Talia told us she once "dreamed of being just like my parents and making the National Team" from as early as she can remember. Talia played for a nationally ranked club team at Bethesda, and competed in the youth Development Academy for the Washington Spirit when Jim was the organization's head coach and director of soccer development. But she also played basketball and lacrosse in high school — and rarely missed proms and

Tiffany Roberts Sahaydak, celebrating a championship at the University of Central Florida

homecoming dances. While many of her club team members jumped on the recruiting bandwagon early, Talia held off on committing to the University of Central Florida until midway through her junior year. "My daughter didn't just focus on one thing; I'm pretty much an advocate for having a life outside of soccer," said Carin. "I am an advocate for making sure you're well-rounded."

Talia's college coach figures Carin has succeeded just fine in passing along those family values to her daughter. Yet another one of the National Team connections, Tiffany Roberts Sahaydak laughed when she recalled Talia's recruiting visit. One of her first questions involved an assessment of the young player's weaknesses. "My work ethic," answered Talia, speaking as bluntly as her parents. Tiffany, known for having the highest level of fitness of any National Teamer during her 112-game career, nearly fell out of her chair. "I thought, 'Oh, God, how can you be on my team if you're going to say work ethic?' But what I learned very quickly is that she sets a very, very high bar for herself." Tiffany said she learned, too, that the daughter of such noted players and coaches was also highly self-aware. Coming off a torn anterior cruciate ligament in her knee and a herniated disk in

her back, suffered during her senior year in high school, Talia was honestly not sure if she would ever reach the level of physical effort and output required to become a truly elite player. "I still love soccer so much, but . . . just . . . at some point I realized soccer wasn't everything I wanted to do with my life," Talia said.

CARIN GABARRA DIDN'T HESITATE WHEN asked to name the most commonly held trait of Kim Kammerdeiner and Linda Hamilton, or Mia Hamm, Kristine Lilly or any of the other soccer

Talia Gabarra, with her parents, Jim and Carin

Making the Decision of a Lifetime

We asked National Teamers for their perspective on the most important factors when considering which college to attend. Here are some of their replies:

TAKE THE GOLDILOCKS APPROACH — Don't say yes to the first college that offers a scholarship; find the school that's most comfortable and offers what you're looking for. "I didn't go to (North) Carolina because I didn't feel comfortable; that Competitive Cauldron wasn't for me," said Penn State graduate **Christie Welsh** (USWNT 2000-2006). "I didn't go to Clemson because, in the end, I just felt like it was too far away from my family even though I thought the people were great. I thought the talent was great. I looked at UVA (Virginia) and I just didn't feel like the culture of the school was me. It wasn't blue collar enough for me."

DON'T CHOOSE JUST FOR SOCCER — Four years is a long time and so much can change, including injuries, so make sure the school has plenty of other things to offer you. "You need to know this is a great place for your overall being, because you could go in the first day and tear your ACL and never play soccer again," said **Shannon Boxx** (USWNT 2003-2015). "If the only reason you went to the university was for the coach, or for the soccer program, you're going to be miserable."

FIND THE RIGHT MATCH — The school's offerings are important, but so too is the fit between the player and the coach. Have an open conversation, ideally several, prior to committing. "I really do look for the person behind the talent," said **Sam Baggett Bohon** (USWNT 1998-1999), the head coach at Embry-Riddle. She asks recruits, many of them engineering students, to take the Myers-Briggs personality indicator to help her decide.

KEEP PARENTS OUT OF IT — Mothers and fathers may guide choices of colleges, especially as it relates to family finances and other practical decisions. When it comes to the soccer part of the college decision, parents need to step back. "I've been really lucky with parents," said **Amanda Cromwell** (USWNT 1991-1998). "There was one mother. She was telling me how hard her daughter works and she wanted me to guarantee that the daughter would play in at least half of every game. I said, 'What, are you kidding me?' The daughter ended up transferring."

DON'T GIVE UP — Ella Masar (USWNT 2009) didn't get any scholarship offers growing up outside Chicago, but decided to go out for the soccer team at the University of Illinois as a walk-on for the school's legendary coach, Janet Rayfield — who had been the first player ever recruited to the University of North Carolina by Anson Dorrance. "Janet said, 'I can't offer you money, but what I can offer you is the opportunity for your dreams to come true.'" By her junior year, Ella was receiving a full scholarship.

FIND ROOM FOR FUN — Women's college soccer has one of the highest attrition and transfer rates of any sport, primarily because players find soccer is no longer fun after high school. If you're being recruited, check with current team members to assess their enjoyment level. "One of the things I'm really conscientious of is trying to create a hard-working culture — and soccer can feel like a job at times — but I also try to make it a fun environment," said **Lauren Orlandos Hanson** (USWNT 2001), the head coach at San Jose State in California. "We are here to have fun together and I don't ever want my players to forget that."

playing legends whom she and her daughter call friends. "They're all incredibly driven," said Carin. "My generation was from the Title IX era where there was no team and then it was, 'Maybe we'll have a team. Maybe we'll have a World Cup. Maybe we'll have an Olympics.' None of us played for money; none of us played for anything other than the love of the game, and love of competing." The biggest payoff for most players, then and now, is the requisite college education that opens so many doors when soccer is done. Purely in terms of soccer, however, some people within the game are beginning to wonder if the most driven and talented players should be provided a different option outside the university system. Yes, the National Team won the 2015 and 2019 World Cups, and four of eight since 1991, but the talent gap with England, Spain, France, Germany and many other nations appears to be closing. "We have success now, and we had success in our day, both psychologically and physically over all those other countries, because we believed we could do anything," said Kim, whose 1991 team only faced 11 opponents in the World Cup. In 2019, 24 teams participated and the tournament will soon have 36 teams. "You can see from the last World Cup that all these teams from around the world are catching up. The women's game is amazing now."

COURTESY OF CARLYN BALDWIN

Carlyn Baldwin, with her father, Steve

The highly visible canary in the coal mine, the American men's national soccer team, has struggled to compete viably in Olympics and World Cup tournaments in all but a handful of years in the past half century. In Europe and elsewhere around the world, boys and young men have had the option of turning professional as teenagers — without the constant rigors of high-level academics required by colleges — and those foreign teams typically dominate the U.S. In recent years, some of America's best teenage male players have been going to Europe and, in 2012, current National Team standout Lindsey Horan cracked the door open for women by joining a professional team in France right after finishing high school in Golden, Colo. She came back nearly four years later, both with money in her bank account and seemingly a better player than she would likely have been had she attended the University of North Carolina, where she had been offered a full scholarship. Even Anson Dorrance reluctantly agreed that, in Lindsey's case, it was the right decision. "What I really enjoy is how complete she is," Anson told the *New York Times* in 2019. "She can create goals, she's a playmaker, an outstanding defensive presence. At her peak right now, she checks every box."

Olivia Moultrie, a professional at 13

MEDIA PUNCH/TONY FORTE/ALAMY STOCK PHOTO

Lindsey's move was duly noted by Carlyn Baldwin, who left Tennessee a year early in 2017 to sign a professional contract in Switzerland, and also by her father, Steve, a highly successful businessman who acquired majority ownership of the Washington Spirit in early 2019. He credits Larry Best, his daughter's youth coach and the president of the Spirit, with a vision for a minor soccer league system for women in America that flips the current college equation of academics first, sports second. Baseball, with its minor leagues, has lured youth right out of high school for generations. NBA basketball has had a developmental league for the past decade. "We should be supporting the elite female athletes who want to see how far they can take their game," said Steve. "Ironically, the success of our National Team has spurred many countries around the world to start investing in their women's teams. They have a very rich history with the men's soccer academies around the world and they're starting to offer those opportunities to women. It's only a matter of time before our women will be surpassed, unless we start to do something about it." He acknowledges that American girls have access to superior training and coaching through their clubs teams and the newly formed Girls Academy — which replaced U.S. Soccer's Development Academy in 2020. But asking the best players to simultaneously worry about SATs and other college entrance exams can be an unfair burden. "Something has to give, and in most cases it's going to be a girl's soccer development. Rightfully so. But the window closes on soccer opportunities very, very quickly. The academic opportunities will always be there."

One girl's family, notably, forged its own soccer pathway without moving to Europe. Olivia Moultrie made national headlines when she signed a letter of intent to accept Anson's full scholarship offer to one day attend North Carolina, even though she was just 11 years old at the time. She made an even bigger splash when she rescinded the commitment two years later and turned professional. Signing a six-figure sponsorship deal with Nike through representation with the Wasserman Media Group that signed Mia Hamm, post college in 1999, immediately stripped Olivia of any future college eligibility and placed her at the center of a raging on-line debate about out-of-control parents. "My crazy dream is that I want to be the best soccer player ever. Period," stated Olivia, then age 12, in a video posted to her father's YouTube channel.

Even her private coach, Fredo Sainz, said he initially questioned K.C. Moultrie's ambitions for his daughter when he brought her to train with Fredo for multi-hour sessions at age 9. "Honestly, when we first met, I used to think, 'K.C. pushes her way too much and it's too forced,'" he said. In time, however, Fredo said the girl became a revelation. If he asked her to do 10 repetitions of a drill, she would do 20. When she dribbled the ball through cones, seemingly to the point of exhaustion, Olivia would go five minutes longer. Fredo would try to get her to relax, but she wouldn't have it, whether her father was watching, or not. "Even if I want to goof off and say, 'Let's go play basketball or something, let's just mess around,' she'll look at me like, 'OK, hold on, let me perfect this first and then let's go play.' There's something about that girl that she needs to put in work every single day and I realized that's true even when she's on her own. That's where I realized this girl is so, so in love with this sport that she truly wants to get better on her own."

COURTESY OF FREDO SAINZ

Olivia Moultrie, with her private trainer, Fredo Sainz

In 2019, the Moultries moved to Portland, Ore., so Olivia could begin training full-time with the Portland Thorns, one of the Washington Spirit opponents in the National Women's Soccer League. Though she's not allowed by rule to appear in games for the Thorns' senior women's team, she works out regularly with its players and appears in Thorns' youth academy games while she home-schools and bides her time until age 18, or a league rule change, or a National Team invitation, whichever comes first. It's an unprecedented project, said head coach Mark Parsons, that deserves close scrutiny. His background is both playing and coaching in the boys' soccer academies in England, and he believes that if the Thorns and Olivia are both successful, the idea for an entirely new girls' training model may reveal itself in the U.S. "When I was made aware that the family was willing to make this commitment, I got asked the question, 'Is this a player that you would want in the training environment with the goal of developing her to be a better player and a better person?'" said Mark. "Of course, you do a bit of homework and then the answer is, 'Yes, I would love to be involved because that's my DNA, that's what makes me tick.' But we have to do it properly. We have to do it intelligently. No one's ever done this before, so the question becomes, 'How do we build a system or process to evaluate our progress?' Because we know all eyes will be upon us and we want to do right by this young girl."

MALLORY PUGH KNOWS FULL WELL THE PRESSURE OF ATTENTION. Some in the game say that, thanks in part to her experience with recruiters in middle school and high school, a new 2019 NCAA rule states that college coaches can no longer contact recruits until June 15 after their sophomore years. When she accepted the offer to attend UCLA as a sophomore in 2014, America's youth national teams were already calling. Mal reaffirmed her commitment to the Bruins throughout high school, but in the meantime became the second youngest female soccer player ever called into a U.S. Olympic team not long after she tossed her graduation cap into the thin Colorado air at the Red Rocks Ampitheatre. Without any seasoning in Europe, or any exposure to college soccer, she proved almost instantly she belonged on the field with the best players in the world. Her would-be college

Mallory Pugh, feeding the frenzy of girls with dreams of their own

coach was salivating. "She ran the show every time I saw her," Amanda Cromwell told ESPN at the time. "She made the players around her better, for sure, and that's something that really caught my eye. But it wasn't going to be like sharing the ball. I think from an early age, she knew she was a Michael Jordan or Kobe Bryant. She wanted the ball." Rather than matriculate in September of 2016 — after years of soccer media speculation asking, 'Will she, or won't she, go pro full time?' — Mal traveled with Horace, her mother, Karen, and her belongings to California in January of 2017.

Few campuses in America are more lovely by comparison than UCLA in January. Amanda and her players couldn't have been more gracious in their attempt to make Mal feel at home. Early that spring, however, Mal was called back into a National Team training

Lindsey Horan, left, with Mallory Pugh, heroes of their hometown in Denver

camp after just three unofficial spring season college games. She was instantly stunned by the pace of play, far faster than back in Los Angeles, and called her father to question her decision to be in college. "I can't get this type of training in college and I can't get that type of competition in college," she told Horace. He advised his daughter, as always, that it was her decision. On April 17, 2017, Mal became the first player in history to turn professional in America without playing an official game in college, or a professional game in Europe. In the spring of 2020, when she would otherwise have been graduating from college, she had already logged 63 National Team appearances, more than 40 appearances with professional teams, and numerous lucrative endorsements.

At an age when most 22-year-olds begin paying back student loans, Mal knew she was at the epicenter of a national college debate. Some say she's a once-in-a-decade prodigy, a mental and physical anomaly blending speed, technical finesse and spatial awareness, and not too much should be made of her unique ascension. Still others see Lindsey Horan, Olivia Moultrie and Mallory Pugh all skipping college in their own manner, and figure it's about time to simply make it easier for any girl who has the talent and drive. Count Mal in that camp. "I do believe that if the opportunity is there, and that's 100 percent what you want to do — not what your coaches think that you should do, or your family thinks that you should do — then you should go ahead and take that opportunity," she said. "During my process, I spoke to a lot of people. I finally realized that this is my life and my career, so it really only matters what I think. And therefore, I made a decision to leave UCLA and go pro. UCLA was like a second family and that made it one of the most stressful decisions of my life — just like the decision to go there in the first place — but I knew something deep down was telling me I needed to leave. In the end, it was the most growth that I feel like I experienced for myself."

15 : INJURIES

Not If, But When

Overcoming Aches, Pains, Breaks and Tears is a Fact of Life for Almost Anyone Who Takes Their Game to the Highest Level

MALLORY PUGH CAN LAUGH about some of the injuries now. She fell off monkey bars in one incident, burst her eardrum in another, and mashed her face and front teeth into a tree while snowboarding. She broke her arm on three different occasions between ages 8 and 13. And then there was the day before her club's regional weekend tournament when she tried hanging herself from her pants, upside down, from a pulley system in the family's Colorado garage used to hoist bicycles 10 feet off the ground for storage. "I was trying to swing from the bike rack like I was flying," said Mal, who told us she was 12 at the time of the high-wire act that ended on the concrete floor with a bone protruding from her wrist. When Horace Pugh told his daughter she would have to skip the tournament, she panicked: "He did NOT just say that!" Proper bone placement and a firm cast would have to wait. Looking her father straight in the eye with her tears flowing, Mal set the bone back into place herself, made a quick trip to urgent care with her mother Karen for a bubble-wrapped splint, and proceeded to score six goals in six games. Or maybe it was eight or nine goals, depending on who's telling and re-telling the well-worn story with a happy ending.

No one was laughing, however, two years later. Mal had taken a hit during a hard tackle

My favorite memory of 6th grade was Outdoor Ed.

I want to be on the USA soccer team and win a gold medal.

Mallory Pugh

COURTESY OF MALLORY PUGH

Young Mallory Pugh, already dreaming big

Rose Lavelle, center, and Mallory Pugh, celebrating a World Cup victory in France in 2019

in an early season game for her club team Real Colorado and came away with what felt like just a sore leg for the next month. Horace and Karen prescribed ice and Advil. A tournament game in Arizona brought another awkward tackle in the exact same spot as the previous hit, where doctors later surmised Mal had suffered a stress fracture from overuse. This time she screamed. "Mal's pain threshold is off the charts, ever since she was a little girl," said Horace. "So when you hear your daughter make that kind of sound, you say, 'Oh, wow. Something's really wrong this time.'" With Mal writhing on the field, her club coach said he had to look away from the gruesome break; many trained observers thought the injury — a snapped femur just above the growth plate in her knee — could be career-ending. At age 15, with her bones still growing, all she could do was wait it out for seven months of healing and pray for no long-term damage.

DR. SARA WHALEN HESS was once the Mallory Pugh of the National Team. Having made her first appearance in 1997 while still enrolled at the University of Connecticut, she was supposed to be one of America's answers to who's up next when perennial stars like Mia Hamm, Michelle Akers and Julie Foudy retired. A member of the storied 1999 World Cup championship team, Sara played a key role in the final when Michelle left the game both exhausted and concussed in the 100-degree heat, and Sara was soon thereafter included among the 20 foundational players who launched America's first-ever female professional league, the Women's United Soccer Association. Poised for a long career with 65 National Team appearances already on her resume, along with 31 games for the WUSA's New York Power, Sara endured what has become a rite of passage for a vast number of female soccer players — as well as female and male athletes in many other sports: torn knee ligaments. On June 26, 2002, in a game against the Carolina Courage, Sara's knee absorbed the full force of a collision with Birgit Prinz of Germany, a three-time honoree as world player of the year. "Almost everyone tears their knee in soccer at some point, so no big deal," Sara thought to herself as the trainers carted her off the field, and even days later after the seemingly successful surgery was complete. With a typical athlete's recovery — most players are back on the field within nine months to a year, though her

Soccer Injuries:
An Epidemic at a Glance

P LAYING SOCCER IS LOADED WITH BENEFITS that cross physical, psychological, and social boundaries. Soccer is also violent, with injuries to the brain, neck, knees and ankles a fact of life — especially for girls, who are more likely than boys to suffer concussions and sprained or torn ligaments. Our family started visiting Stacy King, a physical therapist who specializes in treating soccer players, when my daughter, Angie, had her first knee injury at age 8. "Now that we have made soccer a year-round sport, the injuries have really become an epidemic," said Stacy. "We are seeing more of a broad spectrum of problems, especially from overuse injuries." Here are the three biggest injury issues with girls who play soccer 10 to 12 months of the year:

CONCUSSIONS — An average of 11,670 girls in the U.S. are treated in the emergency room every year for soccer-related brain injuries, according to a study released in March of 2019 by the Centers for Disease Control and Prevention. Head contact with the ball, the ground, the goal post, elbows and other players' heads needs to be watched closely. Some doctors have recommended an outright ban on teens and pre-teens striking the ball with their heads, but U.S. Soccer rules only forbid players under the age of 11 from heading the ball. "I think we've made a lot of strides in awareness of concussions," said U.S. Soccer president **Cindy Parlow Cone** (USWNT 1996-2004). "When I was coming through it was pretty much considered normal to see stars, or just to have to shake it off. We now understand that if you get hit, or head the ball incorrectly and you see stars, that's not normal. It needs to be checked, with the proper protocols, immediately." **Brandi Chastain** (USWNT 1988-2004) and several other players have pledged to donate their brains for research into chronic traumatic encephalopathy, which occurs when repeated hits to the head lead to a buildup of an abnormal protein called tau. Girls, especially, are encouraged to engage in exercises aimed at strengthening neck muscles to reduce the incidence of concussion.

ACL INJURIES — Research shows that the incidence of torn anterior cruciate ligaments (ACL) of the knee is four to six times greater teammate Shannon MacMillan once set an unofficial National Team record by returning in little more than two months after surgery in 2003 — Sara figured she'd be ready for the start of WUSA's third season.

Alone in her Manhattan apartment, however, the pain didn't subside. After a couple of weeks with no progress, doctors didn't see any evidence of swelling, advised patience, and sent her home. By the second month waiting for recovery, she came down with what she thought was the flu. By eight weeks in, she had become an invalid. "At that point my fever was severe, with nausea and vomiting, body aches, and rashes, but we still didn't know it was my knee," said Sara, who also didn't know her most dangerous symptom of all, liver failure, was in advanced stages. When Sara couldn't even get out of bed on her own, her cousin Dr. Beth Shubin Stein, who also happened to be the New York Power's team physician, showed up at her door. The visit saved her life.

REUTERS/SYLVIA BUCHHOLZ/ALAMY STOCK IMAGE

Cindy Parlow Cone, left, in close contact

for females, post puberty, than it is for males, according to a 2017 study by the National Institutes of Health. Four members of the 2019 U.S. Women's World Cup team have suffered the injury, which may require a year or more of recovery. Stacy told us that girls need to learn to "play lower, with knees bent" to reduce the likelihood of injury, though not all experts agree that the risk of ACL tears can be alleviated through proper training. Early specialization in soccer may be the biggest culprit. "It's crazy the amount of soccer some young kids are playing," said **Thori Staples Bryan** (USWNT 1993-2003). "Using one specific set of muscles, doing the same type of movement earlier and way too often, is just asking for trouble."

OVERUSE INJURIES — Certain injuries such as concussions, ankle sprains and bone breaks occur during contact. Often the more problematic injuries, including tendinitis of the knees or ankles, occur as a result of overuse. "Your body absolutely needs training seasons and cycles to help avoid injuries," said Stacy, who recommends cross-training. Tennis, and especially getting into the pool, lake, or ocean, are the activities most recommended by National Teamers. "Swimming was my first sport, and I've kept it with me all my life," said **Danielle Garrett Fotopoulos** (USWNT 1996-2005), who lettered in six sports at Lyman High School in Longwood, Fla. — P.T.

"She tapped my knee and pulled out the grossest, slug-like, sickest fluid you can imagine," said Sara, with the memory still vivid nearly 20 years later. "A staph infection had spread nearly everywhere in my body by that time. She got me into the hospital that night for what would be the first of many, many antibiotics and surgeries." Having learned from doctors that she had only been hours from dying and, at age 26, had played her last soccer game, Sara spent months in and out of the hospital. With her career and life as she knew it gone, she said she stopped just short of being suicidal. "It wasn't like I would ever hurt myself, but I also didn't have the energy to live anymore," she said. "I just felt so sick, every single day. I couldn't shake that feeling of just deep, deep despair. None of the meds were working; a lot of things they were trying were making me worse. I lost a ton of weight, I wasn't eating, and I thought to myself, 'Maybe this isn't going to work out.' And I didn't care."

Avoiding and Overcoming Injuries

When it comes to all the various ailments that can be suffered on, or off, the soccer field, we asked National Teamers how they play through, bounce back, and know when it's time to quit:

OWN YOUR OUTLOOK — A year out of college in 2010, **Jessica McDonald** (USWNT 2016-present) ruptured the patella tendon in her knee and was told by doctors she would likely never play again. During recovery, she conceived her son. "It felt like that was it for me," she said. "Here I am rehabbing and I find out I'm pregnant, and society, family, everybody's telling me, 'You're a mom now, you need to settle down.' But I really didn't want to do that."

STAY FIT — **Lori Lindsey** (USWNT 2005-2013) remained remarkably injury free during a nearly 200-game professional career that included 31 appearances for the National Team. "Focus on fitness was a big part of my story because I started lifting weights in high school, and I really believe that was a huge part of the longevity, and being able to step away from the game on my own terms, rather than due to an injury."

FIND INSPIRATION — When **Shannon MacMillan** (USWNT 1993-2005) played a National Team game on a Saturday, then flew across country to play the next day for her pro league team, she tore her ACL just months prior to the 2003 World Cup. Her college coach Clive Charles — then terminally ill — told her she could still recover in time. She did, just 62 days after surgery. "I called his wife and said, 'I know Clive's not up to talking, but please just let him know I made the team.' She called back and said, 'Clive says he's proud of you and he loves you.' He was crazy motivation (See Chapter 16)."

CROSS TRAIN — The Cal Ripken of soccer with 354 National Team appearances, as well as six appearances as the only woman in a men's professional league, **Kristine Lilly** (USWNT 1987-2010) played every sport she could find, rollerbladed, or ran stairs at stadiums or office buildings. "These kids these days are so focused on doing one craft and that's what will hurt them in the long run," she said. The research says she's right.

BE REALISTIC — A full honest self-assessment is essential when faced with any kind of physical setback, according to **Amy Rodriguez Shilling** (USWNT 2005-2018), who played 30 of her 132

KNEE INJURIES, BONE BREAKS, ANKLE SPRAINS AND OTHER maladies from excessive use of joints, muscles, and soft cartilage are the most obvious afflictions of soccer players of all ages — to the point where injuries are considered to be epidemic in the girls' and women's game by many physicians (see Page 178). Michelle Akers figures she's had at least 30 surgeries on her right knee and said she doesn't recall a single time in her 153-game National Team career where something on her body wasn't at least partially injured. "You just learn to play hurt," she said. Current National Teamers Alex Morgan, Megan Rapinoe, Ali Krieger, and Ashlyn Harris have all suffered and recovered from Sara's injury, tearing the anterior cruciate ligaments that flex diagonally in the middle of their knees to keep the tibia (shin bone) and femur (thigh bone) working together. The incidence of women's soccer injuries rivals men's football in frequency, especially in the most concerning, yet perplexing issue of all: concussions.

COURTESY OF AMY RODRIGUEZ SHILLING

Amy Rodriguez Shilling, left, with Tobin Heath and Lauren Cheney Holiday

games for the National Team after giving birth. "Whether you're coming back from a pregnancy or an injury, I do think it is quite important to give yourself grace. Have patience with your body because you can't snap your fingers and all of a sudden be ready. It takes months and months of work, day in day out."

HEAL THE MIND, TOO — A series of misdiagnosed hamstring injuries left **Rose Lavelle** (USWNT 2017-present) frustrated for the better part of two seasons. When her body finally made it back onto the field ready to go, she had made sure her mind was there, too, by reaching out for professional help. "I have no clue if I would have been able to get to where I was mentally by myself," she said. "It's nice to be able to sit down and talk about what you're going through with somebody and not feel like you are going to be judged, and help you get to a different perspective."

GET A SECOND OPINION — When **Lauren Cheney Holiday** (USWNT 2007-2015) was pregnant in 2016, she began to have trouble swallowing and also excessive swelling of her feet. Doctors diagnosed multiple sclerosis, yet opted to put off an MRI until after the baby arrived. Waking with a severe migraine at six months, however, led Lauren to insist on an immediate MRI that revealed a massive brain tumor. "You have to advocate for yourself," said Lauren, who had the tumor successfully removed just 34 days after giving birth to her daughter, Jrue Tyler ("J.T.").

LET YOUR BODY TELL YOU WHEN — She was the "Buehldozer" coming out of Stanford in 2007, a take-no-prisoners player who seemed to dole out more punishment than she received. Approaching the 2015 World Cup, however, a pulled calf muscle followed by Achilles tendinitis became flashing stop lights on the path to retirement. "I went through probably a year and a half of one injury after another," said **Rachel Buehler Van Hollebeke** (USWNT 2008-2015). "That takes a toll on you."

Parents, according to World Cup heroine Briana Scurry, need to fully understand the risks of sending their children onto the field — yet she sees reluctance at every turn. "Nobody wants to talk about concussions. People get squeamish in their chairs when I talk about it. I don't think people who haven't had a hit to their head severe enough to basically disconnect them from themselves, like I did, can truly understand." The scrambling of the brain that can occur whenever the head comes in contact with the ground, or a goalpost, ball, knee, elbow, foot, or another player's head, affects a high percentage of female soccer players, most notably goalies, depending on how often and long they play. Briana figures she's likely had 20 or more skull-jarring incidents during her lifetime in the sport that began at age 12 when a youth coach in Dayton, Minn., stuck her in goal for an all-boys team, ironically, because he figured it was the safest place on the field for a girl. As an adult, she bounced back quickly from her first two diagnosed concussions; the first came in 2007

Concussions: Are Rewards Worth the Risks? One Girl Says 'Yes'

W HITNEY KLEIN, FROM WHAT I COULD OBSERVE from the sideline, was a demure high school-aged assistant coach for my daughter's club team. She seemed to quietly come and go sporadically for two seasons, for reasons left mostly unexplained, except that the effects of her soccer-related concussions were lingering. When Whitney didn't appear at practice at all during the winter and pre-COVID spring of 2020, I reached out. "Soccer is my thing!" Whitney told me in a tone that instantly quelled my impression of her shyness. The game is in her DNA, she said. Her grandmother Elizabeth Phillips Stoddard was a pioneer who filed a formal complaint with the Wellesley school board in Massachusetts in the late 1970s to force the town to add a girls' high school team, which she coached. Her first-ever roster, notably, included future National Team player and coach Dr. Lauren Gregg.

Whitney, still loving the game

Whitney laughed disarmingly when she told me about suffering her first concussion playing goalie at age 10. The fog was so thick she never saw the shot go by, and when she went back to retrieve the ball she also never saw the goalpost. "I grabbed the post with both of my hands and tried to hold myself up, then I kind of just collapsed," she said. That would require a seven-month recovery. At age 13, playing midfielder, she took a shot to the back of the head. She sat out the rest of that game, played the next day, but felt progressively worse. Diagnosed with concussion number two, she missed three months of soccer.

Fast forward to her final soccer practice as a player, Nov. 14, 2017, when she suffered a head-on collision in front of the goal. The result was an Advil for one girl — and nearly three years of emergency rooms, entire semesters of school missed, and trips to the Mayo Clinic for Whitney. During that winter of 2019 and spring of 2020, she was hospitalized for acute migraine headaches, followed by a month of intensive physical therapy. She rattles off just some of her conditions like a med student — acute light-headedness ("postural orthostatic tachycardia syndrome"), swelling of the throat ("idiopathic angioedema"), and chronic fatigue syndrome ("myalgic encephalomyelitis") —

when a close-range shot deflected off the post directly into her forehead. The second came a year later when teammate Abby Wambach came at her with the ball in practice, one-on-one, only to have both tall, physical players wind up in a heap on the ground.

Briana also caused one of the more notable concussions in National Team history when she inadvertently punched teammate Michelle Akers in the head while trying to make a save just as the 1999 World Cup final against China was heading into extra time — the play that would give a young Sara Whalen Hess her first opportunity on a major stage. It would be a minor game, by comparison, that came to consume much of Briana's post-career life. In goal in April of 2010 for the Washington Freedom against the Philadelphia Independence (featuring the co-author of this book), Briana came out of the crease on a seemingly routine play to field a low shot from her left. In the moment she lunged down to scoop the ball into her hands, a Philadelphia player was running full speed from her right to try to beat

Coach Whitney Klein, far left, with her Potomac club team and special guest Elise Kellond-Knight of the Australian national team

yet can no longer do the most basic math problems without a calculator, and has lost the faculties to learn new languages.

Through it all, said Whitney, she was never a crier — except when she tried to come back to the soccer field in those early days of coaching. What I mistook for shyness was actually a barely concealed broken heart. "My greatest joy was taken away from me," she said, still remarkably upbeat. "I have had to learn to love the game again in a different way." When I asked her what I thought was the most obvious question, she reiterated that to be able to play the sport that her grandmother fought for meant everything. "Yes, I had all the doctors discourage me from playing all my life since the first concussion. My parents knew soccer was my one true love, and they let me continue. After the second concussion, I think most everyone wanted me to stop . . . and I'm so grateful that I didn't because I really would not be the person that I am today. I mean, if I wouldn't have gotten that last concussion, I literally would have been a radically different person. But I also would not have been able to play soccer for my freshman team. I wouldn't trade that experience for anything." — P.T.

Briana to the spot. The resulting collision, with the player's knee hammering the right side of Briana's temple, left one of the most iconic players in American history sprawled on the ground. The field instantly went hazy. Briana said she remembers the shot, but not how she rather miraculously held onto the ball. She never saw the player coming, but vaguely recalls the male referee extolling her to keep the game moving: "Get up, keeper, you're all right." With about seven minutes remaining before halftime — she had been nothing if not tough in her 16-year career that included two Olympic gold medals in addition to the World Cup — Briana stayed in the game for what would be the final seven minutes as a professional player on a soccer field in her life. Literally nothing would come easy again for years.

Briana Scurry, with her former coach, Lauren Gregg

To this day, doctors still don't fully understand why some hits to the head can be absorbed, why some players, female and male, rarely if ever get concussions, and why female athletes suffer roughly twice as many as men overall. Doctors can see the internal bleeding and bruising on MRIs, but don't fully know how to predict the cumulative effect of multiple traumas, or the severity of the resulting maladies that can range from memory loss and headaches, to mood disorders, speech impairment and loss of balance. Briana said she suffered from all of the above. Waking each morning with debilitating headaches after nights of Ambien-induced sleep, Briana tried medications and alcohol to numb the pain and launch a post-career life. As a commentator for ESPN during the 2011 World Cup, however, she struggled to remain focused. When she was hired as the general manager for the Magic Jack, a professional women's team, she struggled to recall information as basic as a player's name. Depression, even thoughts of suicide, accompanied the lowest moments when the once cat-quick athlete camped listlessly, interminably on her sofa in Arlington, Va. "All of my career, my success had been based on my mentality, about how I look at something and how I go after it to overcome obstacles," she said. "I know I have physical assets as well, but it all starts with my mind. At that point, my brain was broken. That's how I felt. And I thought, 'If I can't use the number one thing that I used to use to start everything, to achieve and overcome, then what do I do?'"

Even at her worst, though, she retained the fighting spirit that being a National Teamer had taught her. When the insurance company initially didn't want to pay for an emerging surgical procedure — that would release pressure on the occipital nerves that fan across the back of the skull to the ears — she wouldn't take no for an answer. She even invited cameras into the operating room because she felt it was important to share the facts of

The Bigger the Injury, the Smaller the Baby Steps

F YOU PLAY THIS GAME LONG ENOUGH, moments will come that freeze-frame in your mind forever: goals, victories, losses and, yes, injuries. Unless your name is Kristine Lilly, and you play a world-record 354 games for your country across 23 years, you're going to get injured and probably badly. My moment was April 15, 2017, just 11 minutes into what was supposed to be the best season of my life. Without any contact with another player, my left knee buckled oddly, but I got up and ran. My knee buckled again when I tried to turn, but I got up again. One more time. Same outcome. I had, in soccer parlance, "done my knee" — otherwise known as tearing the anterior cruciate ligament, or ACL. To say I was devastated doesn't cover it. I hadn't missed a game in seven years and the required surgery would cause me to miss the entire season. As a player in the latter stages of her career, I worried whether I would even have a job on the other side of whatever a recovery would look like. Had I lost my identity, my purpose?

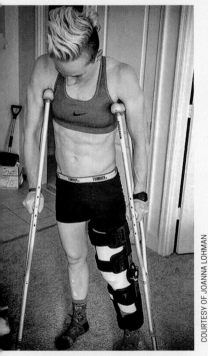

COURTESY OF JOANNA LOHMAN

Joanna, slow going in 2017

To begin, I stared at the beauty statement I had crafted for myself. Did it even apply? I feel beautiful when I am bold, brave, courageous, authentic and strong. I express my beauty through my mohawk, style of dress, physique, physical activity like singing and dancing, my occupation, travel, and energy for life.

Could I feel beautiful if my leg was in a brace and I was stuck on my couch? How could I express my beauty with physical activity and dancing with a bum leg? Honestly, doubt crept in. I cried myself to sleep. And I'm not going to sugarcoat it: the pain sucked. Still, my beauty statement was there in front of me, so I began to break it down. "Bold, brave, courageous, authentic and strong?" Check. I could still do that. "Mohawk, style of dress, physique?" Those were good, too.

Without abandoning the rest of my statement, I did let go of who I thought I "should" and "could" be for the rest of that season — almost as if I mourned the death of my pre-injury self. I promised myself I would love my life for exactly how it was, and not what it might be. For instance, I tried to never say, "I can't wait to run" or "I can't wait to kick a ball again" because those kinds of statements dismissed the beauty of the present and the struggle. I dedicated myself to physical therapy every single day. I put myself through pain and frustration and soon realized that strength isn't measured by how much weight I could lift, but how much weight I could endure until I felt lifted. When I could jump and dance, even a little, I posted videos. And when I kicked a ball (very softly) for the first time, tapping it into the goal with my teammates, we burst into celebration like we'd won the World Cup.

My beauty statement was intact and, in the end, so was my knee, my psyche and my career. When I look back on my ACL injury, I say it is the best thing that ever happened to me. It was hard as hell, but I made it through with an attitude of optimism, gratitude, and appreciation for even the smallest victories. At the other end of recovery, I realized I loved myself, the game — and what it gave me — even more. — J.L.

her surgery and recovery with anyone, especially the next generation, who might need the information. "I once tried to explain what my concussion felt like to a young girl. "I said, 'It feels like you're in the woods by yourself and you're yelling. People are walking by, but they can't hear you.'" said Briana, who endured the procedure at Georgetown University Hospital on Oct. 18, 2013, after suffering the effects of the concussion for three-and-a-half years. With extensive physical therapy after the operation, she told

Briana Scurry, left, inadvertently knocking out her own teammate, Michelle Akers, 10, in 1999

PA IMAGES/JON BUCKLE/ALAMY STOCK PHOTO

us she feels like all of her faculties are restored and she plans to release a book about her life in 2022 now that she can finally recall all the details. "The one thing I am grateful for, now that I look back on it, is that I got concussed at age 38 and not 18. I couldn't imagine if I had been concussed at 18, going through schoolwork and classes, school activities, all that kind of stuff that comes with being a teenager."

AS FOR MALLORY PUGH'S TEENAGE LEG INJURY, she did manage to recover with all the vitality one might expect from a high school freshman. With almost no training to regain skills and timing after the doctors cleared her to play, she nonetheless led her team to a tournament victory in her first games back. On the surface, she made it all look easy, with appearances for youth national teams, breathless accolades from journalists who called her the "new face of American soccer," and even Mia Hamm, who Tweeted, "Speed kills, but technical speed absolutely annihilates defenders. Mallory Pugh is for real." That was July 22, 2016, just three months after Mal's 18th birthday when she was already emerging as the National Team's newest star.

What most people didn't know, however, is that undiagnosed stress fracture that led to the broken leg would continue to cause all sorts of complications. In October of 2017, Mal was sidelined with a hamstring pull. In May of 2018, she sat out with a knee injury, and by August of 2019 she suffered a strained hip flexor, which means the muscles are overstretched. In all cases, she said, the underlying issue is the growth plate in her leg getting impacted when she was still a child. "I grew a couple of inches after that happened, but my two legs didn't grow equally," said Mal during our conversation in 2020 when the nation was shut down due to COVID-19. "I'm starting to realize now that a lot of my injuries have come from that leg-length discrepancy, because all my injuries have been on my right side where I broke my leg."

A lift, inserted into her right cleat, attempts to achieve balance and relieve the pressure on her hip and knee. Stretching, and stretching more — what she calls "prehab" — is a constant way of life prior to practices and games. Most of all, she said, she reminds herself and anyone else facing injuries to maintain the right outlook with baby steps toward full recovery and always resist the temptation to come back too soon. "It sounds so basic and cliché to say you just have to stay positive, but you have to wake up and say, 'Maybe I sprained my ankle pretty badly. Maybe I can't run or touch a ball today. But what can I do?' And then you figure out what you can achieve and you literally attack that. Take those little victories; you're going to be so much happier throughout the whole injury process." She knows some players and parents will hear her story, or the ones shared by Sara and Briana, and wonder if all the pain is worth it. "It is pretty crazy to realize what athletes put their bodies through for a game we love," said Mal. "But I know I wouldn't change it."

Mallory Pugh, with Kelley O'Hara and Emily Sonnett

Horace Pugh, meanwhile, said he believes we have not yet seen the best of his oft-injured wunderkind. He knows, too, that some in the soccer world were beginning to doubt her durability and effort. On Jan. 16, 2020, when Mal received a double whammy of bad news — she had been traded from her first professional team, the Washington Spirit, to the New Jersey-based Sky Blue, and was left off the National Team roster for the Olympic qualifying tournament in February — she called her father while crying at her Denver apartment. "I'll be right there," he said. As Horace consoled his daughter, he reminded her of the primary reason he felt she had not been at her best at the Olympic tryouts. The nagging injuries related to the broken leg aside, Mal was still trying to shake the effects of what he called "the worst flu of her life," which antibody tests later revealed was most likely the coronavirus, aka COVID-19. "I reminded her she was at about 60 percent capacity (at the tryouts)," he said. "After that, she questioned herself for about two minutes and then stated, 'I'm pissed.' I saw that look in her eye, just like when she was a little girl. She said, 'I know what I need to do, and you know I don't like this feeling. I'm going to feed off of this, and I'm going to work even harder to make sure this never happens again.'"

'The Thing About Clive and Self-Confidence'

A Portland Legend had an Uncanny Knack for Drawing the Best Performances from his Players

BY THE LAST DAY OF HER RECRUITING VISIT to the University of Portland in 1990, Shannon MacMillan had nervously almost convinced herself the whole weekend was a bust. Coveted by college coaches everywhere after she led her San Diego youth team to the finals of a national tournament, she had been draped with accolades and promises at her other college visits that fall. Starting positions. Full scholarships. National Team introductions. It had all seemed too good to be true and there, on the shores of the Willamette River in Oregon, she allowed herself to believe all over again that maybe the dream wasn't real. Head coach Clive Charles never said a word to her for nearly two days until about an hour before Shannon, crestfallen, was scheduled to leave for the airport. "We've been watching you," he said quietly, with a distinctive British accent. "We've watched you interact with the team, we've talked to the team, and we think you'll be a really good fit up here." She stole a glance at the man across the desk from her, then looked to the floor. She

Shannon MacMillan, her youth days

COURTESY OF SHANNON MACMILLAN

swallowed hard, desperately trying to fight nerves and hold back tears, then mustered the strength to utter a seemingly simple question. "Am I going to play?" she asked. Clive shrugged his shoulders. "I don't know," he said. Shannon's eyes shot back to the floor as she turned her head to one side, then the other, almost expecting someone from "Candid Camera" to appear from behind his office door. "He's the coach," she thought to herself. "How can he *not know?*"

She swallowed again and surprised herself when the words came out of her mouth: "How do you not know if I'm going to play?" Clive shrugged again, this time waving his hand for emphasis. "All I can guarantee you is that you're going to get an opportunity," he said slowly. This time Shannon didn't look away. "Because I can't tell you how many goals you're going to score, or if you're going to make a National Team, or if you're going to do this that or the other thing. All I know is that I can give you an opportunity. And after watching you here this weekend, we think this could be a home for you. And we'd love to have you." The silent moments just afterward felt like minutes as Shannon studied the man's cherubic face and soft eyes. As her heart welled inside and pounded at the surface of her chest, she clenched her teeth. "I really wanted to say, 'Where do I sign?' Right then and there," she told us 30 years later.

EYE CONTACT WAS NOT SHANNON'S STRONG SUIT in high school. Numerous books, articles and former teammates reference her difficult childhood bouncing between New York and California with soccer — made possible by the goodwill of other families who covered most of her club fees and travel costs — as one of the few constant positives. Terms like "cruelty" and "neglect" are most often used to describe her home life by the time the family settled in Escondido, north of San Diego. When she packed everything she cared most about into a travel trunk at age 17 and hitched a ride with her brother, Sean, to the bus depot so she could buy a ticket north, he simply said, "Don't look back." A sometimes paralyzing lack of confidence followed her, at first, into classes, around campus, and even the sacred space of soccer practices. Shannon recalls a situation with a "free kick" in August of 1992 after she was fouled about 20 yards away from the goal. When she lined up to take her shot, a teammate sent her away from the ball. Clive stopped practice, walked over and put his hand on Shannon's shoulder. "What are you doing?" he asked. "She said she wanted it, so I let her have it," answered Shannon, instantly on the verge of tears. Clive was calm and direct: "I am paying you to go to school here. You're here on a full ride. I don't even know who that other girl is. You're telling me you're going to let her call you off of a free kick?"

COURTESY OF THE PORTLAND TIMBERS

Clive Charles, circa 1975

Shannon froze. "Now, line up, put this ball in the back of the net," Clive said. When she struck the ball and scored, inspiring her teammates to gasp audibly from the power of the shot, the coach called over to her again. "That's what you're here for!"

If North Carolina's Anson Dorrance is the National Team's godfather, and Santa Clara's Jerry Smith its benevolent king, the University of Portland's Clive Charles may have been the magi, an almost mystical sage revered like few others in the game. In Clive's case, that goes for women and men, since he coached both and made minimal distinction between the sexes when it came to coaching styles. "If the school is going to do something for the men, then we're going to do it for the women, too," Clive told administrators when they asked him to add the women's team to his duties in 1989 after having taken over the men's squad three years earlier. Nearly everyone who remembers him references a charismatic aura that expressed itself, again and again, in well-worn, yet profoundly simple phrases. "Be as honest as you can with your players," he told aspiring coaches. "Keep your shirt tucked in and your boots polished," he reminded the children at his FC Portland Soccer

---

INSPIRATION: SELF-WORTH

The Keys to Confidence

We asked the National Teamers for perspective on how to grow and maintain self-confidence for sports and life:

LISTEN UP, MOM AND DAD — The benefits of positive messaging begin at home in the formation of a person's self-image. "My parents never told me I was too small to do something; they never doubted that I could do something and having that confidence coming from home made it easier for me to actually be confident everywhere else," said **Angie Woznuk Kerr** (USWNT 2005-2009).

PREPARE FOR SUCCESS — Staying as fit as possible and practicing repetitively helps the body overcome an anxious mind. "I was nervous every single game, whether it was for the Seattle Reign, for the University of Washington, or for the United States," **Hope Solo** (USWNT 2000-2016) told a group of Girls Academy players in 2020. "What gave me confidence is just relying on my training. How much you train, how much you enjoy it, how detailed you are, and how detailed your coaches are, means you can always fall back on that if you get nervous."

BE OPEN TO NEW EXPERIENCES — **Crystal Dunn** (USWNT 2013-present) originally felt anxiety when coach Anson Dorrance asked her to play multiple positions at North Carolina. Years later, she is acclaimed on the National Team for her versatility. "I was thrown all over the field and I think I really struggled with a lot of different mental issues. I struggled because, even though he believed that I could handle all of those roles, I didn't believe in myself. I remember him always finding time to put his arm on my shoulder and say, 'You're good. You're great.'"

READ, LISTEN AND LEARN — Some people are naturally more outspoken and confident than others, but everyone benefits from knowing the facts — on the field and off. "I have unwavering confidence, obviously, whether it's warranted or not. I'm impossible to embarrass," **Megan Rapinoe** (USWNT 2006-present) told **Julie Foudy** (USWNT 1987-2004) on Julie's podcast "Laughter Permitted." "But I think I did grow into it by having my experience informed by the National Team, by contract negotiations, by coming out, and by educating myself, reading a lot, listening to people and having thought partners and people who challenge me."

Academy. "Have fun. If you have fun, you'll win," he told his would-be 2002 national championship team the day before it played Santa Clara in the cold, Texas December rain. "The thing about Clive and self-confidence is that you left every interaction with him feeling better about yourself," said Lauren Orlandos Hanson, a defender who played a game for the National Team in the 2001 summer prior to her senior year at Portland. "He was just really gifted at teaching the game of soccer, but also his personality was super welcoming and really funny. He had the whole package as a coach. Some can relate to their players; some are good at the Xs and Os. Clive was really both. He understood he was teaching a game, but it wasn't necessarily winning on the field that mattered the most. It was more about bringing a group of people together and helping them to achieve the best that they could achieve individually and then collectively."

A native of the town of Dagenham in England, Clive thought he was headed for Maine

COURTESY OF LAUREN GREGG

Lauren Gregg, with teammate Suzy Cobb Germain, in 1986 and 2019

women now about leadership. I think they see me from the outside and they see all my accolades and they're thinking, 'Wow that was really easy for you.' It wasn't. It came after just being torn down a bunch. My mentality was, 'If this is what I want, I have to put everything in. If I still don't make it, well then I at least know that I did everything possible.'"

ASK FOR HELP — No one can get through the journey of soccer, a job, or life in general without input and support from others. "Even the best player in the world needs confidence, and I think a lot of people don't realize that," said **Lauren Gregg** (USWNT 1986). "You can be the best player in the world and begin to question, doubt and need reassurance and validating. It sounds like a little thing, but if you, in any way, let fissure or doubt creep in, or even entertain a negative thought, that would widen the fissure. I feel like that was one of the things that I did very well as a coach, to be matter of fact, to let players know, 'We're prepared, you're ready, and we need you.' So there's just no time to let it fester."

EMBRACE FAILURE — Fear of failure is the biggest driver of the lack of confidence, but learning to fail, even to lose, on the field of play can actually help build self-assurance in time. "I failed so many times," said **Shannon Boxx** (USWNT 2003-2015). "I talk to a lot of business-

UNDERSTAND YOUR ROLE — The goal may be to be a starter, to score goals and be a star. Learning that all teammates serve important functions, even as supporters, can lead to a bigger role in time. "I knew what my role was and I think that was important," said **Tracey Bates Leone** (USWNT 1987-1991). "You never want to be completely satisfied. That's OK. So you want to keep working hard and you want to be self-disciplined enough to be ready for your own opportunity when it comes."

JUST DO IT — Getting out and playing sports, at any level, has been shown to have numerous benefits for self-image off the field. "When girls play team sports in a socially safe environment, they're more likely to use condoms. They're more likely to delay sexual debut and they're more self-confident," said **Lorrie Fair** (USWNT 1996-2005). "Physical exercise can help you concentrate more in school, which may translate to better grades. There are so many benefits."

in 1978 when he signed a contract to play for the Portland Timbers. He had met his wife, Clarena, while playing for the Montreal Olympique in the early '70s and they were both excited to escape the racism of his homeland and head to a state on the northeastern Canadian border — only to find out by surprise on a map that they would be traveling 3,000 miles farther west. The geography error would come to change the face of soccer in Oregon and, eventually, the National Team. Almost as soon as he began coaching at youth clinics to supplement his income, an 8-year-old girl showed up at one of Clive's first practices. "Tiffeny Milbrett had the greatest soccer mind of anyone I ever met in my life, and that's men or women," said John Bain, an Irishman who was one of Clive's teammates and a record-setting goal scorer with the Timbers. "Her vision and creativity was like nothing I ever witnessed, at least until I saw Tobin Heath play many years later. Clive and Tiffeny were a perfect match, really. He had a way of communicating with players that was just very, very special and Tiffeny was like a sponge, absorbing all of it."

REUTERS/SYLVIA BUCHHOLZ/ALAMY STOCK PHOTO

Tiffeny Milbrett, hoisted by Mia Hamm in 2000

LIKE SHANNON MACMILLAN, TIFFENY'S CHILDHOOD was less than ideal. She never knew her biological father and worked picking strawberries or whatever jobs she could find starting in middle school to help her mother, Elsie, pay the rent at their apartment complex in Hillsboro, just to the west of Portland. After school, when Elsie was still working the local factory assembly line, Tiffeny practiced her soccer spin moves hour after hour on the paved parking lot, or at nearby Shute Park. Some evenings and weekends, Tiffeny tagged along to the new amateur women's soccer league her mother helped form. Some media accounts of the day claim Tiffeny was subbing in for the adult women by age 10, but she told us that was an exaggeration; she played during practices, but not games. "I was good, but not that good. And, besides, I was too small," she said.

Around Clive Charles, though, the diminutive girl was always made to feel as if she had just the right size, speed and demeanor in every situation. As a coach, he never tried to tame her creative instincts on the field. As a mentor and friend, he always leaned in closely with a joke, to offer a stick of gum, and generally let her know she was beloved. "It was a connection, a bond I had with him from a very young age," said Tiffeny, who became somewhat of a local athletic legend despite only growing to 5-foot-2. "I think what maybe people may not truly understand is that Clive wasn't just my coach. He was a life force for me for many, many years way outside of the game of soccer. I don't think I understood until many years later, when I was done with soccer, how much confidence that had given me in my life." She would achieve all-state high school status in basketball and track in addition to soccer — and was offered college scholarships nationally in all three sports — but when Clive asked her to stay home and help him prop up his year-old women's soccer experiment, she didn't hesitate. For the next 15 years, the small Catholic college would be among the top 20 teams in the nation nearly every season and Clive never hesitated to give her the credit. "In the second year, I managed to sign Tiffeny. She single-handedly turned the program around. There's no question about that," Clive told *Soccer America* in 2003. "She was magnificent. I tell our players all the time: 'The only reason you're here is because of Tiff. Because if she hadn't have come, you wouldn't have wanted to be here. 'Cause we wouldn't have won a game.'"

On the strength of an 18-goal freshman season at Portland, Tiffeny confidently joined the National Team as an 18-year-old when April Heinrichs' knees were failing her in the months prior to the first women's World Cup in 1991. April managed to recover in time to help bring the trophy home from China, but retired soon afterward to leave the door open for the game's next great scorer. Tiffeny was all of that and more, with 100 goals in 206 games across 15 years. She entered the national Hall of Fame in 2018, drawing praise as one of the great players in world history, and yet, in 2020, she confirmed a career-long struggle with virtually all the coaches who came into her life after college. "A lot of people said to me through the years, 'You know, not everybody's Clive,'" said Tiffeny, who took a "mental break" from the game for 18 months after the 2003 World Cup. "I wasn't expecting Clive. But after experiencing someone who is so capable and so professional, such a phenomenal developmental coach, somebody who manages a team fairly and treats you with respect — and this is what you experience when you're 8 years old, then 9, 10 . . . 15, 16 . . . and then college — then I would expect something even a little greater when I go to the National Team. The truth is that very few coaches, if any, ever came close to Clive. Those coaches fell way, way short, in my opinion."

One of Tiffeny's bits of advice, all these years later, is for parents and players to consider professional psychological support as a requisite in the high-level sports journey from a young age. "I've honestly come to feel badly for a lot of my coaches through the years, and I got there with plenty of therapy," she said. "If you're a high performer, you almost have to have therapy for your mental health. You have to have support. There's no question. This isn't just me; all high performers are extremely sensitive, finely tuned people and they have to have help managing that. Through the years I have come to terms with the disappointment that I was never again going to have a pure coach who was managing with all the right soccer and life stuff."

THE SOMEWHAT MYSTICAL FORCE KNOWN AS SELF-CONFIDENCE can elude even the best of players, from youth league tears at age 10 and college recruiting anxiety at age 15, to injury recovery doubts at age 25, and wondering if you have another year left in your body at age 30 and beyond. Not a single National Teamer has survived without a crisis of confidence somewhere along the way. Becky Sauerbrunn once called self-assurance "fairy dust" in a 2016 *Washington Post* article about her teammate, Crystal Dunn, tying a record held by Tiffeny and seven others with five goals in one National Team game. "I regret saying that," Becky told us. "Confidence ideally shouldn't be fairy dust; it should be there all the time instead of some mythological thing that you do every once in a while." Becky, who has been one of the most dependable, longest serving captains of the National Team, said her most enduring confidence comes from within, despite an admitted life-long struggle with her self-image. Ideally, she said, confidence shouldn't have to be doled out by parents, coaches and teammates. "I've always been pretty self-critical, and I don't think my parents really quite knew how to deal with it. They tried their best, but there have been times when the external factors were just too much for me." To cope, Becky said she has learned to focus on everything she can control — the intensity of her workouts, getting as much information as coaches are willing to share — and then she frequently escapes into books. She's known to buy stacks of them in a single visit to Powell's Books when she's home in Portland. "It's escapism, and I do use it when it comes to soccer and especially the National Team when things become too much of a grind. I know when I need to get away and kind of refresh my batteries."

COURTESY OF LORI LINDSEY

Becky Sauerbrunn, center, with Megan Rapinoe, left, and Lori Lindsey

Clive Charles, according to his former players and teammates, instinctively understood the link between his players' confidence and performance, and when to push forward with toughness, or pull back with humor. At halftime of a 1999 game against a Santa Clara team that featured Aly Wagner and Danielle Slaton (see Chapter 7), an overconfident Portland team was losing 4-0 at halftime. The embarrassed, angry players sat huddled in silence as Clive slowly erased a whiteboard in the front of the room. "Who thinks we can win this game?" he asked. No one uttered a sound — until freshman Lauren Orlandos Hanson couldn't help herself. "I do!" she said, springing to her feet and expecting others to follow. "No, you can't," said Clive. When Lauren recoiled, the coach explained that on some days, the other team is simply better. "You play hard, you hold your head high when we walk out of here," he said. At the end of the game, which Portland lost 8-0, Lauren was approached by her father, Bob. "You should have gone to North Carolina when you had the chance," he said.

Two years later, back in California preparing to face Santa Clara in a key tournament game, the nervous University of Portland players were unusually quiet. When the bus pulled into the stadium, Clive motioned to Lauren, by then the team captain, as soon as the players stepped outside. With her teammates hushed, Lauren walked slowly toward her coach, expecting to receive information to share about the game. "Hold out your hand," he said. "Why?" she asked. "Hold out your hand," he said again. When she complied, he took the chewing gum out of his mouth, placed it in her hand, and walked away. Stunned, Lauren was soon engulfed by teammates who were laughing hysterically.

Crisis of Confidence?
Look no Further than Home

N 2013, WHEN THE BOSTON BREAKERS FIRED HEAD COACH Lisa Cole near the end of the National Women's Soccer League season and hired National Teamer Cat Whitehill as interim player-coach, we ended the year with three wins in the final four games and finished just one spot out of the playoffs. Optimism abounded. If you've read this far, you hopefully understand I'm a positive person in general. Finding the silver lining in situations and people is the mantra and mission that carried me through surgeries and slim financial pickings for 16 professional seasons. I don't, as a matter of principle, hold grudges — and I had no idea how much that would be tested when we kicked off 2014.

Cat had tried to hire Kristine Lilly as her assistant the previous summer, but Kristine could only stay for one game due to other obligations. Cat offered the job to some others, but a friend of a friend recommended a youth coach, whose closest brush with soccer credibility had come years

Joanna, at a low point in her career

ASHLEY PALMER

earlier as an assistant with the Under-17 national men's team. He seemed OK in a four-game sample carrying around the Breakers' clipboard and running us through a few drills, and apparently made enough of an impression that the team ownership handed him the head job. The fact we started the year 1-6 only tells a whisper of the story that unfolded. Often late to training, he was quick to slam us for mistakes. Pushing a group of women including several National Teamers to near tears daily, he tried to motivate through threats and fear. As the defensive center midfielder, I tended to roam the field and, after a particularly bad loss, he picked us apart one by one in front of the entire team. I'll never forget what he said to me: "You will play in the center circle and you will not move outside of it. If you decide to dribble up the field and you lose the ball, you can slit your own throat."

I felt almost literally cut like a knife. Words matter. And though I've had coaches yell, scream and criticize — and I can ALWAYS take it — that statement will go down as the worst thing a coach has ever said to me. I'm sure it will come as no surprise to anyone that we went on to lose 16 of our 24 games that season. It is said that great teams find ways to win. Our team, incredibly talented on paper, but emotionally battered by our own leader, found ways to lose. In the game of soccer, confidence is key and ours had been shattered. One player simply quit the game of soccer altogether when the final whistle blew that year.

As for me, I left Boston and moved back in with Mom and Dad. I was 32, old enough to know that living with your parents wasn't the hippest thing in the world — but it was the coolest. Who better to show you that you matter, that you are so much more than a game, and everything is going to be OK? They helped me to slowly restore my confidence and put the pieces of my life back together. Getting picked up by the Washington Spirit in the 2015 waiver draft became the silver lining that I always seem to find. As for old whatshisname, he won four games in 2015 before getting fired. After that, I heard he became the soccer director at Club Med. Perfect. — J.L.

Soccer Can Be Tough on the Ego

AS A PARENT OF A WOMAN IN HER 30S AND A MAN IN HIS 20S, I've long since learned that being present and attentive in both key and mundane moments of your children's lives builds all-important, yet often elusive, self-confidence. When my then 10-year-old aspiring actress, Aimee, was on stage on May 6, 2017, I was all-in — with one eye. Just below my seat, to my right, I held my iPhone where my wife couldn't see that I was silently streaming a soccer game. Sure enough, just as Aimee was getting ready to step out on stage as Frieda in the youth production of "You're a Good Man, Charlie Brown," my "soccer daughter," Havana Solaun, took off like a bullet out of a shotgun at midfield, fielded a Franny Ordega pass in stride, and scored a

COURTESY OF GAINESVILLE TENNIS

Havana Solaun, at home on the tennis court

highlight reel goal, her first of the new season with the Washington Spirit. My wife was happy for our houseguest, but also less than amused when I revealed my divided attention. "Havana scored!" I whispered, unable to contain the news.

Aimee has always been remarkably poised. She does things on stage I could never have even imagined, especially at her age. For her sister, Angie, and her soccer sister, Havana, self-assurance on the soccer field always seems far more fleeting which, according to Havana, is simply the nature of a team sport. As a highly ranked tennis player in her home state of Florida, she needed to make a decision when soccer recruiters came knocking. She originally quit soccer for two weeks, but changed her mind when she missed the inventiveness inherent in the sport. "Tennis is a bit cut and dry; you can hit a stroke in only so many ways," she said. "With soccer, once the whistle blows, the game is live and the creativity you can bring to bear is always a lot of fun for me." Individual sports like tennis, however, are also cut and dry in another way: If you win, you keep playing, and no coach can stop it. "There's just a certainty in gauging where you're at in tennis. Whereas in soccer, there can be a coach that says, 'You're useless. You can play right bench.' There can be another coach who says, 'You are the center of my team. We're going to build a team around you.'"

Havana's mother, tennis teaching professional Sandra Brower, sometimes laments her daughter's decision. "I always found it very bizarre, her lack of confidence on the soccer field, because on the tennis court, she would choose not to lose. Losing wasn't an option," she said. "I would have thought that would have transferred more positively into soccer." Havana has had highs — she was the centerpiece of soccer teams at the University of Florida, her first year in Washington, and in Norway in 2019 when she was voted one of the top 11 players of the league — and the lows of coaches and general managers ignoring her during and after the lonely recovery from injuries. As a Mom, it's always hard to watch the satisfaction and confidence ebb and flow, but that's why Sandra is often in the stands for Havana's games, and hugging her afterward, whether she played, or not. Me? I still stream them on my phone. — P.T.

BY HER SENIOR YEAR OF 1995, SHANNON MACMILLAN WAS an All-American selection and universally anointed the best college player in the country. "That woman could do things on the soccer field that I could not even come close to doing," said John Bain, who served as Clive's assistant during Shannon's sophomore year. "The strength and power were off the charts." The new National Team head coach, Tony DiCicco, appeared ready to bring her into the fold for the first-ever Olympics featuring women's soccer, telling *Soccer America*, "She has a good chance to make this team, and we're going to give her every opportunity." For the first time in her life, coming off a senior year with 23 goals, Shannon's confidence seemed rock solid. Just weeks after making that comment to the media, however, Tony left Shannon behind when he moved the National Team to Florida for the pre-Olympic residency camp. Angry, hurt and disillusioned, she flew home and caromed straight into Clive's office.

COURTESY OF SHANNON MACMILLAN

Shannon MacMillan, right, with her wife, Michele, and their son

The coach, who had seen this look before, knew this would be no ordinary cry. He pulled a box of Kleenex out of his desk drawer, the one he always told Shannon he kept around just for her, and then leaned back in his chair. "The coaches are so stupid and the world isn't fair and college is already done and there aren't even any decent leagues overseas and this is what I played for my whole life and you told me I was good enough and how can all of this be happening?" She ranted, in similar fashion, for 45 minutes. "Are you done?" asked Clive. "No, I'm not," said Shannon, who continued her tear-streamed monologue to the point of exhaustion. Clive turned and looked at the clock on his wall. "OK, it's 2:30," he said. "I will see you back here tomorrow at 2:30. Don't even bother bringing your ball and, be ready, I'm going to kick your ass." Shannon wiped her nose one last time. "Why bother?" she asked. "Go home," he said. "You have 24 hours to pout and feel sorry for yourself. And then, after 24 hours, I'm going to kick your ass. Next time you get your chance, you're going to be ready. You're not going to be moping around."

In the weeks that followed, training one on one with Clive, Shannon had no realistic hope of playing in the Olympics. Tony invited more than 20 players to Florida and only 16 would make the final roster. Just a month later, however, Julie Foudy — acting on the advice of Billie Jean King — pleaded with her teammates not to sign the latest contract offer from U.S. Soccer, which locked nine starters out of training camp. Swallowing his pride with gaping holes in his roster, and needing players for a tournament in Brazil, Tony called Shannon to ask her if she was in game shape. Hold that thought, she said. Shannon needed to contact Julie first to see what the National Team leaders thought of her breaking the picket line. "Get your butt on that plane — and this time prove to him you deserve to be on that team," said Julie. Even when the strike ended, Tony kept Shannon this time. "Cutting Shannon MacMillan was the biggest mistake I ever made," he once said.

MILBRETT AND MACMILLAN. TIFF AND MAC. At a campus the locals call The Bluff, the Hall of Famers are forever known simply as "M&M." Though several other National

Teamers have been more famous, and a few have played more games or scored more goals, there's not another story quite like theirs in the game of soccer. From broken families with no realistic prospects for what would come next, they put a small college on the international map almost overnight. They helped win the 1996 Olympics, with Shannon scoring two key goals in the final two games, and the 1999 World Cup, with Tiffeny emerging as the leading scorer. Tiffeny would be the most valuable player in the WUSA, the first women's professional league, and also receive the nation's highest soccer award, U.S. Soccer Player of the Year, in 2000 and 2001. Shannon won the honor in 2002. For all of that, though, both women were carrying a regret: They never won a championship for the man, a British immigrant of African descent, who they both say made it all possible. "He basically turned my life around," Shannon told *Soccer America* years before becoming a mother herself would help her make peace with her parents. "When I took that Greyhound bus to Port-

Clive Charles, with his wife, Clarena, Tiffeny Milbrett and ESPN reporter Ellen Weinberg-Hughes

land, I got off a weak, timid, unconfident little girl who didn't know her potential or how to achieve it. Really, through his teaching, friendship and love, he became the father figure I'd never had."

At the height of their professional careers, however, the news about Clive Charles' health turned grim. He had been diagnosed with prostate cancer and kept it a secret from everyone but his wife in 2000. By the fall of 2002, the world of soccer knew the truth. Treatments were failing and time was running out. The legacy of M&M had helped stack the Portland roster with future American National Teamers Lauren Orlandos Hanson and Lindsey Huie, as well as Canadian National Teamers Wanda Rozwadowska and the incomparable Christine Sinclair, whose uncles had played with Clive and John Bain back in the Portland Timbers' heyday. With Christine off playing for Canada, the season started 0-2, and the team would rack up four losses and three ties for an eighth seeding heading into the tournament that would decide the national championship. Almost unthinkably, Portland defeated top-ranked Stanford with a backup sophomore goalie, Lauren Arase, blocking three of five penalty kicks after a scoreless game. At the Final Four, also known as the College Cup, Portland shut out Penn State, featuring Joanna Lohman, then readied itself for the championship game against its archrivals of Santa Clara.

The day before the game, sensing the tension of his overachieving players, Clive lined up all the young women as if they were about to stretch. "Take off your boots," he said. They looked curiously at him, then at each other, and then complied one by one. "Let's see who can throw them the farthest," he told them. When the 19 pairs of cleats were all in a pile somewhere near the middle of the field in Austin, Texas, Clive ended the last practice of his life with a command, as recounted by Christine in an oral history published by the Portland Timbers: "Go out there and have fun. And if you have fun, you'll win, and you'll make me a very happy man." It was the first occasion in his coaching life, according to anyone who knew him, that he made the score of the game a top priority.

Clive Charles, the legend of Portland

COURTESY OF THE UNIVERSITY OF PORTLAND

When the finals began on a soggy field, Santa Clara scored first. Then Christine tied the game in the 61st minute and, for the first overtime and into a second, the score remained 1-1. Goalie Lauren Arase suffered a concussion in the middle of it all and, with his legacy hanging in the balance, Clive was faced with a choice: Replace her with an experienced senior who had been benched for violating a team rule, or put in an unrecruited walk-on who hadn't played a minute of college soccer in her life. Lauren Orlandos Hanson, the team captain, begged Clive to play the senior; he sent in the walk-on. "Who makes that decision in that situation?" said Lauren, the head coach at San Jose State since 2014. "I look back on that now, as a coach, and I think, 'What an amazing decision to stick with your morals, to do the right thing — instead of doing the best thing to win the national championship — in what is the last game you will ever coach.'"

In the 104th minute, Christine — who would later become the most prolific scorer in international soccer history — scored again. The national championship, the first in any sport in the school's history, was heading to Portland and Clive, who had been too weak to walk onto the field and arrived by wheelchair, stood and hugged all comers. Shannon and Tiffeny were there first, and then came his wife, Clarena, and Jerry Smith, just a year removed from his own national title. In that moment, Lauren sprinted from Clive to her father in the stands. "Still think I should have gone to North Carolina?" she asked. Then ESPN came by and directed its microphone and camera toward the man who had landed in Oregon a quarter century earlier by happy mistake. Clive Charles would pass away less than nine months later at age 51. But in the glow of a victory that still reverberates, he drew Tiffeny into the hug he was sharing with his wife. "Tiff came to Portland when it was not cool to be in Portland," he told the national television audience. "The reason we won today is because of her . . . I hope she knows that."

Turning Adversity Into Opportunity

Every National Team Player Has Overcome Numerous Obstacles to Become the Best Version of Themselves

SOMEONE YOU HAVE HEARD ABOUT, MIA HAMM, was born with a club foot that required special corrective shoes. Someone you may not know of unless you're from St. Louis, named Ruth Harker, became one of the first goalies the U.S. National Team ever signed despite being born blind in one eye and keeping her condition a secret so no one would ever try to stop her from playing. "There are stories after stories like this that I could tell that speak to players overcoming adversity," said University of North Carolina coach Anson Dorrance, the man credited with molding the loose collection of players into a truly enduring program from 1986-1994. By giving a core group of young girls — including Julie Foudy, Carla Overbeck, Kristine Lilly, Brandi Chastain, Joy Fawcett and Mia — more responsibility than they ever thought possible, Anson instilled a culture that would span generations. Those six women played a stunning combined total of 1,557 games for the National Team, most of them together and many for Anson. "We don't share most of the stories, because we don't want to embarrass any of our players. But the one that was made most public was about the day I was driving to work, and out of the corner of my eye, I see a player. It was Mia Hamm's senior spring. I see this figure running five yards and

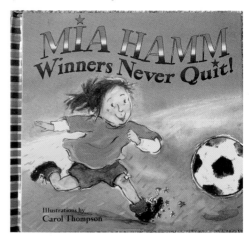

back, 10 and back, 15 and back, 20 and 25 and back. It was our fitness exercise; it's this grueling thing the kids call 'cones,' because they're running back and forth between these cones. It's early February; it's cold out. Between these sprints you can see the sweat flying off Mia's brow, with hot air coming out of her lungs. I was just so impressed."

The coach, who had discovered America's first female team sport superstar as a 14-year-old high school freshman, drove back to his trophy-lined office where he thoughtfully scribed his thoughts about what he had just seen onto a piece of stationery. As he has done hundreds of times, for hundreds of other players, he folded the note into a stamped envelope, dropped it into the outbound mail slot, and went on with his day. More than a decade passed, with Mia leading the American team to World Cup championships in 1991 and again in 1999, before his words would resurface on the breastplate of her

COURTESY OF RUTH HARKER

Mia Hamm, with Ruth Harker in 2019

best-selling autobiography, "Go For The Goal," published in 1999. The coach still keeps a copy of the book just an arm's length from his desk all these years after he memorialized his thoughts — that also adorned countless posters on young athletes' bedroom walls — from that morning: "The vision of a champion is bent over, drenched in sweat, at the point of exhaustion, when nobody else is looking."

If you're a soccer fan, and even if you're not, you have probably heard about Rose Lavelle by now, too. In her coming out party that was the 2019 Women's World Cup, Rose scored the final goal of the championship game and earned the Bronze Ball awarded to the third best player in a tournament filled with all the best players on the planet. Having come of age in the Internet era when highlight reels are now reduced to Twitter posts and seconds-long memes, the Cincinnati native plays the game as if there are two sets of goals on the field: the ones mere soccer mortals try to shoot the ball into to score, and the second ones that involve utterly embarrassing, and breaking the will of, an opponent by kicking the ball between her legs. The move, in soccer parlance, is called a "nutmeg," or "meg" for short. The sport's historians debate the term's origin; some say it originally described kicking the ball under a male opponent's testicles (aka "nuts"). Author Peter Seddon attributes the expression to historically shady export deals between North America and England involving nutmeg that was "such a valuable commodity that unscrupulous exporters were to pull a fast one by mixing a helping of wooden replicas into the sacks being shipped to England. Being nutmegged soon came to imply stupidity on the part of the duped victim and cleverness on the part of the trickster."

PUT DOWN THIS BOOK, GRAB YOUR COMPUTER OR PHONE, and Google the simple phrase "Rose England nutmeg." The meme you'll find viewed millions of times, dated July 2, 2019, depicts the singular World Cup moment in the semifinal match — ironically against England — when America's newest sports darling nearly broke the Internet. Dribbling the ball frantically, seemingly with nowhere to go against one of world's best defenders, Rose simply took the most direct route to the goal by dribbling the ball between Millie Bright's legs. Never mind that Rose barely missed her shot on goal just afterward, or that it came only four minutes into the contest, it was already game over for England. "There is something about a nutmeg that brings out a kind of childish glee," wrote Molly Hudson in the *Times of London.* "When Rose Lavelle slipped the ball between Millie Bright's legs in the opening four minutes of their World Cup semi-final against England, the Stade de Lyons gasped as one. It was a signal of what was to come."

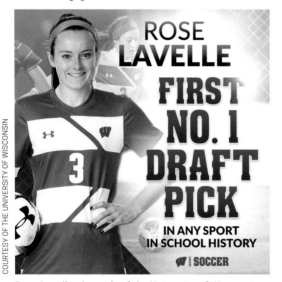

Rose Lavelle, the pride of the University of Wisconsin

For Rose, though, it was just another result of the lifelong affliction she has had to overcome: her size. The third of Janet and Marty Lavelle's four children has typically been the smallest player on every field she's ever been on, from the time she joined a Cincinnati YMCA team at age 5 and scored a goal in her first game — and immediately ducked behind a much larger teammate to hide her immense satisfaction from her opponents. Her mother and father had never played soccer, didn't consider themselves to be overwhelmingly competitive, and were as amazed as anyone at Rose's survival instincts against taller, heavier players who initially saw Rose as easy prey. "She'd kind of hang toward the outside of the group waiting for the ball to get popped free, rather than be in the crowd," said her mother. "She'd get a break-away and then maybe she'd run into two defenders and she would just stop and wait for them to move. And then she would move around them. So she kind of did her own little thing and she would refer to it as 'tricking them.' She'd say, 'I tricked them, Mom. Mom, I tricked those people. That's how I got by them!'"

If Rose's agent, Remy Cherin, was right years later when he described his shy slight client as "fucking ruthless" to the media, it was an edge honed in those early days living in fear of the heights and feet of others who were constantly pushing, kicking and mocking her. "I had to figure out ways for them to not be able to knock me off the ball," Rose told us.

Rose Lavelle: Keys to Success

TURN YOUR CHALLENGE INTO YOUR ADVANTAGE — "I was the smallest player on the field, but I used that to my advantage. While I could not bowl over players to get past them, I could outmaneuver them because I was low to the ground, elusive, and impossible to catch!"

EMBRACE THE GROWTH MINDSET — "I spent hours and hours by myself in my backyard trying to beat juggling records and master new skills. I knew eventually, with all of this practice, I would conquer the challenge."

Rose Lavelle, with the late Neil Bradford

COURTESY OF SAY SOCCER

GET COMFORTABLE BEING UNCOMFORTABLE — "Leaving my friends behind and joining Cincinnati United Premier was a very hard decision. I lost some friends over it. I knew however, it was the best step for my development."

RIDE THE ROLLER COASTER — "There were some serious low moments in my career, for example, my hamstring injury in 2017 when I spent months on the sideline. There were also some serious highs like scoring a goal in the 2019 Women's World Cup Final. Experiencing those low moments made me truly appreciate the highs."

IT'S OKAY IF IT'S HARD — "I tore all three of the muscles in my hamstring without fully understanding the severity of the injury. Spending months in rehab and working my way back slowly was one of the hardest points in my career."

PRACTICE DELIBERATELY — "My footwork is one of the best parts of my game. I was only able to develop this footwork over time and hours and hours of practice. Each time I practiced, I worked on moves, skills, and drills that challenged me as a player and person."

SHARE THE STRUGGLE — "When I tore the third muscle in my hamstring, I was at home in Ohio practicing at a local park. I came back to the house and shared the news with my mother. I broke into tears and allowed my Mom to help me through the pain. It's so important to lean on those around you who support you the most."

FAIL AND FAIL AGAIN — "For all the amazing moves I have pulled off in a game, there are hundreds of failures. Hundreds. Whether I trip over the ball in my backyard with no one around to see, or I misplace a pass in front of thousands of screaming fans, each failure was pivotal to my development."

BE ACCOUNTABLE — "It wasn't until college that I realized how important nutrition was. My diet was out of balance and I wasn't giving my body what it needed to perform at the highest level. At the end of the day, you are responsible for being your best. How many hours are you sleeping, what are you eating, how many hours are you practicing? These are all parts of the game that matter immensely."

AVOID THE BLAME GAME — "When I make a pass that does not reach my teammate, I don't blame her. When I lose a game, I don't blame the ref. When I have a bad game, I don't blame my coaches. Take ownership of your game and you will grow from every experience that doesn't go your way."

We Lost, But I Won

O N OCT. 7, 2016, I WAS SHOCKED TO LEARN I WOULD NOT BE STARTING in the championship game of the National Women's Soccer League. The 2016 season had been the best of my 16-year career. I was the second leading goal scorer for the Washington Spirit, my hometown team, started 18 of 21 games, and played in every match. I didn't miss a day of practice due to injury, contributed off the field in a massive way by connecting to the fan base, and — most importantly — I cared about this team tremendously. It pulsed through my veins. From that moment until game time, two days later, I was heartbroken. Devastated, actually. With only three substitutes allowed in a professional soccer game, my chances of contributing were slim. Maybe I would not step on the field at all in the biggest game of my life. To make matters worse, my parents had flown to Houston. They had provided a lifetime of support, through injury, illness and the poverty borne of my career choice, but they had not seen an away game in more than a decade.

Still, up 2-1 in the first overtime — thanks to two goals by our U.S. National Team superstar Crystal Dunn — things were looking good. Though I had still not stepped on the field, we were close to winning. I warmed up with the hope of at least getting subbed in by the time of the final whistle when we would be declared champions. On the field, my teammates were holding strong with literally moments to go. The players on the bench, including me, were in starting-gate sprinter position ready to rush the field. That game was ours. I thought to myself, "At least if I am not going to play, we're winning a trophy!"

Ten seconds left. Somehow the

COURTESY OF THE WASHINGTON SPIRIT

Joanna, happiest on the field

last kick of the game sailed into our defensive box. Out of nowhere Lynn Williams — one of those annoyingly talented National Team players! — smashed it with her head into the back of our net. Euphoria turned to panic as we were suddenly forced to prepare for a penalty kick shootout. And since I was not one of the 11 active players on the field, I would not be allowed to participate. Five seemingly simple shots later, we lost 3-2. I was shattered. This was my best shot at winning a championship. My greatest season was over. And in the world of sports, especially this young league, the turnover rate is immense; I knew the team would never be the same again. As tears started streaming down my face, my parents looked on in agony from the stands.

I began a slow walk in their direction. My Mom embraced me, then Dad, too. In my sadness and devastation all I wanted to do was apologize to them for coming all that way to watch me sit on the bench — for wasting all that time and watching us lose. When I feel like I have disappointed my parents, it shakes me to my core. "I am so sorry. I am so sorry you traveled all this way to watch us lose." I cried harder still, but Mom pulled me even closer. "Jo," she said. "*This* is exactly why we *are* here." In my weakest and most vulnerable moment, my parents were there to reassure me. When it seemed like my identity was shattered, they showed me I am loved. Unconditionally. Not for what I accomplished, the minutes I played, or didn't, but for exactly who I am. Their daughter. Period. — J.L.

"Ways for me to feel like they can't touch me, they can't get the ball, which is one of the reasons I got so good with my feet." Rose's dominance would even bring taunts from parents on the opposing sidelines of youth games. "Let her dance! She's not going anywhere," yelled one mother. Undeterred, Rose responded: "I'll beat your daughter, and I will beat her again and again." And so she did. With the ball practically glued to Rose's foot as she spun away, the defender swung at the air with her leg in desperation. Rather than going for the goal, Rose turned back to dribble around the girl again, and then again. "Parents were always trying to get into my head. But I had so much confidence when I was younger," she said. "It came from the desire to prove you wrong."

PA IMAGES/RICHARD SELLERS/ALAMY STOCK PHOTO

Rose Lavelle, with Millie Bright at the World Cup

At age 9, when an Englishman, Neil Bradford, invited Rose to join his team of 11-year-olds, he almost immediately declared she would be on the National Team one day, if she put in the work. If most girls on the team were challenged to complete 20 "juggles" — which is bouncing the ball off your foot repeatedly without it hitting the ground — he would ask Rose to do it 40 times. If teammates were asked to do 40 toe-touches — tapping the ball with the bottom of your cleats in rapid succession — in 20 seconds, the coach would expect Rose to do 80 or more. She bristled at first, but then headed to her backyard hour after hour, day after day. Long before Rose would flog Millie Bright in that viral meme, she could be found on-line, in that backyard, in her coach's video stating: "I'm Rosie Lavelle and I'm 11 years old." She was putting on a soccer juggling and ball-control clinic that, to this day, most other adult professional players in the world couldn't begin to match.

By high school, at all of 90 pounds as a freshman, Rose had moved to the Cincinnati United Premier travel squad. Feathers were ruffled when she left her long-time friends behind. "I needed something new," said Rose, in a call-out to younger players facing similarly tough decisions. "I loved my team so much and they were so influential to me, but I was like, 'I don't want to shy away from a new challenge just because I want to stick with my friends.'" Less than a decade later out of high school, still one of the smallest players on any field, she would be a World Cup champion, sitting on a stage of a conference center in Gaithersburg, Md., dispensing more advice to a room full of girls who desperately wanted to be her. "You've got to get comfortable being uncomfortable," she told them. "That has really been the key to whatever success I've had in my life."

THOSE WORDS WOULD HAVE BEEN EASY FOR RUTH HARKER to take to heart had she heard them a half century earlier. A child of the 1960s, she can't remember a day she ever truly felt at ease since the day her father said he was leaving her St. Louis home for a loaf of bread and never came back. Ruth and her three older siblings persisted with their mother on dehydrated milk and WIC allocations of food stamps. Though Ruth compulsively ran everywhere, her mother never allowed her to play sports — opting to dress Ruth in cheerleader outfits instead. Every morning before school, she would be ordered to put on one of the few dresses she owned, but as soon as she got to the school restroom Ruth would pull the same pair of patchwork red pants out of her backpack. "This went on for the whole semester until parent-teacher conferences," said Ruth, with a laugh. "The teacher asked my Mom if we were having financial problems, which we probably were, because I was wearing the exact same pair of pants every single day."

COURTESY OF RUTH HARKER

Ruth Harker, goalie in the making, circa 1980

She certainly wasn't a bit relaxed in high school, at the same age Rose Lavelle was a self-described 90-pound freshman weakling, when Ruth was a broad-shouldered tomboy ready to attack the world of high school sports — never having played a minute prior. She cut a deal with her mother; she'd work two jobs to pay for her own taxi rides to practice so she could join the soccer team and basketball teams. But she also carried her secret; she was born blind in her right eye. "I didn't want anyone to think I had a handicap, so I never said a word," she said. If the lack of peripheral vision proved challenging, the lack of experience as a field player on the soccer field was insurmountable. That led her to try out for goalie, where she says she still can't quite explain her almost immediate success. "It was probably more difficult to deal with monocular vision in goal than even the field position would have been, because you have to have good depth perception and understand the angles of incidence and trajectory. But I just took to it. It's a very cerebral position, I guess, and it suited me."

Just a year later, she was already getting invited to international tournaments. A full scholarship to the University of Missouri-St. Louis was next, where her team would even take down North Carolina during her freshman year, followed by an invitation to participate in the nascent Olympic Sports Festival in Baton Rouge, La. It was 1985 when — much to almost everyone's surprise — the players for the first ever U.S. Women's National Team would be selected for that now infamous four-team tournament known as the Mundialito in Italy. Ruth, who had been playing soccer for only eight years, not only made the team, but was selected as most valuable player of the Festival. For all that success, however, she was still harboring another secret: "I was telling myself and everyone else including my college boyfriend that I was saving myself for marriage. The truth is, I just wasn't interested."

HAVING ADOPTED MAX, AGE 10, AND ALI, 19, with Hallie, her partner of many years, Ruth Harker sees the humor in life more easily than ever these days. She laughs at the memory of herself in dresses. The head mechanical engineer of a plastics firm, she even laughs at the memory of the day she went to Busch Stadium for a Cardinals game a few years back with a bunch of male employees and a male fan, unprovoked, punched her in the face for looking too masculine. "I punched him right back in the face, in the nose, and he went down," she said. "You do it to defend yourself, not because you're provocative. I mean, I'm a pacifist. I'm a Buddhist, and I just think about those times in my life where I wish I had Buddhism already, because life has always been about fear and survival and talking in pronouns, so you don't get caught talking about someone you care about."

She'll never forget 2019. It was the year she was inducted into the St. Louis Sports Hall of Fame and the year Megan Rapinoe and the U.S. Women's National Team lifted a lifelong weight of adversity off her shoulders — hers, and she suspects, legions of others — by infamously stating aloud during the team's march through the

COURTESY OF RUTH HARKER

Ruth Harker, with Megan Rapinoe and their friend, Preston

World Cup, "You can't win without the gays, baby. That's science right there." When you hear that, said Ruth, you breathe a bit easier in your own skin. "What I see and think about is kids are out there thinking about suicide and not fitting in just like me. I thought all those things and sport helped me get through that. When you have these high-profile people like Megan out there, overcoming ignorance, it's putting us on the same bell curve as heterosexuality on some level, and even maybe a little more glamorous at this point. I don't want glamour. And I don't think any gay person really wants glamour about their sexuality, but they want acceptance. Just, hey, let's all live and let live."

Something else happened in 2019 that put all those challenges in perspective. Knowing Ruth had a penchant for helping others in need, her friend told her about a 12-year-old boy, a fellow goalie from Illinois named Preston Klug, who could use a boost. Without hesitation, Ruth flew the boy, who was battling a brain tumor, to Los Angeles for the National Team players association reunion meeting that included the 20-year anniversary celebration of the 1999 World Cup champions. Player after player, generation after generation — the Julie Foudys and Carla Overbecks and Mia Hamms, along with the Megan Rapinoes, Carli Lloyds and Alex Morgans — made Preston king for a day. "I had bought Preston this golden ball," said Ruth. "Brandi Chastain came over to Preston and said, 'You're a friend of Ruth's? Well come on down.' She introduced him to every single player in the room; they all autographed his ball and gave him gifts. If you look closely, you'll even see Preston in the press picture for the event. I mean, that's the kind of stuff they do, the kind of women they are."

NATIONAL TEAMERS FEATURED IN THIS SECTION

Michelle Akers

Denise Bender

Brandi Chastain

Joy Fawcett

Danielle Garrett Fotopoulos

Julie Foudy

Mia Hamm

Emily Pickering Harner

Ashlyn Harris

April Heinrichs

Lori Henry

Tisha Venturini-Hoch

Lauren Cheney Holiday

Angela Hucles

Ali Krieger

Alex Morgan

Heather O'Reilly

Leslie Osborne

Carla Overbeck

Megan Rapinoe

Briana Scurry

Hope Solo

Abby Wambach

Holly Hellmuth Wiles

The Final Analysis?

The rewards of playing the game go far deeper than medals

Focus on the Journey, Not the Destination

Aiming for the National Team and Not Making it May be the Best Outcome of All

MARC GOODSON DIDN'T KNOW WHAT sport his daughter would play, but he knew from Day 1 she would become an athlete. Courtney, nicknamed CoCo almost since birth, was already playing tennis and softball, with competitive swimming mixed in for good measure, when her godmother suggested CoCo might also excel at soccer. Instead of signing her up for the recreation entry level at the Ramona Soccer League in California, Marc figured his then 8-year-old daughter wouldn't need any introduction to a game that seemed simple enough to him — even though he had never played himself — so he placed her on a club team from the start. The other girls were even a year older. On one of the first plays, in CoCo's first game, the referee called for a "drop ball," where, much like it sounds, the ball is dropped between two opposing players who then typically try to beat the opponent to the ball and pass it to a teammate. On this particular play, the opponent kicked the ball squarely into CoCo's stomach, leaving her writhing on the ground. Realizing CoCo didn't understand the scenario, that she was supposed to try to kick the ball, too, the referee let her try again — with the same result. "I didn't have the first clue what I was supposed to do," said CoCo. "But after she kicked the ball into my stomach the second time, I just turned to the referee and said, 'Please just let her have it.'"

COURTESY OF COCO GOODSON

CoCo Goodson circa age 10, with her father

CoCo soon improved; Marc made sure of it. Racing home from the office wearing his suit with his tie still knotted tightly, he would often dash off with his daughter to the local park, remove his socks, shoes, tie and coat, then roll his pants up to his knees and put his daughter through the drills he had seen on the videos he studied night after night. He began to recognize varying styles of different coaches and countries. The Brazilians, he found, like to kick the ball long distances from the back of the field and have the forwards run after it. The British preferred a finesse passing game based on triangular movements up the field. The Germans were strong and poised. Marc, a .279 hitter for the South Alabama University baseball team in 1978, made it his mission to find

HOWARD C. SMITH/ISI PHOTOS

CoCo Goodson, left, head to head with Abby Wambach

private coaches for as many of those styles as possible to indoctrinate his daughter. "I wanted her to see all of this to incorporate it into her game, but also to recognize it in other players," said Marc. "I knew how important it was. I knew she was a gifted athlete. Her great grandfather was a gifted athlete, her grandfather was a gifted athlete, her mother and I were both Division I full-scholarship athletes. At a very young age, we identified that CoCo was going to be 5-foot-11 or 6 feet tall and fast and strong and very coordinated. So we got the very best possible training for her, and I trained her myself. I showed her what it takes to be an athlete."

Marc Goodson can reel off his daughter's soccer highlights as if they happened yesterday. Captain of her high school team and star of her club team, CoCo was recruited by April Heinrichs at the University of California at Irvine when she was only a freshman. CoCo was eventually signed by Chris Petrucelli when he coached at the University of Texas and, after transferring back to UC Irvine and becoming one of the top college players in America, she was picked as the 12th player overall in the 2012 Women's Professional Soccer league draft and, a year later, 21st overall in the first-ever draft of the National Women's Soccer League. Days before she played her first game for Sky Blue of New Jersey, CoCo received a call from Jill Ellis, then the assistant coach, asking her to report to the National Team's camp to join the Under-23 squad — the players just one level below the top team — so Jill and other coaches could more closely evaluate her for potential future promotions. When the Sky Blue coach, Jim Gabarra, said, "No, we need you here," CoCo complied. That moment still eats at her father. "I don't want to say anything to convey disappointment about my daughter," said Marc. "But if there's one thing I regret, one thing I would do over, it would have been to advise my daughter to take that chance when she had it."

BY ALL MEASURES EXCEPT ONE, COCO HAD SUCCEEDED. But when she retired from Sky Blue three years later, never having received another call from the National Team, she joined the largest soccer sorority of all: the millions of girls and young women who don't buck the approximately half-a-million-to-1 odds and crack one of the toughest, most coveted rosters in sports. Once upon a time, Skye Eddy Bruce, just like CoCo, seemed like a lock to make it. Still included in various lists of the greatest college goaltenders of all-time,

COUTESY OF GEORGE MASON UNIVERSITY ATHLETICS

Skye Eddy Bruce, in 1993

Skye began her quest in earnest as a freshman starter at the University of Massachusetts, one of the pioneering powerhouses in the women's college game in the early 1990s. Prior to her sophomore year, however, the pathway got a lot more crowded when a freshman from Dayton, Minn., arrived on campus and started alternating games. By the College Cup championship tournament of 1993, Briana Scurry was starting full-time in goal for UMass — and Skye had transferred for her redshirt senior season to George Mason. When Briana's team lost 4-1 to Mia Hamm and North Carolina in the semifinals, Skye's heroics during a penalty kick shootout against Stanford carried George Mason into the championship game with a chance to write history, both hers and the National Team's.

It could have been a fairytale. North Carolina had never lost in 136 prior games at Fetzer Field, where a then national record of 5,721 fans were in attendance for Mia Hamm's final game. If the Tar Heels were the home field and sentimental favorite, George Mason was Cinderella trying to crash the queen's party, having been unranked and unnoticed until their goalie gave the team instant national credibility. Knowing that North Carolina coach Anson Dorrance, still also coaching the National Team, was watching from just a few feet away, however, was more than Skye's nerves could handle that day. She was a half-step late on her practice dives. Balls she would normally grab easily were slipping through her hands in the warmup. "What's wrong with me?" Skye asked her former UMass teammate and close friend, National Teamer Holly Hellmuth Wiles, when Skye tried to steady herself on the sidelines before the game began. The game was barely two minutes old when another future National Teamer, Keri Sanchez, came at Skye to launch an unrelenting North Carolina onslaught. "The first goal was totally my fault from a decision-making standpoint," said Skye nearly three decades later. "I went forward for a breakaway that I should have stayed back for. I had made that decision hundreds of other times and made it correctly." Thirty-seven shots on goal later, Skye was named the most valuable defensive player of the College Cup, but she also allowed five more of those shots to go in during what turned into a 90-minute dissolution of her dream and a 6-0 loss. Early the next year, when Anson was looking for

The Game is the Best Teacher

We asked National Teamers about some of the intangible benefits from playing sports, whether you make it to the National Team, or not:

JUST PLAY — "Even if my daughter doesn't become a super player, I want her to play sports because of what it brought me," said **Shannon Boxx** (USWNT 2003-2015). "Even if she doesn't get to the level that I got to, it will still bring her joy, it'll bring her persistence, it'll bring her perseverance. It'll bring the teammate relationships, it'll teach her how to be a teammate, how we can be a good team, how to lose and how to win. And it will teach you to follow your dreams. That's everything."

INSPIRE OTHERS — "I feel like the women from the National Team before me had such a positive influence on my life, that they're the reason why I chose soccer, the reason why I kept trying when it was hard," said **Sam Mewis** (USWNT 2014-present). "The reason I didn't get into any trouble ever really is because I just always put soccer first and it was always my number one priority. There's a DNA, a culture that they created for the National Team through just working together and working hard. I think that if I can play any part in inspiring the next generation to continue on that kind of tradition of winning and having a strong culture that's an honor and a responsibility. If people are looking to me, I'm very proud that I've had the opportunity to do it."

EXPERIENCE HIGHS AND LOWS — "Outside of sports, you can't recreate an intense moment where everything is on the line and your kid has the penalty shot and they're shooting it, and then they miss. You can't recreate the disappointment. Grief is a part of being human," said **Abby Wambach** (USWNT 2001-2015). "And then you can't recreate the way that kid gets through it. I just think that sports is one of the greatest teachers of life that we can experience. It will send us tools to deal with

COURTESY OF DANIELLE GARRETT FOTOPOULOS

Abby Wambach, with college teammate Danielle Garrett Fotopoulos

whatever life has coming for us — especially when your kid doesn't hit the lottery and doesn't get the college scholarship and doesn't make the professional team or doesn't get to the national team. They're still going to be able to utilize all the tools that they learn playing youth sports and transfer that into whatever comes next."

OVERCOME ADVERSITY — "Look at what you can do through sports. I'm dyslexic, I'm half black, I'm a lesbian and I'm a woman," said **Saskia Webber** (USWNT 1992-2000). "Look at what I did and look at what I achieved. And anybody can do it at their own level."

EMBRACE YOUR ROLE — "Being a player who starts and plays every minute and is the leader is extremely valuable. So is being the player that never sees the field and is only there to help the team," said **Andi Sullivan** (USWNT 2016-present). "You can gain something from any experience and any role, it depends on how you look at it. If you're too closed off, too stressed or too unhappy with a situation, then you're not going to get anything out of it. But if you say, 'This is an opportunity to learn something about the game, or something about team culture and dynamics and I'm going do my best to learn, then you'll get something out of it. I've had all those experiences for those roles and I think they're all tremendously valuable."

One Game, One Universal Language

I N MY VIEW, THE EARTH AND THE SOCCER BALL ARE ROUND for a profound reason, with about six countries dotted across each of the 32 interconnected panels. It turns out that when you can call yourself a National Teamer, you're welcome in just about all of the world's 195 nations whether they're rich, remote or, most especially, impoverished. In a world that can seem so broken, we do have the three universal languages of love, hope and football — the game that only Americans call soccer. And, so, I travel. Restlessly and relentlessly. The world map is littered with my push pins into the major global cities visited, at 45-plus and counting, but it was the nation of Cote d'Ivoire that stopped me cold in 2017. Among the epicenters of Africa's sex-trafficking trade, according to the Human Rights Watch, the nation between Liberia and Ghana on the southern Atlantic coastline has turned a blind eye to scores of young girls viciously lured with the promise of real jobs, only to be forced into prostitution.

COURTESY OF JOANNA LOHMAN

Joanna, catching a plane

I was, somewhat ironically given my lifestyle and orientation, treated as an absolute rock star due to my National Team resume. Feeling dignified in my U.S. Soccer apparel, with my larger-than-life Jo-hawked image splashed across billboards seemingly everywhere in Abidjan and surrounding areas, I was the celebrity working on behalf of a State Department initiative known as Sports United. It was my boy-band moment in a soccer-mad community. Each daily festival seemed to bring thousands of people out of the remote villages asking for photos and autographs — yet the connections I was trying to foster were the subtle ones. Encourage a girl to play soccer, maybe she joins a team. Get her on a team, maybe a teammate notices when she's gone missing and, just maybe, the teammate can find an adult who cares enough to help. The life lessons shared that week in Africa are as universal as the game itself, the same there as here: Football teaches you how to lead, how to lose and that it simply feels good to play. On the Ivory Coast, though, being on a soccer team can literally save a girl from being pimped out, impregnated and possibly even be tortured, murdered, or forced to marry her assailant.

So I'll keep moving. In the universal language of football, a conversation begins immediately at every airport when you ask any individual, "Who do you support?" Some will say Man City, Barcelona, Real Madrid, and much to my chagrin, Manchester United — my least favorite team — and I make it known, officially, I am all about Tottenham. Either way, the universal game never ceases to open doors. "Just play," I tell the children of Silver Spring, Md., where my journey began. "Just play," I say to the children of Malaysia, Bangkok and Uruguay at my stops along the way. I believe with all my heart that the game, the greatest teacher on the planet, offers everyone hope for fixing what's broken. Maybe, if we're really open to the possibilities, the game will even get us to love. — J.L.

a new goalie for the National Team, Skye was the reigning college All-American, but he called Briana instead. "Of course I aspired to play with our National Team," said Skye. "That was always a dream of mine that didn't happen for a variety of reasons — a lot of them probably having to do with that game."

Rather than dwell on that outcome all these years, Skye has made it her life's mission to help American families understand that no one — not the players, nor the mothers and fathers — should judge their soccer experience on whether or not they made it to the highest level, or even if they received a college scholarship, or not. Through her work at her Soccer Parenting Association, founded in 2014, she constantly focuses her non-stop lectures, essays and interviews on the life lessons of the soccer journey as it unfolds, rather than the evaluation when a career ends. She wants children to be playing soccer in as good an environment as possible for as long as possible. "I'm really happy for everything that soccer has given me," said Skye, whose daughter Cali, became a starting midfielder at Emerson College in Boston. "I've been able to travel the world; I've met so many incredible people and still have such a connection to the game, so I think things work out the way they're supposed to work out. I'm proud to say I competed with Briana Scurry day in and day out, and

Skye Eddy Bruce, one of 31 saves against North Carolina

COURTESY OF GEORGE MASON UNIVERSITY ATHLETICS

alternated games with her, for three years. I learned so much from that, and feel I have so much to share."

Deploying all the same work ethic and competitive fire she learned in soccer, Skye now calls herself "a cultural architect doing what I can to impact change in our youth sports landscape." When Cali came home from a game during her freshman year in high school, Skye was equal parts mortified and bemused at her daughter's story of a parent of an opposing player who flashed her middle finger toward Cali after a hard tackle. Her daughter's mid-field response to the woman — "You do realize you're, like, 42, and I'm 15" — would become fodder for one of Skye's parenting advice columns, titled

"Soccer Parent Verbally Abusing Players is Unacceptable." When Holly Hellmuth Wiles talks about her friend's unrelenting mission, and its positive impact on the game, Holly is equal parts awed and humbled. "I think when you coach soccer, you really quickly recognize how poorly informed most of the parents are in terms of their own athletes, in terms of what they expect from coaches, and how to navigate the very complex world of soccer," said Holly, who has become both a coach and parent since her one National Team appearance in July of 1990 on a day when Hall of Famer Carla Overbeck was away at a wedding. "The soccer world is set up to focus on the players, but it's Skye who's doing an incredible job of giving parents a platform where they can learn the ropes. Educating the parents is, in many ways, more important than educating the kids."

DR. EILEEN NARCOTTA-WELP HAS ALSO MADE it her mission to educate — with a focus quite unlike any other PhD in America. Whereas Skye's goal is to modify parents' behavior in their sometimes unhealthy quest to position their children for a college scholarship, a pro contract, or a spot on the National Team, Eileen's research for the past decade has investigated why parents care so much and what's truly in it for the girls who strive for — and then realize — the dream. Some of her work manifests itself in details: Eileen, an assistant professor of exercise and sports science at the University of Wisconsin La Crosse, can talk expertly about the exponential growth in soccer since 1972, when Title IX mandated scholarship equality on campuses that made it possible for women like Skye to play. Some of Eileen's efforts, including her 2016 doctoral thesis titled "The Future of Football is Feminine: A Critical Cultural History of the U.S. Women's National Soccer Team," simultaneously tackles racism, feminism, sexism, sexual preference and gender identity in the context of the women who have won four World Cups. "How can Briana Scurry, the U.S. women's National Team

Hope Solo, backed up by Briana Scurry in 2006

goalkeeper and the only black player in the starting lineup (in 1999), be understood within a white, postfeminist and post-racial discourse?" she wrote. "I contend that Scurry's black body is tempered by postfeminist ideals and a homogenized team culture that protected white, middle-class values."

Long before her 347-page study was published by the University of Iowa, Eileen was a soccer player herself. She dreamed, too, and like so many young girls growing up in the dawn of Mia scoring goals and tossing her hair back in Pert commercials, Eileen found the National Team to be a vague, yet fascinating, even thrilling notion. "I wanted to be on the National Team when I was 9 or 10, but frankly I knew by the time I was in high school that I probably wasn't quite that good," Eileen told us. "But I really, really loved to play."

Dr. Eileen Narcotta-Welp, right, with her wife, Stacy, and their son

COURTESY OF DR. EILEEN NARCOTTA-WELP

The native of East Bridgewater, Mass., ended up traveling the Interstate 89 corridor as a goalie at the University of Vermont, where her 1997 achievement of only allowing 0.25 goals per game remains a school record for a single season. Injuries, the ones to knees and hips that plague soccer players of all levels, robbed her of two of four varsity seasons. She figures society, at a time when females' professional sports opportunities were virtually nonexistent, cheated her out of the game after that. "I had a lot of mixed feelings about the time of the 1999 World Cup because that is also right around the time that I was graduating from college," said Eileen. "My own career was finishing. There were no opportunities to play outside of some summer semi-professional leagues unless I was willing to go to Europe. I was also probably angry, and jealous, at the National Team because they could still play, but I was still completely enamored with the 99ers and what was going on — angry, but elated, at the same time."

As much as she loved to see the women beating the rest of the world in the buildup to the seminal game in the Rose Bowl, Eileen said she was disillusioned by the media's late '90s construct of a white, suburban girl-next-door image in which Briana was often included as "the fly in the milk," but rarely celebrated for her intellect and individuality. Eileen sensed there were lesbian members of the team whose true identities were still being quashed by a code of silence. And, as years passed by, she also came to believe another fellow goalie, Hope Solo, was unfairly ostracized — not only by the team, but by the resulting media coverage that Eileen saw as deeply gender biased. In 2007, Eileen believes the National Team and the nation were still clinging, albeit barely, to a certain set of outdated values. "We were all contained into this very nice white middle-class heterosexual westernized ideal of a woman. It was all about playing by the rules, about containment, about acting a particular way with femininity," said Eileen. "Then Hope Solo comes along and just blows that all up." Eileen believes Hope when she said she wasn't intentionally badmouthing Briana in her comments after the World Cup loss to Brazil (see page 154). In Eileen's view, the team's actions, in banning Hope from its meals and bus rides, along with the negative media barrage, ultimately handed Hope even more power in shaping national discourse and perceptions. "This was the first controversy of the National Team that became a significant media event," said Eileen. "In that moment, Hope becomes a really important figure to kind of explode the idea, or the containment, of a women's soccer player — and of women in general. The rules have changed, and I think we needed that disruptive force to create real change. That's why I have a lot of respect for Hope in regard to her ability to step up and step out."

"WITHOUT HOPE SOLO, THERE IS NO MEGAN RAPINOE IN 2019," said Eileen. "Without Hope, I don't think you could have someone on the National Team talking about and calling out the President. I don't think you could have someone kneeling on behalf of Black Lives Matter. But because Hope Solo had already taken the brunt of all of that criticism for being different, for being considered selfish, for thinking about herself as an individual, that opened the door for Megan and others to step right through. Thanks to the 2019 World Cup team, that individuality is what we now actually expect from the players."

Briana Scurry, celebrating her historic penalty save against China's Liu Ying in 1999

REUTERS/SYLVIA BUCHHOLZ/ALAMY STOCK PHOTO

With Megan becoming a transcendent celebrity and the National Team arguably more popular than ever after consecutive World Cup victories, the dream of one day making it that far in soccer can be even more tantalizing for the girls of America and their parents. Marc Goodson can occasionally still find himself thinking about what might have been, especially since his daughter would have been at her athletic peak by the time the National Team arrived in France in the summer of 2019. Marc knows this, he said, because at about that same time Megan and Alex Morgan were scoring all those goals, CoCo was rucking up hillsides with a group of men — with a 55-pound backpack strapped to her shoulders. "It turns out that all those years of soccer training come in pretty handy when you decide to join an elite combat unit," said Marc with a hearty laugh. "Most of

A Side Road to the World Cup
Part 1: The Choice

O N THE FACE OF IT, WHEN HAVANA SOLAUN ENTERED OUR HOME IN 2017, there was only one long-term goal left for her to attain. As a third-year women's soccer professional making so little money that she needed to live with a host family just to make it work financially, she might have seen making the National Team as the only viable career path forward. She had been, it seemed, tantalizingly close. When coaches scouting future National Teamer Morgan Brian Gautrat noticed that her club teammate, Havana, could also play, the invitations to National Team youth camps started in high school and continued after Havana's graduation from the University of Florida. She traveled internationally. She scored a few goals. But it had been more than a year since

COURTESY OF HAVANA SOLAUN

Havana Solaun, seated with her mother and father, and other family and friends

Havana's last call-in to the national Under-23 team by the time we met — and doubts were creeping in.

"The truth is, I have been called into national camps six, maybe seven times and I have always felt like the outsider," Havana told me. "That feeling never really went away. To me, it was just a very unwelcoming environment and I think, at that level, the cliques among the girls can be very strong." That was a sentiment shared by many others, including players who made the National Team and some who came close. "I think the times are definitely changing where it's a little bit more welcoming now," said National Team starter Crystal Dunn, who is about eight months older than Havana.

"I will say when Julie (Ertz) and I went on to the National Team, it was rough. We still had Shannon Boxx and Abby Wambach and Christie Rampone around. All these legends. Not to say they were not welcoming, but these were some intimidating all-business women. You had to do everything in your means to even get one second on the field with them."

Havana's lineage makes her a unique case. Her mother, Sandra Brower, is a Canadian-American born in Jamaica. Her father, Felix Solaun, is an American born to Cuban immigrants — and Havana was born in Hong Kong. That gave her eligibility on five different potential World Cup teams if the nations qualified and she could prove she belonged. But when she moved out of our house after one great season in 2017, and another plagued with injuries in 2018, she was still holding out hope of playing for the nation she had called home for virtually all of her life. "I always just wanted to play at the top level, and the United States is the best team in the world," she said. "So to say that you want to go play for somebody else . . . " She stopped talking in that moment, but the tears in her eyes finished the thought.

Just a few months later, Jamaica called. — P.T.

Hope Solo and Abby Wambach, with David Letterman in 2011

the men in her company only wish they were as fit as she is."

Army 1st Lieutenant CoCo Goodson laughs, too, when she hears her father's often gushing appraisal of virtually anything she has ever done since childhood. "He's always been my biggest supporter," said CoCo, just after returning from a four-month deployment in Iraq in the winter and spring of 2020. She is the only female among 12 soldiers in an elite group within the historic 82nd Airborne based at Fort Bragg who received a drop-everything-and-go alert, known as a "Green Corvette," on New Year's Eve 2019. In soccer, she was a center back, often the last line of defense. In the middle of the desert in the Middle East, as a fire support officer, it was her job to be on offense, to spot enemies or their assets and help guide American field artillery onto its intended targets. The first job in sports, she said, prepared her for the second one on the battlefield. "First off, it's very physical. It's very demanding and nerve-racking; you have to push your body further than the average person could probably imagine, but also do it with a smile on your face. No matter what, you're not letting it knock you down, you're staying composed, and all the while you're going through this miserable stuff."

Like millions of others in America, CoCo watched the World Cup. Cheering on her New Jersey teammate Kelley O'Hara, as well as several others who were opponents through many years of college and professional games, she said that, unlike her father, she never felt even a tinge of disappointment — nor does she hold any ill will toward Jim Gabarra for telling her to decline the invitation to a National Team training camp that could have changed the course of her life. "I have played with and against the best people in the world, and not many people can say that," said CoCo. "I'm happy for the people still playing, but I know I tried, I did my best, and I can move on, feeling very proud of myself. As for Jim, he was the person in charge. He said, 'No, we have a game this weekend' and that was that. I let it go. I've always been a team player; that's what comes first."

FOR ALL OF THE JOY SHE PROVIDED HER FATHER ALONG THE WAY, CoCo knows she ultimately accounted for two of the sadder moments in his life. Saying no to the National Team in 2013, followed by her outright retirement from the game just three seasons later, ended an almost 20-year dream that was as much his as it was hers. By the end of her career, CoCo said the game just wasn't as much fun any longer — and maybe it hadn't been quite as much fun along the journey as it could have been. In a page straight out of one of Skye Eddy Bruce's columns at the Soccer Parenting Association, CoCo and her father clearly experienced certain situations from somewhat polarized perspectives. "We had 99 percent really, really great times together," said Marc. "The car rides home were the worst," said CoCo. "We would turn on the radio, and we would sing songs," said the father. "The last thing I wanted, especially after a loss, was to have my parents dissect the game," said the daughter. She told us the story of traveling home from a game during her fresh-man year in high school with her best friend and younger sister in the back seat and her parents in the front. Pulling up to the drive-thru window at McDonald's, Marc placed everyone's burger order — but purchased a Happy Meal for CoCo. "If you're going to play like a child, you're going to eat like one, too," he told her.

CoCo said she and her father eventually learned to laugh about that moment. "It's funny, a good family story," she said. "But at the time it was not; it was mortifying." It was the experience of coaching in youth leagues after her retirement, however, that made her realize that — compared to some mothers and fathers — her father was a picnic. "Parents are crazy," she said. "Parents are the worst part of the game because they are so hard on their kids and their kids already have so much pressure going on. It's especially bad in high school when kids are

Army 1st Lieutenant CoCo Goodson in 2020

trying to be recruited. They want to go out there and play their best and parents putting that extra pressure on them doesn't help at all. It actually hurts."

After three years of coaching, she had had enough. "I needed a new challenge, something with more meaning," said CoCo. "Soccer had set me up for success, but I knew there had to be more to life." With her father cheering for her every step of the way, CoCo enlisted in officer training school and, thanks to her fitness level, she aced every single test the Army could throw her way. Among West Point graduates at Fort Bragg, the soccer player became a bit of a celebrity, thanks to a commanding general who tipped off her new teammates within the 82nd Airborne. "Does everyone here know that we have a professional athlete in our midst?" asked the general. A roomful of men's eyes darted throughout the room. When CoCo's secret was revealed, 1st Lieutenant Ahmad Bradshaw, the starting Army quarterback in 2017, led an impromptu parade of soldiers — with 1st Lieutenant Goodson on their shoulders. "That scene gives me chill bumps," said Marc, ever the father full of pride. "They're saying, 'This is CoCo Goodson. This is a professional athlete. This is an officer in the United States Army.' I mean, my goodness. Even a World Cup couldn't beat that."

Authority is Best Earned, Not Awarded

The National Team's Most Powerful Examples of Influential Behavior Often Happen Off the Field

EVERYONE IN SOCCER SEEMS TO HAVE an Abby Wambach story that has little to do with her record 184 National Team goals. It was 1998 when Becky Burleigh's four-year-old soccer program at the University of Florida was somehow clinging to a 1-0 lead against North Carolina, which had not lost in an NCAA championship final in 13 years. As soon as the whistle sounded for the second-half television timeout, she stood off to the side while her players gathered wearily. "Words . . . I need words," Becky thought to herself as the 120 seconds of break time started racing by, seemingly so much faster than they did during game time. "This is so important," she thought again. Just then, team captain Danielle Garrett Fotopoulos, already a National Teamer who had toppled a Mia Hamm college scoring record for goals and assists that most thought would never be touched, broke the silence. "We got this!" she said to her teammates loosely huddled into a wet circle. But Becky determined there still needed to be more. She knew North Carolina players would be coming at Florida like uncaged animals in the final 17 minutes, so the head coach stepped forward, drew air into her lungs and opened her mouth to speak — only to

Abby Wambach, at the University of Florida

COURTESY OF UNIVERSITY OF FLORIDA ATHLETICS

be interrupted by a towering freshman in the back row: "We are not fucking losing to these bitches!" The stunned Gators' heads whipped around in unison toward Abby, then back toward Becky, who was once again rendered speechless. "Well, OK then," said Becky. "What she said."

It was 2008 when Lauren Cheney Holiday's dream of playing in that summer's Olympics had been crushed by the cruel math of a small roster size. The 20-year-old was back at home in Indianapolis packing for summer school when the 18 chosen players took the field against Brazil in the final exhibition match before traveling to Beijing, but couldn't even bring herself to join her parents in the living

BARNARD

Abby Wambach, a speech gone viral

room to watch the game. Barely a half hour after it started, Lauren's father called to her. "Something's wrong with Abby," he said. Lauren continued folding her clothes. "Dad, Abby's very dramatic," she said. "I'm sure she'll be fine." Less than 15 minutes later, however, Lauren's pulse quickened when Abby's number appeared on her cell phone. "Chen, I'm 98 percent certain that my leg is detached from my body," said Abby, by then inside a San Diego ambulance and heavily medicated, yet still coherent enough to lead. "I don't know if I'm the one who's supposed to be calling you, but you need to get yourself ready.

You're going to the Olympics. And you deserve it. I love you and I believe in you... You've got this."

It was 2018 when a *Chicago Tribune* columnist named Heidi Stevens happened across a speech online when she was looking for a way to connect with her middle schooler. Abby, who once received a T-shirt from her older teammates that read, "Help! I'm Talking and I Can't Shut Up," was brief in her graduation remarks that spring to the seniors of Barnard College. But the words, less than 3,000 of them in total, went viral and eventually spawned two books about life and leadership titled "Wolfpack," one for adults and one for children. "She offered four rules and how to live by them: 'Make failure your fuel. Lead from the bench. Champion each other. Demand the ball.' Each one left me cheering," wrote Heidi. "But my favorite passage was this: 'You will not always be the goal scorer. And when you are not — you better be rushing toward her.'"

LEADERSHIP, IN THE CONTEXT OF THE NATIONAL TEAM, was historically conveyed like it has been on many other sports teams through the years: via the man in charge. For Denise Bender, the oldest living National Teamer, her two-week, four-game stint as captain all centered around those historic first games in Jesolo, Italy, in 1985 when team members needed to iron on USA patches to hand-me-down men's uniforms. Denise's primary

The Overbeck Rules: Elements of Leadership

A National Team member for 12 years from 1988-2000, Carla Overbeck is recognized as one of the most influential captains in sports history. Here are just a few takeaways from her career:

BE WELCOMING — Cindy Parlow Cone (USWNT 1996-2004) was just 15 when she was invited into her first National Team training camp in 1994, only to soon find Carla knocking on the door of her hotel room. "She came in, sat down, and talked to me for 30 minutes. I remember thinking to myself, 'I have never done anything like that for another player.' Here's the captain of the National Team taking the time out of her life to be in the room of a little 15-year-old kid."

STAND STRONG WHEN NECESSARY — Carla considered Tony DiCicco to be one of the best coaches in American soccer history, but stepped between him and her teammates on two key occasions. In April of 1995, an on-field argument between **Mia Hamm** (USWNT 1987-2004) and the coach during a game in France continued when Mia kicked the locker room door open at halftime and the two began shouting at each other. In May of 1999, Tony blew up at **Shannon MacMillan** (USWNT 1993-2005) on the field during a scrimmage, shouting, "When are you going to start scoring?" In both cases, the coach apologized after Carla intervened. "I just wanted to defuse the situation as quickly as I could; I didn't want them to say things that they would regret later," she said.

ACCEPT DIFFERENCES — Years before **Saskia Webber** (USWNT 1992-2000) came out publicly, she was able to speak comfortably about being gay. "A long time ago, Carla and I sat in a locker room together and she's asking me, 'What can we do better as a team, knowing that you're gay and knowing that Briana's gay.' She treated us all as equals. I could talk about my girlfriend like she could talk about her boyfriend. It was always fine."

Canadian national teamer Carrie Serwetnyk, left, with Carla Overbeck

COURTESY OF CARRIE SERWETNYK

LEAD BY EXAMPLE — Carla was never the fastest player, but **Michelle Akers** (USWNT 1985-2000) still calls her out for being able to do 50 pushups and beat everyone in most fitness drills. "She was tough, man," said Michelle. Numerous players, even rookies, recall finding their luggage carried to their hotel room door by the team captain. "She set the tone for that generation, really helped build that culture of never being too big to do the little things," said Shannon MacMillan.

ADMIT YOUR MISTAKES — On March 11, 1993, **Thori Staples Bryan** (USWNT 1993-2003) received one of the few red cards from a referee in National Team history, which meant she was ejected from the game. Carla acknowledges she should have received the red card instead. In reality, Thori was simply trying to hold back a player from Trinidad and Tobago who had sucker-punched Carla in the back of the head. The captain lost it, punching the Trinidadian repeatedly, even on the ground. "Everyone was like, 'That was awesome,' and I'm like, 'No, it wasn't,'" Carla told author Sam Walker in his 2017 book "The Captain Class: The Hidden Force that Creates the World's Greatest Teams," in which she was one of the few women profiled for her leadership qualities.

job, she said, was to act as intermediary between the players and their controlling, foul-mouthed and cranky Irish coach, Mike Ryan, who she knew from her days in amateur soccer before, during and after her graduation from the University of Washington. "I think he picked me as captain because he knew that I could handle his tirades," said Denise, who has had a long career in the biopharmaceutical industry while maintaining lifelong ties to soccer as a player and coach.

In 1986, however, Anson Dorrance declined to invite Denise to try out for the National Team, stating in an offseason letter that she lacked the self-discipline to achieve the proper level of fitness. "Let's just say I didn't agree with that assessment, or the way it was delivered," said Denise, who took great satisfaction in burning the letter in a backyard

CAPTAIN
DENISE BENDER

Denise Bender, the first captain

bonfire years later. "It's always stuck with me — what women had to put up with. Back then, if you wanted to excel in a sport, you had to put up with this kind of shit from mostly male coaches. But I also can't argue with Anson's success, who could? I just didn't fit the physical image of the player he wanted for his team." At the beginning of his eight-year run as National Team coach, Anson anointed a series of North Carolina players, including Emily Pickering Harner, Lori Henry and April Heinrichs, as American captains. There was a strong common denominator, according to Michelle Akers, known as possibly the toughest National Teamer of all-time. "They were badass," she said. "Emily was the one, for me, who started the whole mentality; I credit her with that every time I see her. Lori was the toughest player I ever met and I absolutely hated playing against her in practice. Then there was April, the only player who ever scared the hell out of me. That's how I got the nerve to be a great one-on-one player myself, by pretending to be April Heinrichs."

The National Team was, figuratively and almost literally, Anson Dorrance's team in those early years. He was the one with the vision of American women playing in a World Cup nearly a decade before such a thing existed, and he also had the foresight to add three young girls to the team, Mia Hamm, Kristine Lilly and Julie Foudy, when all the other established male soccer coaches in America thought they had better ideas for how to fill the roster. "He set the foundation. His mantra was, 'I respect talent, but I'd rather have courage and fighters on my team any day,'" said Julie, who might have been the most curious choice initially among the three team "babies," as they were called in soccer circles in the summer of 1987. By Anson's own admission, the girl from Mission Viejo High School wasn't quite ready for prime time on

Emily Pickering Harner, the second captain, in 1986

the field — Julie's official on-field National Team debut wouldn't come until July of 1988, 11 months after Mia and Kristine — but he recognized what he called "the presence" of a champion. "Julie is one of those human beings you build a program around," said Anson, who tried almost desperately to recruit her away from Stanford. "Such a born leader."

Just like Abby Wambach, everyone in soccer has a Julie Foudy story. Mia recalls countless on-field verbal battles imploring Julie to pass her the ball sooner, or faster, or the time when Julie timed a give-and-go pass perfectly against Japan, allowing Mia to knock in an easy goal, her first after a rare scoring slump in which the media — and Mia herself — questioned what was wrong. "Can you get a 500-pound gorilla off my back?" Mia breathlessly asked her teammate during the post-goal celebration against Japan. Julie obliged, pretending to grab the beast off Mia's back and fling it to the ground. Years

Billie Jean King, with Julie Foudy

before Leslie Osborne won her national championship at Santa Clara and joined the National Team for the Olympics and a World Cup, she met Julie at an indoor soccer game in Milwaukee. "She was electric!" said Leslie, still sounding like the teenager she had been at the time. "She was passionate and energetic and I felt like, 'Oh, my god, she's real. Authentic.' It honestly made my dream of playing soccer that much more attainable in that moment I met her."

JULIE CRIED LIKE ALMOST EVERYONE ELSE on July 29, 1994, the day Anson revealed he would be giving up coaching the National Team to concentrate full-time on his duties at North Carolina. She thought she might be leaving soon, too, and the whole program seemed at a crossroads while existing in the shadow of the U.S. men's National Team, which was hosting the World Cup that summer. With the National Team still treated as less than a full-time job and no professional league to play for, Julie was in her 20s by then and tiring of being constantly poor — and had the option of Stanford medical school waiting in the wings. "We used to joke that playing for $10 a day builds character, but at some point you realize you're up to your eyeballs in character," she told us. By 1995, intrigued by the idea of the first-ever Olympics to include women's soccer — based in Atlanta in

1985 first-teamers in 2019: Ann Orrison-Germain, Ruth Harker, Kim Wyant, Linda Gancitano, Emily Pickering Harner and Denise Boyer-Merdich

Making a Difference, One Hug at a Time

"LET ME TELL YOU, THERE IS NOTHING TRIVIAL about being unable to look at pictures of my younger self — because all I can see is the hurt in her eyes." That comment, from a woman named Emma Sturz, stopped me on social media in 2020. We had met in 2013 when I was playing for the Boston Breakers and was one of the few publicly out athletes in the National Women's Soccer League. Most of the time, honestly, my orientation never seemed to matter inside the locker room and — while I knew my visibility was my own form of demonstrating leadership in society — I didn't necessarily think a player with my humble platform would make that much of a difference. Then, after a game one night, I heard Emma call my name in the autograph line. Standing next to her mother, Emma was visibly shaking, clearly overwhelmed and nervous at the chance to meet and speak with me.

"I just want to thank you for helping me to come out to my family," she said softly, confidently. Emma went on to explain how much of an impact I had on her life, even though we had never met. Our friendship grew from that moment. She and her family even provided a safe haven for me at the end of the 2014 season when I was struggling enormously both on and off the field. She provided me a roof over my head, warm food in my belly but, most importantly, she instilled in me a sense of acceptance in my exact form and reassured me I was worthy of love. I reached out to Emma after her post on Facebook, and she responded with a note. I share it here with her permission:

COURTESY OF JOANNA LOHMAN

Emma Sturz, no more pain

"I believe people are most beautiful in their purest, truest, most stripped-down form. Safety to own and live that beauty to the fullest is, to me, one of the most precious gifts you can give someone. I was a fledgling then. I wanted so badly to fly but didn't quite trust that I could yet. To see Jo out there flying, unapologetically living her truth, showed me that I could, too.

"That night after the game I was so nervous, as anyone would be when meeting their hero. My heart was bursting with gratitude. I called out to her not really knowing what to expect, but her response exceeded any expectations I might've had. I thanked her for being out and proud, and, before even asking my name, she wrapped me in a huge hug and said, "Thank you for saying thank you!" It is a moment I will never forget, and a moment that confirmed to me that this woman was indeed a hero. Her sincerity was undeniable; it was unmistakably clear that knowing she'd made a difference in someone's life meant the world to her. Her genuineness and open heart are what make her so strong in a world that tells us being real is a weakness, and she encourages us all to find the strength in our own truth.

"Really, there's no adequate thank you in the world for what she has given me, but the best way I know how to express my gratitude is to pay it forward. I have since learned to fly with the freest heart I have ever known. I am out and proud and unapologetic about it. I do so not only in celebration of my freedom, but with the hope that I may help even one fledgling feel safer, just as Jo did for me." — J.L.

COURTESY OF AMY ALLMANN GRIFFIN

The 1987 team: Back row, Lori Henry, Carin Jennings Gabarra, Michelle Akers, Chris Tomek, Debbie Belkin Rademacher, Joy Fawcett, Linda Hamilton, Wendy Gebauer Palladino; front row: Megan McCarthy, Lisa Gmitter-Pittaro, April Heinrichs, Tracey Bates Leone, Kim Wyant, Amy Allmann Griffin, Shannon Higgins-Cirovski, Mia Hamm, Kristine Lilly and Sandi Gordon. Anson Dorrance, standing, second from right.

1996 — Julie was still hanging around the game when an invitation came in from the Women's Sports Foundation to join a roundtable discussion, hosted by Spalding sporting goods in Chicopee, Mass. Billie Jean King did most of the talking, regaling eight other women from the sports world with stories of the female tennis professionals who bet on themselves and started their own organization, which became the Virginia Slims Circuit in 1970. The more the tennis champion spoke, about sticking together and demanding specific rights in the name of women everywhere, the more the passion swelled inside the soccer player. "Billie Jean's story was our story, mine and Mia's and Kristine's and everyone else's," said Julie. "It was crystal clear to me what we needed to do in that moment."

Flying back from that meeting, in the age before ubiquitous cell phones, Julie got to her

COURTESY OF TISHA VENTURINI

Tisha Venturini, with her daughter, Sadie

teammates just in the nick of time and implored them not to sign a new contract with U.S. Soccer that had read a lot like the old one, with far less compensation and worse accommodations than men were receiving. With the start of the Olympic training camp just months away, the players who had been working under an annual contract were prepared to go on strike — but were instead preemptively locked out of team facilities by U.S. Soccer, which assumed the women would cave in and take whatever was being offered. The world of women's tennis had the infamous "Original Nine" players of the Virginia Slims tour, who celebrated the 50th anniversary of their collective achievement in 2020; in that moment in 1995, women's soccer also had its own nine leaders for all-time. Briana Scurry, Michelle Akers, Joy Fawcett, Carla Overbeck, Carin Jennings Gabarra and Tisha Venturini-Hoch joined Mia, Kristine and Julie in solidarity in the first official women's soccer labor war. Because the players all stuck together, the all-male hierarchy within U.S. Soccer blinked first. The new contract still didn't offer anywhere near the perks and values of the men's contracts, but the women had earned numerous financial concessions and a huge moral victory.

"It still gives me chills sometimes to this day to say I was associated with this group of leaders," said Tisha, who scored the first American goal in the Olympics on the way to the gold medal that summer and now shares those stories with her daughter, Sadie, who aspires to follow in her mother's footsteps. "I want my kid around as many of those women as possible, as often as possible, and I would tell any parent to have their children soak up the essence of these ladies wherever and however they can. They're smart, they're funny, they work hard and they're loyal. It's been a constant challenge with the same burning question for more than 30 years: 'How can we give back and how can we help the next generation?'"

BY 1999, JULIE HAD GIVEN UP THE DREAM of medical school, figuring she could do more for the world as the "Voice of America," as dubbed by *Sports Illustrated* magazine. The National Team, spurred by a summer of sold-out stadiums and a World Cup victory, was America's darling. And though the team wasn't any one person's to own, it was clear that the women of the team were the ones in control of the things that mattered most: their voices and choices. When Julie traveled to Sialkot, a city near the Himalayan Mountains where her sponsor, Reebok, utilized marginalized laborers to hand-stitch soccer balls, she came home and put the conversation of human rights on the table. When goalie Saskia Webber came out as gay to the *New York Times*, it pushed the door incrementally further open in the issue of sexual orientation. And when Brandi Chastain posed nude with her soccer ball for *Gear* magazine, and Julie skipped across the beach with her husband in *Sports Illustrated*'s 1999 swimsuit issue and coined the sarcastic phrase "booters with hooters," it didn't end the discussion of sexism in sports — but it put the women in charge of their own narrative for their families and friends to accept, or not, and for future generations to debate.

In 2011, Alex Morgan was faced with a decision of her own. The pages of years' worth of *Sports Illustrated* swimsuit issues were spread across her parents' kitchen table in Diamond Bar, Calif., and American

WENN RIGHTS LTD/ALAMY STOCK PHOTO

Alex Morgan, painted and proud

soccer's fresh-faced second-coming of Mia Hamm was contemplating something far more aligned with Brandi Chastain's lane in life. "Aye yai yai," offered Alex's mother, Pamela, looking at the nude models who had their bikinis literally painted on. "I don't want to look at that stuff!" said her father, Mike, before leaving the room. Mother and daughter talked about the magazine's offer for hours, weighing every pro and con, as Pamela had known her daughter to do since childhood. Alex, having once considered breast enlargement surgery, was insecure about certain aspects of her body. She also knew that her agent, the man in charge of marketing her increasingly popular image to the masses — just as he had done for Mia years before — was not a fan of the idea for his new girl-next-door client. "She's very savvy and mature for her age," Dan Levy told *ESPN* magazine, but the body painting "wasn't ideal" in his view. Alex also knew that young girls would either see the images, or hear about them from friends, and those minds mattered to her, almost as much as her parent's or her own.

Well into that evening, Pamela had settled on the advice that her daughter accepted; if Alex could endure the actual painting, with artists working so intimately with every detail of her body, then her mother thought she should go for it. "I thought it was going to be beautiful," Pamela told us. "I think it shows the strength and the effort that she had been putting into her body for her whole life. I told her I understood her feelings; I was athletic also and I had the same type of body that she does. Not everyone is a Barbie doll. Bodies come in all shapes and sizes and you need to learn to feel confident in the body that you're given, or the one you're willing to work for. And, as for doing the shoot, I don't think you can live by other people's rules. All of that, the example it sets for others, the confidence factor for herself, she considered all of it."

ALI KRIEGER HAD LONG BEEN PONDERING HER OPTIONS, TOO. Much like her father, who told us, "We are private people, a private family," during a series of quiet conversations about his life as a soccer father, Ali never liked being the center of attention unless a penalty kick was on the line. Ken Krieger wasn't shy in telling us about body-checking his daughter into the hallway walls during raucous soccer games with Ali and his son, Kyle, when they were children growing up in Virginia. "My wife would holler upstairs and tell us to stop when she heard the crashing, but I told her, 'We'll fix it.' Both my kids know how to use spackling compound to repair walls," Ken said with no small amount of pride. He was still hobbling around when we spoke, recovering from the effects of a devasting car accident suffered after watching Ali play in Washington, D.C., in August of 2019. On Oct. 3, 2019, he made it to mid-field with the help of Kyle and a walker for the ceremony when Ali was honored for her 100th National Team appearance. Less than three months later, however, he tossed his cane to the side of the dance floor at the palatial Vizcaya Museum & Gardens in Miami. It was his daughter's wedding, after all . . . his healing could wait, but Ali's heart couldn't.

She met Ashlyn Harris in 2010 when the goalie from Florida, by way of the North Carolina Tar Heels, arrived in her first National Team camp. It was virtually love at first sight, but that privacy gene kicked in and Ali resolved to keep the existence of their intimate relationship private from everyone except team members, family and a few friends for much of the next decade. It was Megan Rapinoe who finally convinced Ali that, as a National

A Side Road to the World Cup
Part 2: The Purpose

AFTER A 2017 SEASON IN WHICH SHE LED the Washington Spirit in points with five goals and four assists, Havana Solaun never played at full health in 2018. Her living area at our home was on the second floor and my wife and daughters and I would cringe on many days when Havana could barely ascend the stairs to her room, much less perform well at practice. Playing in the 2019 World Cup seemed impossible. A world away, meanwhile, a small soccer miracle was unfolding on the Caribbean island of Jamaica. Cedella Marley, the daughter of Bob, the nation's most famous citizen, pledged the funds to re-form a national team and, against long odds,

Havana Solaun, in Jamaican colors, at the 2019 World Cup

the "Reggae Girlz" emerged from a competition among 19 island nations — places like Martinique, Suriname and Barbardos — to become the first women from the region ever to qualify for a World Cup.

Havana, whose mother was born in Jamaica, was healthy at last when a Jamaican coach tracked her down and invited her to try out in early 2019 on the way to her breakout season with 11 goals in the Norwegian league. "Why not?" she thought. It was freezing in Norway and Havana hates the cold. Instead of great soccer and beautiful sandy beaches, however, a developing nation awaited where team members weren't even supplied three meals a day. "It was generations, eons behind the U.S. team," she said. "We're talking basic human needs aren't even being met. One of the players in our eligible pool was stabbed to death on the street."

Even still, she said, an instant bond with her new teammates surprised her. "I was really torn, because I could continue to fight to maybe someday play for the greatest team in the world back in the U.S., or I could play for a country that supplied the blood in my veins. The connections I felt with those girls after one week of camp were really eye-opening for me. I felt more at home than I had at any National Team camp in the U.S. Ever." Her mother agonized while Havana characteristically weighed all her options. "When you compare the islands to here, you're dealing with people who sort through garbage for scraps vs. Wall Street. To some degree, I know Havana felt like she was settling — giving up a dream," said Sandra Brower. But when Havana made up her mind, her mother was filled with the pride of her homeland. "I realized I had found a such a bigger purpose in playing for Jamaica, and not just about helping to lead the girls on the 2019 team," said Havana. "It's about the generations of women left behind, about women's equality. It's about paving the way for these young girls who don't have the basic needs in their home life, but maybe soccer gives them an avenue — a chance at something better." — P.T.

Teamer with an immense social platform, she would serve a higher purpose if she shared their truth. Not long afterward, *Sports Illustrated* was carrying the story of the "wedding of the decade," just as it had with championship games and painted-on bathing suits. "You know, it's fine to be private and not put yourselves out there, we totally get it," Megan told Ali and Ashlyn. "But if you guys do, then you would be helping so many young people who are struggling with feeling the same way, and making sure that they're comfortable in their own skin and being their authentic selves. It would be so powerful if you guys announced that you are together."

His daughter was stunning that night, Dec. 28, in a classic white gown just like Ken had always imagined. Ali's spouse was in a custom black tuxedo — but anything else Ken might have long ago dreamed ended there. With *Vogue* magazine on hand to cover every detail, tables were themed in honor of cultural gay icons, from comedian Ellen Degeneres, to journalist Anderson Cooper, to Marsha P. Johnson, an activist involved in the Stonewall riots — a stained event in American history that saw New York city police

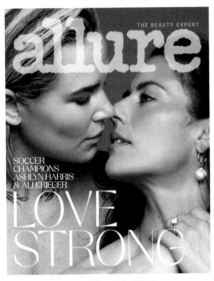

Ashlyn Harris, left, with Ali Krieger

raid the Stonewall Inn, a mafia-owned gay night club in the heart of Greenwich Village. That homosexual behavior was once considered abhorrent was not lost on Ali's brother in his speech as best man. "It has been a gift to watch you grow together," said Kyle, who is also gay. "It's amazing, because you guys are like a beacon of light for all young queer LGBTQ women and men who just need someone to look up to, like we get happy endings too. In the media and the movies, so often . . . you know, queer stories have a devastating ending, but not here. In real life, we get to see you guys live the dream." Months later, Ken had a hard time putting his daughter's impact into words. It was far easier, he said, to talk about the time Ali scored that penalty kick against Brazil in the 2011 World Cup, or the day she started throwing her Cheerios on the floor from her highchair and then laughed at him when he demanded she stop. "I'm not going to tell you I understand every choice my daughter has made," said Ken, pausing to fight back tears. "But I can tell you I always knew she had her own mind, and that I love her with all my heart no matter what those choices have been."

ABBY WAMBACH'S 2008 REPLACEMENT FOR THE OLYMPICS was once private with her companion too, at least as discrete as you can be when he is a 6-foot-4 NBA All-Star point guard. Lauren Cheney Holiday had a surprise waiting for her when she returned to UCLA for her junior season with her gold medal; Jrue Holiday was the star freshman player on the basketball team who Lauren "happened to be seated behind" during a women's basketball game. When another woman approached Jrue for his autograph, mistaking him for another black player before walking away, Lauren seized the moment. "You're much cuter than he is anyway," she said. By the time Jrue became a first-round draft pick of the Philadelphia 76ers in 2009, starting one of the league's most durable and

productive careers of the past decade, Lauren was well on her way to becoming a National Team regular. They would go weeks, sometimes months, without seeing each other due to their travel schedules, but they made it work. Their outdoor wedding, July 7, 2013, in Malibu, would come a year before Lauren earned the honor as U.S. Soccer Player of the Year.

For all that soccer had given her, however, Lauren began to have long conversations with her husband about her possible retirement in the middle of her best season. "There's got to be something more to life," she told him when she was just 26. "All my life has consisted of trying to get to the next level, to prepare for

THE PLAYERS JOURNAL

Lauren Cheney Holiday, with her husband, Jrue

the Olympics, or a World Cup." The more she spoke, of wanting to lead mission trips to impoverished areas, of aching to serve others instead of having people dote on her, the more Jrue encouraged her to be truly introspective. "I cannot make this decision for you because you will never forgive me, you will always resent me," he told her. "This is totally your decision and I will support whatever you decide." When Lauren made her decision

The Holidays, going all in

COURTESY OF LAUREN CHENEY HOLIDAY

to leave the game, win or lose, after the 2015 World Cup, she told us she cried for two weeks. "Are you sure?" her husband asked, again and again.

Lauren's new dream of helping lead the world in a new direction, as well as her husband's career, would be sidetracked just a year later. Pregnant with her daughter, Lauren's debilitating headaches proved to be caused by a benign, but dangerous brain tumor that required emergency surgery in October of 2016, just a month after giving birth. Jrue took a leave of absence from the NBA for the beginning of that season to be home for his family. "I'm blessed," he said at a news conference after his return. "Blessed to have my family back, blessed that we're OK." With her health restored, Lauren set out to share those blessings, that have included her husband's hundreds of millions of dollars in career earnings. At first, she volunteered, albeit quietly, in her community. When the COVID-19 crisis hit in 2020, however, she allowed the couple's donations of catered meals to healthcare workers in New Orleans to become more public. "Jrue and I never really talked about what we do; it's just not our nature," she said. "But one of the things I've learned is that when you do good things for the world, it can inspire others to do good things, too."

WITH THE COVID CRISIS AND OTHER SOCIAL ISSUES emerging as the year progressed, Lauren sat up in bed one morning with an idea. "We need to do more," she told

Jrue. By then, the Black Lives Matter movement was sweeping across the world and she had been inspired by her former teammates taking knees and speaking out. "We should donate the rest of your salary this season — all of it," she said. In Jrue's case, that was more than $5 million, which the couple used to launch the Lauren and Jrue Holiday Foundation. "The year 2020 has affected thousands of lives and local businesses across the nation in unfathomable ways, due to the uprisings

2019 National Teamers: Tobin Heath, left, Ashlyn Harris, Carli Lloyd, Ali Krieger, Crystal Dunn and Christen Press

of the global pandemic and the epidemic of racial and social injustices," they wrote on their website. Lauren also took up writing in a different manner, penning a column titled "I've Stayed Silent for Way Too Long," for *The Players' Tribune*, an online magazine featuring articles by professional athletes.

She began her story by quoting one of her former soccer teammates, who was speaking about her husband: "Jrue is the *whitest* black guy I know . . . I don't think she knew that she was being racist." As she continued, Lauren revealed the story of the day she was pulled over by police, only to realize she had left her license at home. After she called Jrue and asked him to bring it to her, he was immediately handcuffed by white police officers for no reason, she said, other than the color of his skin. "Even though the officer knew in advance that Jrue was my husband, and that he was coming to the scene . . . And even though Jrue could not have been more careful, or more deferential, in how he made his approach. All the cop saw was this large black man getting out of a car."

Lauren told us she was soon expecting a son. She told the rest of the world in *The Players' Tribune*, too, writing: "I've been thinking a lot lately, as I guess a Mom does, about the world our kids are going to grow up in. I've been thinking a lot about the meaning of certain things. About what it means to raise a daughter growing up to be a black woman in America — and soon a son who will grow up to be a black man in America." Despite her fears, she's an optimist who still believes minds can be changed, that perceptions can be altered through honest conversations and the kind of leadership that will require relentless hard work. Soccer, said Lauren, taught her that. Once upon a time when she was a teenager, a coach told her she was never going to make it beyond college. "Just two years after that, I'm on the Olympic team," she said. "I'm living proof that you just never, ever give up."

The Next Mia Hamm

Anything is possible when you make the decision to be the best version of yourself in whatever you do

T WAS THE SUMMER OF 1987 AND ANSON DORRANCE called Carolyn Rice with a favor to ask. He knew of a high school player moving to her area of northern Virginia and Anson figured Carolyn — a rare woman coaching in the almost exclusive male world of soccer — would be a good choice to mentor and coach this young girl, who had already committed to North Carolina. She was a military brat, who sometimes struggled making friends. "She's shy," said Anson. "A quiet kid. But she'll be able to help your soccer team, and I think you'll be able to help her, too." Carolyn, whose daughter, Emily, had already decided to become a Tar Heel, agreed on the spot. Carolyn had seen this girl play once. She might have been 12 or 13, playing with 14- or 15-year-olds, and stood out like a bee trapped inside your car with the windows closed. "It was if she were shot out of a cannon, just remarkably better than all the other girls around her," Carolyn told us. "When someone calls you and asks you if you want that player on your team, it's not a difficult decision." It was almost verbatim what Anson himself had thought the first time he saw the girl, too.

In a dorm room, meanwhile, that same girl was as welcome as a bee near April Heinrichs' ear, a 15-year-old jumping up and down on her bed while the undisputed 21-year-old badass co-captain of the National Team was trying to sleep one bed away at 6:30 a.m. on a Sunday. The girl was just so happy to be playing soccer, around other females who tried as hard on the field as she

COURTESY OF JEN MEAD

Mia Hamm, with lifelong friends, Brandi Chastain, left, and Kristine Lilly

did, that she couldn't contain herself. The recollection still makes Tracey Bates Leone, the third roommate, laugh like hell, but April has a different first memory of this new teammate being crammed down her throat. "In one of our first games, she steals the ball somewhere near midfield and I work to get myself absolutely wide open with a clear shot in front of the net — and she doesn't pass it to me!" said April, also laughing more than 30 years later. "Instead, she fires a rocket shot into the upper corner of the net. I thought to myself, 'OK then. That was a pretty good second option.'"

Girls' and women's soccer might have existed in the world prior to the arrival of Mariel Margaret Hamm, but it has never been the same since. She taught the world that size doesn't matter — she is all of 5-foot-5 — but speed and savvy are often what wins games. She showed us that no matter how much you try to be humble about your obvious mental and physical gifts, and attribute your success to everyone around you, perception is reality. The truth, and fans, will find you on the field of play. And Mia Hamm, ultimately, could never shield legions of little girls from the fire in her own eyes, the ones that drew a business card from that referee after the championship game back in college in 1992. "What do you want to do with your life?" asked the Nike visionary Joe Elsmore, holding a cocktail napkin, upon which he would write down the cost of Mia's worldly needs as a precursor to her first endorsement contract. "I just want to play soccer," she said. Nothing more, nothing less. That would be one of the few things in soccer that didn't work out the way she planned.

EVEN AS MIA FELT INCREASINGLY UNCOMFORTABLE with all the fanfare surrounding her accomplishments and media exposure by the mid 1990s, her teammates knew they were blessed. She had a way of creating space for people, both on the field and off, that allowed them to find success in their own manner. "People always thought I must be mad at Mia when people started calling her the best player in the world, as if that was something she took away from me," said Michelle Akers, who was the beneficiary of a lion's share of Mia's 144 National Team assists — a record that no one ever has, or likely ever will, even come close to equaling. "The truth is, her success was my success, and vice versa. We made each other's life easier." Some social scientists, a few players and even some fans of the game have argued that National Team era's girl-next-door image was a too-good-to-be-true media fabrication, but even if any of

Michelle Akers, center, with her son, Cody, and Amy Allmann Griffin

that were accurate, decades later most of the members of the 1999 World Cup team stay in contact regularly with cell phone group texts. They really were, and are, friends. "Can you imagine how much it would have sucked if our superstar was an ass----?" asked Julie

To My Sisters:
Without You, There is No Me

BEFORE WRITING THIS BOOK, I UNDERSTOOD I WAS A BENEFACTOR of Title IX legislation and there were thousands of women who bravely fought for the rights that I — and millions of girls everywhere — so literally and freely get to exercise now. I knew I was lucky to be born after June 23, 1972, and therefore have an equal opportunity to engage in the fundamental human right of playing sports, one that my own mother never got to experience. A trail was blazed, and has been widened in the past nearly half century. What has been so amazing about this book is that as Paul and I interviewed so many National Team veterans — all the way back to their first game in 1985 — it was as if I could see individual match sticks being lit one by one.

From Michelle Akers to April Heinrichs, to Mia Hamm and Julie Foudy, and onward to Abby Wambach, Megan Rapinoe, Mallory Pugh and so many others, they all set gender equity issues ablaze and earned the right to be taken seriously, both on the field and off. Hearing Michelle tell the story of standing up in third grade and pronouncing to her class that she wanted to play in the NFL just like "Mean Joe Greene" relit a match in my own mind. Two more matches ignited when Michelle clapped back at her provincial teacher and her mother subsequently forced the narrow-minded school principal to stand down. As we built our book, with the quilted fabric of these stories, I couldn't help but feel like I was penning my own personal "23AndMe," a DNA test that traces ancestry and compares traits. As if studying my own genealogy, I began to understand how and why I came to be. As you can imagine, this is a profound experience when you start to put the pieces together and comprehend the evolution of the female soccer player.

Ricky Skelton, sporting his own "Jo-hawk" with his idol

I am more proud than ever to have carried that torch, to have chanted "Ooooosa, Ooooosa, Ooooosa . . . Ah" in a huddle with the best players in the world and represented my country on the international stage. I know, like my National Team ancestors, I have made an impact and continued to burn this indelible trail so that those who walk behind me walk tall in their own skin. I hope this book has shown girls everywhere just how powerful it is to dare to dream, even if you don't one day make the team. Good things will come from the act of playing, of striving, of winning and losing and just plain having fun.

For my last words of my first book, I feel the overwhelming urge to shout out to my sisters, the 241 women who have donned the USA jersey — and everyone, the mothers, fathers, coaches and administrators, the team owners and investors, who dedicated their lives to making our dream possible. Thank you . . . because without you, there would be no me. — J.L.

Foudy on her lively and provocative podcast known as "Laughter Permitted," where her most frequent guests are past and present members of the National Team.

Numerous players have stepped up through the years to help Michelle in her passion for fostering abandoned animals, especially horses. "She was our warrior, our everything," said Mia, but Michelle has had to be even more ferocious at times on her underfunded and undermanned farm in Georgia where — during a flood a decade ago — she literally had to swim with the horses across a raging creek to get them to higher ground. Michelle fantasizes about a Michael Jordan-esque documentary film project about her life of overcoming adversity that continues to this day. Having survived on the National Team for 15 years, with countless concussions and more than 30 surgeries on her knees, she represents the longest and arguably most important link in the chain that binds the original 1985 National Teamers of Jesolo, Italy, to the team of women of 2019 who stormed France. She believes little girls, and boys, would benefit from her story. "I would like to do a film like that because most people still don't know me," said Michelle, still nicknamed "Mufasa" in honor of "The Lion King" character and her own long mane of curly hair. "My legacy, kind of like the team's legacy, can't be confined to soccer. The way I played the game was just how I put out a visible expression of who I am every single day; that was my heart that you saw out there. And you would have thought that after winning the Olympics in 1996 and that World Cup in 1999 that the doors would just be kicked open for women everywhere — but they weren't. They were just kind of edged open, or maybe people just began to notice that there was even a door that needed to be opened."

APRIL HEINRICHS TOLD US SHE HAS NEVER felt the same urge to share her own story, unless you keep it in and around the white lines. Like so many of the National Teamers who grew up in less than ideal settings, she has learned to reconcile with the mother who abandoned her, but figures the full story of her Colorado childhood is best left untold.

April Heinrichs, the first trading card

"My Mom is my Mom," she told us. "And I love her . . . and I feel a sense of responsibility toward her. And that's probably why I've never written a book myself, because I don't need to hurt her." Instead, she said, soccer has provided the family she never really had, complete with arguments around the dinner table, spats that become full-on arguments, and lots of hugs later. "The success of the Women's National Team is first and foremost for me," she told the *Baltimore Sun* newspaper when it announced that she had been named head coach when Tony DiCicco stepped down after the 1999 World Cup. "It's in every cell in my body."

If the National Team had a female Forrest Gump, a savant with the knack for being involved with so many key moments of the game, it would be April — as a player, coach, Olympic official and then U.S. Soccer administrator in a span of nearly four decades. Four years after coming home with the first women's World Cup trophy, she remembers standing in Dallas as one of Tony's assistant coaches, when the National Team played Canada on May 19, 1995, for one of the largest crowds ever assembled for a

COMMON DENOMINATORS

April Heinrichs and Dr. Matt Robinson surveyed 256 female players, ages 13 to 23, who were invited into a National Team youth training camp.* Here is some of what they found, as compared to what we learned from conversations with more than 100 National Teamers who played from 1985 to 2020:

GETTING STARTED — April and Dr. Robinson offered up all sorts of data on the average age of soccer evolution: 1) First time playing, 5 years; 2) Entering organized recreational league soccer, 5.4 years; 3) Entering club soccer, 9 years; 4) Began dreaming of making the National Team, 9.5 years; 5) Starting to specialize in soccer, 12.5 years.

PLAYING WITH THE BOYS — More than 80 percent of the girls and young women in April's survey reported playing regularly with boys through adolescence. We only found two National Teamers who played exclusively with girls through their own childhoods.

FAMILY MATTERS — April's research showed that 84 percent of players on a National Team track come from two-parent homes where the birth parents were still together. Notable among National Team exceptions include April herself, as well as **Tiffeny Milbrett**, **Shannon MacMillan**, **Hope Solo** and **Jessica McDonald**.

SIBLINGS RULE — Maybe the most astonishing statistic relates to the prevalence of siblings among National Team hopefuls, and the National Teamers themselves. April's paper states that 95 percent of the girls in her survey had siblings. Meanwhile, we only found two, **Sydney Leroux Dwyer** and **Rita Tower**, who didn't have at least one brother or sister.

PLAYING UP — In addition to having at least one sibling, a whopping 74 percent of the players in April's survey had siblings who were, on average, three years older. That correlates with our findings of National Teamers. That means "players were struggling, fighting, competing and enduring 'fits of failure' on a

April Heinrichs, in 2013

consistent basis at home and that very training against their older sister or brother prepared them for success in our elite women's soccer environment," wrote April.

PLAYING TIME — April found that elite-level girls, ages 6-12, trained with their team about three days per week and played 1.66 games per week. By age 13-17, that rate moved to 4 days per week of training and two games per week on average. Players in both age groups took about three weeks off from soccer in each calendar year, usually in the winter.

OTHER SPORTS — April's overwhelming data shows that, until high school, girls bound for National Team youth camps played all sorts of other sports. About 90 percent played basketball and 77 percent competed in track and field. By high school age, those percentages dipped dramatically, to 37 percent on track teams and 24 percent still in basketball.

*—Data is derived from the report titled "Finding the Next Mia Hamm and Alex Morgan" by April Heinrichs and Dr. Matt Robinson, Aug. 2014, on behalf of U.S. Soccer.

women's soccer game by that point, all of 6,145 people. "The little girls screeching, absolutely ear-piercingly loud when Mia's name was announced, made it sound like there were tens of thousands more," she said. "That's when I began to understand the social change that was taking place in America." It was April who, already National Team head coach by then, wandered by a youth tournament game in Rhode Island in 2001 and heard parents cheering for a goal. She was there to scout older girls, but was instantly captivated by a buzz saw of a player named Heather O'Reilly, the closest April had ever come to seeing herself

PHOTOSHOP ILLUSTRATION BY PAUL TUKEY

April Heinrichs, with the first World Cup trophy

play. Within a year, Heather would be the first in a long procession of "next Mia Hamms," some like Heather, Alex Morgan and Mallory Pugh who came close, and some who didn't

A Side Road to the World Cup
Part 3: The Goal

HAVANA SOLAUN WAS FURIOUS. On June 18, 2019 at Stade des Alpes in Grenoble, France, in front of more than 17,000 fans, three weeks of lost luggage, excessive training, non-existent expense money, virtually sleepless nights and lopsided losses were coming to an end. With the Jamaican Reggae Girlz ranked 64th in the world, and the Australian Matildas 6th, the game had all the markings of a massive blowout. Still, Havana hadn't traveled more than halfway around the world to sit on the bench in what could be the final World Cup match of her life. "She was pissed off," said her mother. "That's when I knew . . . "

With her team down 2-0 at halftime, Havana finally entered the game just as my family and I walked into a Chicago supermarket in the middle of a family vacation. We hadn't even found the milk aisle yet when the score flashed 2-1 on my iPhone. I was frantic. Was it Havana? Was it Cheyna Matthews of our hometown Washington Spirit? Maybe it was Khadija Shaw, an immensely talented athlete who liked carrots so much as a little girl she was nicknamed "Bunny" by one of her four brothers who had been either murdered or killed in a car accident in the first 20 years of her life in the Jamaican slums. At the checkout register, I found the Fox Sports highlight video and instantly started weeping. "What's wrong, Dad?" asked Angie, my then 9-year-old World Cup wannabe. "It was Havana!" I shouted, making strangers' heads turn in the crowded store. "Havana scored!" Back in France, team benefactor Cedella Marley cried tears of joy too. So did Havana's college coach, Becky Burleigh, along with Havana's mother and step-father, her father and his husband, her two sisters, her brother and two friends from home. "I said to her, 'Why do you have to be so angry to play your best?'" said her Mom, Sandra Brower, laughing at the memory.

Jamaica lost 4-1 that day, but as anyone who has ever played on an overmatched team knows, sometimes even a single goal — in this case the only one in Jamaican World Cup history — constitutes winning. Months after the headlines, interviews and celebrations had ended, I had a chance for a quiet reflection with my soccer daughter who was now a national hero, just not America's. I asked her to tell bear the weight of lofty expectations. "You want a life lesson? It's that you play your butt off every single game because you never know who might be watching," Heather told us. "I wasn't on any special team. Just totally bizarrely by chance, April walks by during this epic comeback when, we're down 2-0 and I score a couple of goals and have an assist and we win 3-2 and, suddenly, I'm on the National Team's radar. When luck and opportunity meet, you just never know."

AS A HEAD COACH, APRIL WAS INSTRUMENTAL in launching the National Team careers of numerous future icons, from Heather, Hope Solo and Cat Whitehill, to Abby Wambach, Angela Hucles and Shannon Boxx — even as April jostled from time to time with the members of her team who used to be her teammates. Everything from successful jockeying in labor relations, to filling stadiums with World Cup fans, to getting their own first professional league started, had provided the players with unprecedented leverage. It was their team now, and they occasionally put their foot down with a coach they sometimes found too controlling with curfews and overly demanding workouts and other restrictive rules. After winning the Olympic gold medal in 2004, several older players

Havana Solaun, the post-goal celebration with Bunny Shaw

DPA PICTURE ALLIANCE/ALAMY STOCK PHOTO

me about the goals, the one she scored and also the one she attained. "As soon as I saw Bunny steal the ball at midfield, I just took off toward the goal as fast as my body would let me run. I didn't even look back," she said. The highlight video will forever show Havana receiving Bunny's perfect pass in stride, dribbling past a defender, leaping over the goalie's outstretched leg, and then shooting the ball between two defenders into the net. "There was no conscious thought from when I took off running until I was off the ground in Bunny's arms. I think that was just a purely instinctual moment for me, the result of every bit of training I had ever done."

When the stadium erupted for several minutes, the only thing Havana heard were the voices of her teammates, her Jamaican blood sisters. She had given them hope and dignity. "These girls are such fighters, fighting so that they can make a better life for their family," she said. "I really hope that game is fuel for their future." It was for Havana, whose vagabond career brought her to three more teams in three different nations in 2020 alone. "I still love it every time I lace on my boots — and I still have more to prove. I would like to think that some point down the road, the U.S. coaches will watch Jamaica play and say, 'Dang, we missed out on that one.'" — P.T.

met with April and asked her to resign — and she reluctantly agreed. "I learned so much about communication over time," she told us more than 15 years later. "Coming off the '99 World Cup, I was focused on the importance of teaching and evolution and change. And I wasn't apparently sophisticated enough at that time to understand that there's no finish line to being a good communicator. I could have one good communication, or three good communications with a player, but you have to keep having good communications with that player. As a coach, we don't get to check that box, because it's ongoing."

April also encountered another universal truth about coaches and parents, or friends and co-workers: Your words don't always come out as intended. "You can walk into a locker room and say something at halftime. You think you're direct; you think it's clear, but there can be at least three different interpretations of what you just said. One player will think, 'Oh, my God, April just said I'm the reason we gave up those goals!' Another player's like, 'April just said we all suck!' And then there are the ones who heard what I thought I was saying, 'We just have to get a little bit tougher and we'll be better.' I was aware more as time went on that I needed to be a bit more nuanced in things I would say. And I also think it was tough to play for a peer. I said at the time and I say today, 'If Michelle Akers was the head coach and I was the player, or if Carla Overbeck was the coach, if the roles had been flipped, I'd be thinking to myself, 'What are *you* doing coaching *me*?'"

COURTESY OF TRACEY LEONE BATES

April Heinrichs, with Tracey Bates Leone in 2004, the second U.S. gold medal

After she left the National Team, April landed at the University of California at Irvine, where she tried unsuccessfully to recruit the future Army Lieutenant CoCo Goodson. Just a year later, she moved to the U.S. Olympic Committee, then eventually returned to U.S. Soccer, where she took control of youth programs. Among her quests? She tried to develop an efficient, predictive system to help unearth more American players like herself and Michelle Akers and, especially, that 15-year-old with whom she once shared a dorm room. "In a sense we are trying to identify triggers of ignition for those who have reached the National Team level," states a report titled, "Finding the Next Mia Hamm and Alex Morgan," that April co-authored with Dr. Matt Robinson, a professor of sport management at the University of Delaware. "Of the hundreds of thousands of girls who play (high school) soccer, only a small percentage will achieve National Team status. Again, the question being, 'If she can do it why can't I?'" April and Dr. Robinson found all sorts of common denominators among players who were invited to National Team training camps — including supportive parents, two-parent households, older siblings, and frequently playing with and against boys — but also found outliers (see April's Findings, Page 239). "Our soccer community could do a better job of being more inclusive and supportive of those players without a two-parent household," noted the authors.

THE MATH PORTRAYS WHAT COULD BE A SOBERING REALITY for the millions of girls who share the National Team dream. Of the approximately half a million girls still playing soccer by high school and college age, less than one-tenth of one percent of them,

Joy Fawcett, paying it forward

about 400, will get invited to try out for the youth National Team program from ages 13 to 23 in any given year — and only about 30 women, and the occasional young girl, make it into the player pool for the senior level team that competes for Olympics and World Cups. A much bigger emphasis, for April and Mia and so many others, is in talking about the value of just playing the game and having fun. Period. "One of the things we do at the Mia Hamm Foundation is to encourage and empower girls through sport, and it doesn't mean you have to be on the National Team," Mia told us. "At the end of the day, it's not about who plays at the highest level, it's just about all those life lessons you learn through sport and how that can impact your life going forward."

Those lessons, both simple and profound, are what compel Mia's teammate, Joy Fawcett, to focus her efforts on a non-profit organization known as Pure Game that works with southern California schools to bring soccer to inner-city and often underprivileged children. The students, notes the program's founder, Tony Everett, typically have no idea that their coach for that day starred in four World Cup tournaments and won two. "You'll see the boys start talking, this and that, about how girls can't play," said Tony. "So then Joy, quiet and reserved as ever, stands up and takes their challenge — and absolutely schools them. The boys learn very quickly, 'Oh, girls *can* play, too.'" It's safe to say there's not a single

National Teamer who hasn't paid it forward to grow the game in some manner, from Briana Scurry's work with #SheCanCoach and Kicks to the Pitch, to Danielle Slaton, Julie Foudy and Brandi Chastain's championing of the Bay Area Women's Sports Initiative, to Megan Rapinoe lending her name and voice to Play Proud, a coach-mentor program created by streetfootballworld to provide safe soccer spaces for LGBTQ+ youth. "I would have loved, when I was a kid, for these things to even be talked about, or to even sort of have the space for them to live," Megan told *The Advocate* on the day of Play Proud's launch. "Not only for the LGBTQ+ kids, but for the straight kids as well, I think it's really important to give them this information and this education so they know how to talk about things and they know the right way to make sure that soccer is an inclusive environment."

Yasmine Sanchez was a beneficiary of the Play Proud program through New York City Football Club's

Yasmine Sanchez, with Megan Rapinoe, tears of joy

Saturday Night Lights (see Page 23). Before that, Yasmine had survived a lifetime of physical and emotional abuse, and it was the soccer program that she credits with pulling her through. In July of 2019, Billie Jean King presented Yasmine with one of four national Youth Leadership Awards. When the ESPN cameras cut to a commercial break inside the packed auditorium at L.A. LIVE!, just after Billie Jean had asked Yasmine to stand and be recognized by the national television audience, Yasmine made a break for the front row to show Megan just how much her support had mattered in her life. "Would you mind a selfie?" Yasmine asked the woman who gave her the courage to be out, and proud, and play her favorite game. When Yasmine examined the picture, with her eyes filled with tears of joy, she ran back to her hero as the cameras were about to come back on. "I'm so sorry, I was crying. My eyes are red and puffy, can we do another one?" she asked. Megan, tearing up herself, obliged.

HEATHER O'REILLY RECALLS CRYING, TOO, hiding in the bathroom at age 12 prior to her first-ever tryout for the Olympic Development Program evaluation where she didn't know another girl in the mix. "Dad, I just want to go home!" she said through the door. Like many

COURTESY OF ANGELA HUCLES

National Team parents, her father was an athlete and he wasn't having any part of his daughter's meltdown. For the only time in her life, he led her into the open air next to the field, put his hand on Heather's back, and physically forced her toward the other girls. "He literally shoved me out there," Heather told us in 2020, the year she gave birth to her first child with her husband, Dave Werry. Now an assistant coach for Anson Dorrance at North Carolina, Heather is aware of all the stories of overbearing parents, the mothers and fathers who force their children to play soccer and other sports either more often than they'd like, or against their will entirely. In her case, though, she said her father really did know best. "He understood I had the talent and that I would be fine if I just got out there and met a few people. I do think about that now, because making that team, in turn, led to

Heather O'Reilly, with Angela Hucles

the New Jersey state team, then the regional team and then the National Team. I mean, It could have gone very, very differently if my father had said, 'OK, let's get in the car and go home.' I do think that when parents make decisions for their kids, sometimes they do know a little bit more than a 12-year-old about how the world works."

Steve Baldwin and Alexis Ohanian knew something of the world, too, and they didn't like it very much: Their daughters live in a world where girls aren't getting a completely fair shake compared to boys, especially as it relates to soccer, and both fathers decided to do something about it. Steve, the technology guru who had watched from close range as his daughter, Carlyn, lived on meager wages playing in Europe, became a silent partner in the Washington Spirit in 2017. Mild-mannered and thoughtful, he mostly watched from a

Aubrey Bledsoe, left, and Havana Solaun with some young fans, Megan, Angie and Scout

distance at first. Then, up close and personal at a Panera Bread lunch with National Team hopeful Aubrey Bledsoe at the end of the 2018 season, he listened to her laundry list of observations. The goalie and her teammates weren't paid a living wage, weren't provided their own apartments, didn't have their own training facilities, and only had the bare minimum of qualified coaches and trainers — and yet they were the one one-thousandth of one-percenters who start playing soccer at age 7 and demonstrate the ability and will to call themselves professional soccer players 15 years later. After nearly four hours of Aubrey talking, Steve was sold. He has invested almost all of his time, and a lot of his money, ever since. Wages are creeping higher; the days of his players staying with host families to make ends meet have mostly ended. "The Washington Spirit will not ever be the reason you do not get to follow your dream of making the National Team," Steve told Aubrey. "We will get you the coaching, we will get you better facilities . . . I am all-in."

Alexis, meanwhile, was new to the game. The co-founder of Reddit was a new father, too, when a buddy told him he needed to hit the next plane to Paris to experience the spectacle of U.S. vs. France in the 2019 World Cup. Watching the finals at home a few days later with his wife, he dared to dream out loud, just like millions of other soccer Dads around the nation: Could his daughter one day play for the National Team? "Without missing a beat, my wife was like, 'Not until they pay her what she's worth,'" Alexis told CNN. "And she was half joking, but not really." Alexis took the comment as a challenge and made his investment in the Angel City women's soccer team a family affair. His wife, tennis legend Serena Williams, their daughter, Olympia, and Alexis are part owners of what will be the 11th franchise of the National Women's Soccer League in 2022. "As someone who spends hours kicking around a football with my 2-year-old daughter, I want her to have a front-row seat to this revolution," he posted to social media in July of 2020. "I'm personally investing on behalf of my family because creating more opportunities in women's sports is important to my wife @serenawilliams and me, and we want to be a part of making a better future for our daughter."

Megan Mangano, left, with her wife, Angela Hucles and fellow National Teamers Tiffany Roberts Sahaydak and Lorrie Fair

Last Words

We talked to so many players throughout 2019 and 2020 in interviews that generated millions of words of commentary and memories, far too many for just one book. Here are a few final thoughts from some of the women we met along the way:

SHANNON LITZ/THE RECORD-COURIER

Lorraine Figgins Fitzhugh, a high school coaching champion

FUN FLOWS FROM EFFORT — When the Douglas High School girls team struggled to field competitive teams for many years in Colorado, it turned to its math teacher who had grown up going head to head in the Seattle area with **Michelle Akers. Lorraine Figgins Fitzhugh** (USWNT 1986) said she often received negative feedback from parents who thought she was training her players too hard, but two state championships and eight years later, she retired back to anonymity with her principles intact. "I had huge, huge pushback from a small community here with all those parents involved," she said. "I was able to look myself in the mirror and I felt that we had a good time. Yes, we practiced hard and it was painful. You have to go through a lot of pain in soccer to win. We also had great team camaraderie, great captains, great preparation and I believe that's why we were successful."

SCOUTING YOUTH IS EASY? — **Rita Tower** (USWNT 1993-94) played with **Mia Hamm** for the entirety of their careers at North Carolina and said that experience set her up for significant success as a real estate executive. "You're good enough to play at that level? That makes you a different level of human," she said. "These girls are more successful in life, whether it's in business, whether it's in their education. They are more confident. It's profound." Rita asserts that the difference between the average club player and a girl capable of an elite Division 1 scholarship reveals itself even prior to puberty in most cases. "It sounds so pretentious and rude, but it is the fact of the matter. I coached hundreds of kids, and I can tell who's going to do what at a very young age. Of course, there are a few surprises, but not many. An elite soccer player is just a different level of person, more driven, more resilient. And they go after things harder. That's easy to see."

YOUR MOM DOES WHAT? — As one of the 12 women in the history of the National Team who returned to play after giving birth, **Amy Rodriguez Shilling** (USWNT 2005-2018) gets a kick out of it when her oldest son, Ryan, or his brother, Luke, is asked what their Mom does for a living. "The boys say, 'She plays soccer.' And then the kids in the school yard and the teachers laugh," said Amy. "It's like, 'No, my Mom actually PLAYS soccer!' Most parents work 9 to 5 in an office and I obviously have a unique experience. I'm proud of that. I think I've taught them what hard work looks like, and what it looks like being challenged, going through hard times and having to sacrifice. I'm glad my boys get to see that."

Michelle French, with an icon

GONE, BUT NEVER FORGOTTEN — Clive Charles (see Chapter 16) left a lasting impression on many people who knew him at the University of Portland. Seventeen years after his passing, few people feel the impact more vividly than **Michelle French** (USWNT 1997-2001), who came back to her alma mater to coach in 2017. "A big reason I took this position was because I wanted to have an opportunity to do what he did for me and do the best that I could to represent who he was as a coach," said Michelle. "I feel his presence. In the hallway, there's a picture of him. In my office, there's a picture of him. There isn't a day goes by that I don't think about him."

MICHELLE, APRIL OR MIA? — For fun, we asked the earliest National Teamers the same question: "If you had first pick for a two-on-two game, who would you choose to play with against the other two? The choices are **Michelle Akers**, **April Heinrichs** or **Mia Hamm**." As a defender, who had to try to stop all three of them in practice for many years, **Debbie Belkin Rademacher** (USWNT 1986-1991) had a nuanced perspective. "I'd probably take Michelle,

because she could just physically pound you into the ground," said Debbie, who coached women's soccer at the University of Michigan for many years. "But two-on-two? Mia was so quick she would twist your ankles in knots. And, April, she was slippery and sneaky, just coming at you 100 miles an hour." For the unofficial record, the majority of players we spoke with picked April. "This woman, she just finds a way to win," said **Tracey Bates Leone**. "It's too bad America never really got to see April Heinrichs, the player, before her knees gave out."

Danesha Adams, an all-time UCLA great

PEOPLE CAN LEARN FROM MISTAKES — **Danesha Adams** (USWNT 2006) will never forget the day a teenage opponent called her the N-word — twice — on the soccer field. She fought back by shoving and received an instant red card and ejection from the referee; her own mother was then assaulted by the girl's mother. When the dust settled, though, an entire community seemed to grow from the experience. "I will say the (opposing) coaches were great; they came up with an apology," said Danesha. "I got a letter from the girl and my Mom got an apology from the other Mom, too. And the funny thing now, to full circle this, the young lady is married to an African American man that I know. I went to UCLA with him." The refs even rescinded the red card.

Women's soccer, now played in most nations around the world . . . in Nike gear

IN JULY OF 2020, ANGELA HUCLES RECEIVED AN email from two women who had always made her drop what she was doing. They had an opportunity for fellow Californians, including Angela, Shannon Boxx, Saskia Webber and several other National Teamers who live in the area: How would you like to be part owners of a women's soccer team — in partnership with Serena Williams, actresses Uzo Aduba, America Ferrera, Jennifer Garner, Eva Longoria and Natalie Portman? Angela, who had just given birth to her second child with her wife, couldn't say yes fast enough to the emailers in question: Julie Foudy, who had been one of Angela's first National Team captains, and Mia Hamm, who was, well, Mia Hamm. "I hold them in very high regard and I trust them implicitly," Angela told the media soon afterward. "I definitely wanted to say a very strong verbal, 'Yes!'" As news of the new team spread across America and around the world, just as the National Women's Soccer League was the first professional sports entity in America to resume playing in the midst of the COVID-19 crisis, expanding opportunities for women seemed like a rare bright light on the horizon. Angela reflected, again, on her own journey through soccer. "I'm a woman. I'm Cuban. I'm black, and I'm a part of the LGBTQ+ family and I'll be forever grateful for the gift of the women who came before me and held the door open for someone like me."

Mia told us she was looking more in hindsight, too, given the gift of time at home in the year of 2020. She was thinking of her own mother and father, who never once told her she couldn't do something because she was a girl. She said she thinks all the time about her late brother, Garrett, who invited his little sister to tag along to all of his games and, sadly, was taken from her before he could share the glory in all of hers. She's thankful for Anson Dorrance. His vision. His humor and, especially, the day she sat alone in his office at the beginning of her sophomore year in college. "Mia, what do you really want?" Anson asked, according to the great biographer, Tim Crothers. Mia couldn't think of anything to say at first, but as the coach waited, she blurted out a question that fans around the world would answer for themselves. "To be the best?" Anson knew he had her then. North Carolina was home free, but he clicked the lights off, and then on, for emphasis. "It's just a decision, a light-switch decision. That's all it takes, but you have to make that decision every single day. You can't make it today and then say, 'Whew, glad that's over.' You have to make it tomorrow and the next day and the day after that for the rest of your career."

She is thankful, too, for that referee, the man drawn to that fire in her eyes like a moth to a flame. Three decades later, Joe Elsmore still chides Mia from time to time with an email of the photo, the one hanging in his office that will eternally depict her as being offsides. "Joe, you were too slow, you could never keep up with the play!" she always replies. Together, the shy young woman with a dream and young man with an audacious idea opened doors, sold some soccer gear and christened a giant building at Nike — but most importantly they opened minds to possibilities. Millions of them, in America and around the world. "Girls soccer reaches virtually every corner of

Marian Dalmy Dougherty, with the former referee who helped start a revolution

the earth now," said Joe, the company's global director of soccer marketing. "It's grown and changed so much, I don't even have words to explain it. But the one constant has been Mia, all the way through."

Those kinds of comments, the ones that can sound like they're giving one person too much credit in an 11-player game, still make her uneasy. It's just so much more comfortable for Mia to talk about Michelle Akers' power, Julie Foudy's leadership and Briana Scurry's focus, or Mallory Pugh's speed, Alex Morgan's tenacity and Megan Rapinoe's right to celebrate and express herself however she damn well pleases. "Megan has obviously been unapologetic — and she should have been," said Mia. "People need to be able to be their authentic selves, whatever that means. The world is different now." As if to emphasize the point, the doorbell rang at the home of the girl next door who became an American icon. Mia's brother, Martin, was stopping by to help her children with their on-line classes in the middle of a pandemic — so we asked her one final question before saying goodbye: "Is it fair to say the world has changed because of you, your team, the National Team, going all the way back from 1985 'til now?" She paused, much longer than she ever did on a soccer field. "I think so," she allowed. "I'd like to think that young girls saw the image of strong women then, and they see strong women now, and there will be more strong women in the future as a result."

JOANNA'S ACKNOWLEDGMENTS

I WANT TO THANK MY PARENTS, NANCY AND STEVE LOHMAN, for your unconditional love, constant encouragement to dream, and instilling the belief that I could achieve greatness. I want to thank my sister, Molly, for being a guiding light in the writing process and my brother, Peter, for making me the athlete I am today — chasing you and your friends around all my youth was a gift and a privilege. To my nieces, Mariel and Soraya, I hope this book shows you a better world so you have every opportunity to pursue your version of success.

I want to thank my best friend, Charlotte, for always helping to tie up loose ends and being a sounding board for all my crazy ideas. And most importantly, I want to thank my partner, Melodie, for always inspiring me to push my limits and holding my hand through it all.

Thank you to the Washington Spirit for providing some of the best years of my life, retiring my jersey, and constantly providing a professional environment for young girls who have big dreams. And to all the soccer players and parents I have had the pleasure of working with, thank you for providing the foundation for this project. Thank you, Paul, for being the best writing partner, a dear friend, and a magician with words. Your energy and passion is remarkable and you motivate me every day to keep going. To each and every girl out there who dreams of making the USWNT, you are already a champion in my eyes.

OUR ACKNOWLEDGMENTS

SO MANY PEOPLE WERE INSTRUMENTAL in bringing this project to life, we couldn't possibly name them all. Our first collective thank you, however, goes out to Steve Baldwin, the soccer Dad who loved the game so much that he bought a team. Kudos to Shannon, Meg, Sean, John and the talented, efficient stylists at O'Brien Design of Freeport, Maine, for making these pages clean and easy to read. To Laurie Lane, soccer club president extraordinaire, for one of the first interviews and for setting Paul straight, and Mark Cantor, for explaining the lay of the soccer land when the idea for this project was just a spark. To our promotional team, Chryssa, Amy, Scott and many others, now the real work begins.

Thanks, too, to Alex Chew and all the other advance readers, one chapter at a time. In those early days of the marathon, the encouragement kept us going. To our editor, Allen Lessels, you were as ever a consummate pro. To John Silbersack: All those phone calls, and all that positivity, meant a lot to us.

Finally, a giant bear hug (with masks on!) goes out to the entire soccer community of players, coaches, referees, administrators and, of course, parents. More than 150 people were interviewed in total for this project, many of whom aren't even quoted in the book due to space considerations. Will there be Volume II?! To Carli Lloyd, our friend and hero, what a gift to be able to literally affix your name to the top of our book. To Lauren Gregg, April Heinrichs, Becky Burleigh, Anson Dorrance, Jerry Smith, Chris Petrucelli and other coaches, thank you for giving the profession such shining examples of dedication, not just to winning, but to the utter devotion of yourselves toward molding lifetime champions. Lilli Barrett-O'Keefe, you are an angel; thank you for bringing us two of the most remarkable characters in our story.

Thank you, ultimately, to Angie. You brought us together, a soccer Dad and a Rainbow Warrior, and spurred us to create something truly special — in hopes of helping young people like you dare to dream higher than ever.

SOURCES

A Word About Our Sources

THE VAST MAJORITY of this book is derived from more than 150 recorded interviews we conducted throughout 2019 and 2020 with people from around the game of soccer, National Teamers, as well as their parents and coaches. In cases where direct quotations are utilized from other sources, including books, magazines, newspapers, on-line sites or Julie Foudy's podcast, "Laughter Permitted," those are noted in the text. Within the stories we presented, in which direct dialogue is quoted and we were not in the room, the words are based on the recollection of one or both parties involved in the conversation. We realize memories don't always agree; we sincerely did our best to verify facts and the general tone of the moment in question.

Our research for this book also involved reading dozens of other books in advance, as well as thousands of articles from newspapers, magazines and on-line sources including Soccer America and the Players Tribune. Special thanks go to Caitlin Murray and her book, "The National Team," which we found to be the most thorough representation of the history of women's soccer since 1985. In our search for accurate historical facts, we note other key authors in our Advance Reading List, at right, including Tim Crothers and Anson Dorrance, Hope Solo and Ann Killion, Tim Nash, Dr. Lauren Gregg, Jere Longman, Gloria Averbuch and Brandi Chastain, and Abby Wambach.

Advance Reading List

"Breakaway: Beyond the Goal" by Alex Morgan. Simon & Schuster. 2015.

"The Captain Class: The Hidden Force that Creates the World's Greatest Teams" by Sam Walker. Random House. 2017.

"Catch Them Being Good" by Tony DiCicco and Dr. Colleen Hacker with Charles Salzberg. Viking. 2002.

"Choose to Matter: Being Courageously and Fabulously You" by Julie Foudy. ESPN W. 2017.

"The Champion Within: Training For Excellence" by Dr. Lauren Gregg with Tim Nash. JTC Sports. 1999.

"Forward: A Memoir" by Abby Wambach. Dey St. Books. 2016.

"Game On: The All-American Race to Make Champions of Our Children" by Tom Farrey. ESPN Books. 2008.

"The Girls of Summer" by Jere Longman. Harper Collins. 2000.

"Goal!: The Ultimate Guide for Soccer Moms and Dads" by Gloria Averbuch and Ashley Michael Hammond. Rodale Press. 1999.

"Go for the Goal: A Champion's Guide to Winning in Soccer and Life" by Mia Hamm with Aaron Heifitz. Dey St. 2000.

"It's Not About the Bra: Play Hard, Play Fair, and Put the Fun Back into Competitive Sports" by Brandi Chastain and Gloria Averbuch. Collins. 2004.

"It's Not the Glory: The Remarkable First Thirty Years of U.S. Women's Soccer" by Tim Nash. 56th Minute LLC. 2016.

"The Man Watching: A Biography of Anson Dorrance, the Unlikely Architect of the Greatest College Sports Dynasty Ever" by Tim Crothers. Sports Media Group. 2006.

"The National Team: The Inside Story of the Women Who Changed Soccer" by Caitlyn Murray. Abrams Press. 2019.

"Powerhouse: 13 Teamwork Tactics that Build Excellence and Unrivaled Success" by Kristine Lilly, Dr. John Gillis Jr. with Dr. Lynette Gillis. Greenleaf. 2019.

"Solo: The Memoir of Hope" by Hope Solo with Anne Killion. HarperCollins. 2012.

"The Sports Gene: Inside the Science of Extraordinary Athletic Performance" by David Epstein. Current. 2013.

"Standing Fast: Battles of a Champion" by Michelle Akers and Tim Nash. JTC Sports. 1997.

"The Vision of a Champion: Advice and Inspiration from the World's Most Successful Women's Soccer Coach" by Anson Dorrance and Gloria Averbuch. Echo Point Books and Media. 2002.

"When Nobody Was Watching: My Hard-Fought Journey to the Top of the Soccer World" by Carli Lloyd with Wayne Coffey. Houghton Mifflin Harcourt. 2016.

RESOURCES

PART OF OUR MISSION, VISION AND GOAL in creating this project is to draw attention to underserved communities and marginalized would-be athletes. A portion of the proceeds of the sales of Raising Tomorrow's Champions will be donated to support causes near and dear to the hearts of the soccer community. Here is a list of just some of the organizations we believe to be doing great work in North American and, in some cases, around the world:

USWNT Player-Supported Foundations

Bay Area Women's Sports Initiative, BAWSI.org (Julie Foudy, Brandi Chastain, Danielle Slaton)

Ertz Family Foundation, ErtzFamilyFoundation.org

Jrue and Lauren Holiday Foundation, JLHFund.org

LA84 Foundation, LA84.org (Amanda Cromwell, Angela Hucles, many more)

Lupus Foundation of America, Lupus.org (Shannon Boxx)

Mia Hamm Foundation, MiaFoundation.org

Michelle Akers Horse Rescue and Outreach Inc., MichelleAkers.org

Pure Game, thePureGame.org (Joy Fawcett)

Together Rising, TogetherRising.org (Abby Wambach)

Black Lives Matter

Black Alliance For Justice Immigration, BAJI.org

The Color of Change, ColorofChange.org

The Movement For Black Lives, M4BL.org

NAACP Legal Defense and Education Fund, NAACPLDF.org

UndocuBlack Network, UndocuBlack.org

LGBTQ+ Supporting Organizations

Athlete Ally, athleteally.org

Federal Triangles Soccer Club, FederalTriangles.org

Human Rights Campaign, HRC.org

International Gay and Lesbian Football Association, IGLFA.org

LGBT SportSafe, LGBTSportSafe.com

North American Gay Soccer Association, uslgbtsoccer.org

Play Proud, beyondsport.org/project/p/play-proud/

SMYAL (Supporting and Mentoring Youth Advocates and Leaders), SMYAL.org

You Can Play Project, YouCanPlayProject.org

Girls (and Boys) In Soccer

America SCORES, AmericaScores.org

Aspen Institute Project Play, AspenProjectPlay.org

Changing the Game Project, ChangingtheGameProject.com

Charity Ball, CharityBall.org

Common Goal, common-goal.org

DC Scores, DCScores.org

Girl Boss Sports, GirlBossSports.com

Goals for Girls, GoalsForGirls.org

Grassroot Soccer Inc., GrassRootSoccer.org

Julie Foudy Sports Leadership Academy, JulieFoudyLeadership.com

Kicks to The Pitch, kickstothepitch.com

Positive Coaching Alliance, PositiveCoach.org

Saturday Night Lights, nycfc.com/comunity/saturday-night-lights

She Can Coach, WeCoachSports.org

Soccer 4 Hope, Changemakers.com

Soccer Parenting Association, SoccerParenting.com

Soccer Shots, SoccerShots.org

Soccer Without Borders, SoccerWithoutBorders.org

streetfootballworld, StreetFootballWorld.org

US Soccer Foundation, USSoccerFoundation.org

Women and Girls in Soccer, womenandgirlsinsoccer.org

Women's Sports Foundation, WomensSportsFoundation.org

INDEX